Hunger by Design

Hunger by Design

The Great Ukrainian Famine and Its Soviet Context

edited by Halyna Hryn

Distributed by Harvard University Press
for the Ukrainian Research Institute
Harvard University

The Harvard Ukrainian Research Institute was established in 1973 as an integral part of Harvard University. It supports research associates and visiting scholars who are engaged in projects concerned with all aspects of Ukrainian studies. The Institute also works in close cooperation with the Committee on Ukrainian Studies, which supervises and coordinates the teaching of Ukrainian history, language, and literature at Harvard University.

Publication of this book has been made possible by the generous support of Ukrainian studies at Harvard University by Stefan and Iwanna Rozankowskyj.

Library of Congress Cataloging-in-Publication Data

Hunger by design : the great Ukrainian famine and its Soviet context / edited by Halyna Hryn.
     p. cm. -- (Harvard papers in Ukrainian studies)
  Proceedings of the symposium, held on October 20, 2003, entitled "The Ukrainian Terror-Famine of 1932-1933: Revisiting the Issues and the Scholarship Twenty Years after the HURI Famine Project."
  Includes bibliographical references and index.
  ISBN 978-1-932650-05-1 (alk. paper)
  1. Ukraine--History--Famine, 1932-1933--Congresses. 2. Famines--Ukraine--Congresses. 3. Famines--Soviet Union--Congresses. I. Hryn, Halyna.
  HC340.19.Z9F3116 2008
  363.809477'09043--dc22
                    2008044694

Cover design: Marika Whaley
Front cover photograph: Death record for eight-year-old Iefrosyniia (Khrosyna) Korobii, from the death record book for Antonivka village, Stavyshche raion, Kyiv oblast, 21 June 1932. State Archives of Kyiv Oblast, fond 5634, op. 1, spr. 969, ark. 86. Used with permission.
Back cover photograph: "Exemplary brigadier Fenichev of the kolkhoz 'May 1,' Synelnykovo, Dnipropetrovsk oblast, 1932." Used with permission of the State Committee on Archives of Ukraine.

Contents

Contributors

Hennadii Boriak is head of the Department of Specialized Research and Electronic Resources at the Institute of History of Ukraine, National Academy of Sciences of Ukraine.

George G. Grabowicz is Dmytro Čyževs'kyj Professor of Ukrainian Literature at Harvard University.

Andrea Graziosi is professor of contemporary history at the Università di Napoli "Federico II."

Lubomyr Hajda is associate director responsible for academic programs at the Harvard Ukrainian Research Institute and was the organizer of the HURI Symposium on the Great Famine of 1932–1933, held on 20 October 2003.

Gijs Kessler is a research fellow of the International Institute of Social History, Amsterdam, where he is a specialist in the social history of the interwar Soviet Union.

Sergei Maksudov is an associate of the Davis Center for Russian and Eurasian Studies at Harvard University.

Niccolò Pianciola is an acting professor of the history of Eastern Europe at the University of Trento, Italy.

Foreword

The catalytic role of the Ukrainian Research Institute at Harvard University (HURI) in the scholarly study of the Great Famine in Ukraine in 1932–1933 continues with the publication of this volume, a collection of articles entitled *Hunger by Design: The Great Ukrainian Famine and Its Soviet Context*.

This publication appears on the seventy-fifth anniversary of the Famine—now more and more frequently called *Holodomor*, a compound word combining the root *holod* 'hunger' with the verbal root *mor* 'extinguish, exterminate'. It is the latest in the series of HURI initiatives that reach back a quarter century to the time of the fiftieth commemoration of the tragedy.

The pioneering work that then laid the foundation for all subsequent research in the field captured the essence of the tragedy with searingly memorable imagery:

> Fifty years ago as I write these words, the Ukraine and the Ukrainian, Cossack and other areas to its east—a great stretch of territory with some forty million inhabitants—was like one vast Belsen. A quarter of the rural population, men, women and children, lay dead or dying, the rest in various stages of debilitation with no strength to bury their families or neighbours. At the same time, (as at Belsen), well-fed squads of police or party officials supervised the victims.

Thus opened Robert Conquest's *The Harvest of Sorrow* (New York, 1986), the now classic monograph on Ukraine's tragic "Soviet Collectivization and the Terror-Famine," as the author subtitled it. Amazing as it may seem, this was the first—half a century after the fact!—book-length study of the 1932–1933 man-made catastrophe inflicted on Ukraine that ranks high among the horrors in a horror-filled twentieth century. Until Conquest's book, as several authors in the current volume emphasize, the 1932–1933 Famine was the subject of one major scholarly article; a handful of serious (if limited) and more numerous tangential references in general studies; and a few publications, including eyewitness accounts, published—with an intense sense of mission but little critical analysis—by the Ukrainian diaspora.

Harvest of Sorrow was the product of a special scholarly project undertaken by HURI in 1982–1983 to commemorate the fiftieth anniversary of the Holodomor. In addition to Robert Conquest, engaged in various aspects of the Famine Project were James Mace, who would soon become through his writings and appearances at scholarly forums a major voice in the discourse on the Famine; Leonid Heretz, at the time a Harvard graduate student who was especially active in recording interviews with still living witnesses to the Famine; and Oksana Procyk, librarian for Ukrainian collections at Harvard's Widener Library, who organized a large-scale exhibit whose permanent value is reflected in the published catalogue *Famine in the Soviet Ukraine, 1932–1933: A Memorial Exhibition, Widener Library, Harvard University* (Cambridge, Mass., 1986). The HURI Famine Project turned out, in fact, to be the most important scholarly contribution on the occasion, which otherwise was limited to a number of more modest academic efforts and memorial commemorations in the Ukrainian diaspora community.

How different has the situation become over the intervening period! A critical breakthrough occurred in the late 1980s when, shortly before the collapse of the USSR, the Famine was finally acknowledged where it had been forbidden to even mention it: in Ukraine itself. With Ukraine's independence in 1991, memory of the Holodomor became one of the elements of nation building in the new state. Archives were opened, and the documentary evidence has allowed for a proliferation of studies large and small. Outside Ukraine, too, a substantial and growing scholarly literature has made its appearance, oftentimes stemming from conferences and other forums dedicated to Famine studies. Scholarly (and not only) polemics concerning various aspects of the Holodomor have fueled controversies that call further attention to the Famine and have stimulated even more intense study. In all these enterprises, the products of the HURI Project formed the core and starting point of the evolving scholarly discourse.

In 2002–2003, the seventieth anniversary of the Terror-Famine, scholarly interest in the Holodomor proliferated in the international academic arena in seminars, symposia, and at conferences. The Ukrainian Research Institute shared in this enterprise with the symposium, held on 20 October 2003, entitled "The Ukrainian Terror-Famine of 1932–1933: Revisiting the Issues and the Scholarship Twenty Years after the HURI Famine Project." Most papers from this meeting were subsequently published in a special issue of *Harvard Ukrainian Studies* (vol. 25, no. 3–4), and that volume in turn forms the core of the present collection, with revisions, updates, and the addition of new material.

Of central interest at the 2003 HURI symposium was the lecture by Terry D. Martin, "The Great Famine in Ukraine and the Nationalities Question." Based on archival sources made available since the collapse of the USSR, including papers of some key players in the orchestration of the Famine from Moscow repositories, Martin's presentation offered new insights and interpretations of the still controversial nexus between the Soviet collectivization and nationalities policies in Ukraine. For contractual reasons it could not be published by HURI, but much of the author's evidence and argument is presented in chapter 7 of his monograph, *The Affirmative Action Empire* (Ithaca, N.Y., 2001).

The Italian historian Andrea Graziosi presented at the symposium an overview of the current state of scholarship, and offered a fresh analysis of the historical significance of the Holodomor and the scholars who studied—or ignored—it. Of special interest was the agenda he proposed for researchers on issues that still cry out for investigation. His remarks were published in the *Harvard Ukrainian Studies* (*HUS*) issue as "The Great Famine of 1932–1933: Consequences and Implications." Graziosi has since expanded the original paper, and the new version is offered here (as well as in volume 27 of *HUS*) as "The Soviet 1931–1933 Famines and the Ukrainian Holodomor: Is a New Interpretation Possible, and What Would Its Consequences Be?"

Not part of the symposium but published in the *HUS* volume was an account by Hennadii Boriak, longtime head of Ukraine's state archival system, of the history of the publication of documentary sources on the Famine. Boriak described the early attempts of the Ukrainian emigration in Western Europe and North America to produce analyses and eyewitness accounts; the first collections of documents culled from various Soviet archives in the newly independent Ukraine of the 1990s; and the discovery of the potential of the Internet for publishing documentary materials about the Holodomor. At a symposium held at HURI on 30 November–1 December 2007 entitled "Breaking the Great Silence on Ukraine's Terror-Famine" (which may be viewed on the Internet at www.huri.harvard.edu/na/famine_symp_30nov_1dec_2007.html), Boriak presented a wealth of new material, reflecting the vastly expanded source base unimagined by the pioneers in the field in the 1980s. The article in this volume, "Sources and Resources on the Famine in Ukraine's State Archival System," adds yet more recent findings.

The large study by Sergei Maksudov (Alexander Babyonyshev) of the "Victory over the Peasantry" harkens back to that period of scholarship when sources were scarce and much depended on the methodological ingenuity of the scholar. Maksudov's contribution has the dual value of demonstrating both the difficulties faced by scholars of the time and the still unsuperseded results of so much of their endeavors.

Of great comparative value are two contributions from the 2003 symposium, published in the earlier *HUS* issue and reprinted without change here, which focus on territories outside Ukraine. "The Collectivization Famine in Kazakhstan, 1931–1933" by Niccolò Pianciola analyzes the Kazakh case, which may be viewed as a kind of tragic prologue to Ukraine's Great Famine. Robert Conquest's *Harvest of Despair* (chapter 9) already called attention to the Central Asian and Kazakh tragedy, noting both analogies with the Ukrainian Holodomor and the region's specific features. Pianciola provides further insights on both. Gijs Kessler's "The 1932–1933 Crisis and Its Aftermath beyond the Epicenters of Famine: The Urals Region" is a noteworthy study that provides invaluable material on the contrasts of degree and scale of suffering, ethnic relations in the face of hunger, as well as official policy and responses to food shortages and starvation in the Urals region of Russia. Especially important for scholars of the Holodomor is Kessler's analysis of the post-Famine countryside, an underdeveloped theme in the study of Ukraine's Great Famine.

"Holodomor and Memory" by George G. Grabowicz, the final article in this collection, is offered by HURI for the first time. A translation and updated version of an article first published in Ukrainian in the Kyiv journal *Krytyka* (December 2003), Grabowicz breaks new ground in Holodomor studies by going beyond the usual strictly historical paradigm. Now that the Famine has finally been acknowledged in Ukraine, it becomes imperative to address the tragedy within the context of a twentieth century that saw many such tragedies around the world. The recognition of the Great Famine as a willful act of genocide compels us to fully confront its enduring, painful legacy. Grabowicz's essay is a seminal contribution in this endeavor.

Hunger by Design is offered to the reader as a scholarly milepost. It does not signify the genesis of Holodomor studies—that role belongs to the HURI Famine Project of the 1980s. Nor does it mark their culmination, an unattainable task. But it does offer the reader, lay and specialist, a collection that captures a point in scholarly time. These articles are the product of the strivings of the past decades, and in turn will serve as the building blocks for future endeavors.

Lubomyr Hajda
Harvard University

The Soviet 1931–1933 Famines and the Ukrainian Holodomor: Is a New Interpretation Possible, and What Would Its Consequences Be?*

ANDREA GRAZIOSI

> Sooner or later the Soviet people will put you in the dock as traitor to both socialism and revolution, main wrecker, true enemy of the people, *organizer of the famine* . . .
>
> —F. Raskol'nikov, Soviet Ambassador to Bulgaria, to Stalin, 17 August 1939[1]

Between the end of 1932 and the summer of 1933, famine in the USSR killed, in half the time, approximately seven times as many people as the Great Terror of 1937–1938. It was the peak of a series of famines that had started in 1931, and it constituted the turning point of the decade as well as Soviet prewar history's main event. With its approximately five million victims (I am not including the hundreds of thousands, possibly more than a million, who had already died in Kazakhstan and elsewhere since 1931), compared to the one to two million victims of 1921–1922 and 1946–1947, this also was the most severe famine in Soviet history and an event that left its mark for decades. Its effect was felt in countries inhabited by immigrant communities from the Russian Empire and the USSR, and its importance, political as well as historical, is still strong today. Since 1987–1988, the rediscovery and interpretation of the Famine have played a key role in Ukraine in discussions between supporters of the democratization process and those who still adhere to a procommunist ideology. The *Holodomor* (the word

---

* Oleg Khlevniuk and Mark Kramer commented on and much improved this text, whose conclusions and mistakes are only mine. Ukrainian, French, and Russian versions of this article have appeared in *Ukraïns'kyi istorychnyi zhurnal*, no. 3 (2005), *Cahiers du monde russe* 46, no 3 (2005), and *Otechestvennye zapiski*, no. 34 (2007), respectively.

coined to mean hunger-related mass extermination, implying intentionality) thus moved to the center of the political and cultural debate, becoming part of the process of state and nation building in Ukraine.

Yet until 1986, when Robert Conquest published his *Harvest of Sorrow*,[2] historians had almost completely ignored this extraordinary event. This is not to say that there was no documentation available, as I realized when reading Italian diplomats' reports to Mussolini—in fact such documents prove that it had always been possible to know. Thanks to the twentieth-century mass population movements—migrations, forced or otherwise, displacements, etc.—and the traces that they left, such as diplomatic dispatches, travel accounts, memoirs of witnesses and victims, much was there, ready to bear witness.[3]

In this light it is startling to recall how little we knew before Conquest's book appeared.[4] In the best case, historians such as Naum Jasny and Alec Nove did speak of a "man-made famine" (which was still being treated as a single event) without, however, researching it fully and generally ignoring its national aspect. A few years later, Moshe Lewin analyzed the mechanisms that caused the Famine, but did not deal with the Famine as such.[5] In the worst case, the Famine became the occasion for depressing polemics in which its very existence was questioned or minimized. In the USSR, where historians, even after 1956, could speak only of "food difficulties," the use of the very word *golod/holod* (hunger, famine) was forbidden. In Ukraine it was uttered officially for the first time in December 1987, in First Secretary Volodymyr Shcherbyts'kyi's speech celebrating the republic's seventieth anniversary.

That is why Conquest's book, the outcome of the Harvard Ukrainian Research Institute project, has been of crucial importance: it forced a reluctant profession to deal with a fundamental question, and it did so by stressing the connection between famine and the national question while properly differentiating the Kazakh case. It can thus be maintained that historiography on the famines and the Holodomor starts with Conquest, even though other authors, such as Sergei Maksudov or Zhores Medvedev, were by then seriously dealing with these events.[6] The book's significance is even greater in light of the polemics that it raised. Because their level was much superior to that of previous polemics, they grew into a positive phenomenon, which may be viewed as part of the process through which historians finally became aware of these events' extraordinary human and intellectual dimensions. This process was, and still is, especially painful because it took and is taking place *after* a historical judgment had already been made and a "collective memory" had set in, all *without* the Soviet famines entering the picture. This was both a consequence of the successful Soviet attempt at concealment and a manifestation of one of the European twentieth century's key features—the logic of "taking sides" that dominated the discussion. Therefore, the famines had to, and today still have to, be brought into our representation of the past at the price of a complete restructuring of commonly held beliefs.

Then came the 1991 archival and historiographical revolution. It allowed the accumulation of new knowledge and caused a leap in the quality of polemics, which, with few exceptions, then grew into serious controversies. True scholarly spirit and a firm moral commitment, born of an awareness of the immensity of the tragedy they deal with, animate the two camps in which it is possible to group today's existing positions at the price of some simplification and much schematization. One can thus contemplate these past few years, during which Conquest's conclusions have been integrated and in part surpassed, with a sense of satisfaction and find in them some reason for optimism.

By means of yet more simplification, the positions of these two camps may be summed up in the following way (I am paraphrasing from a letter that a brilliant young Ukrainian scholar recently sent me). On one side there are what we could call "A" people. They support the genocide thesis and see in the Famine an event artificially organized in order to: (a) break the peasants and/or (b) alter (destroy) the Ukrainian nation's social fabric, which obstructed the transformation of the USSR into a despotic empire. On the other side we have "B" people, who, though fully recognizing the criminal nature of Stalin's policies, deem it necessary to study the Famine as a "complex phenomenon," in which many factors, from the geopolitical situation to the modernization effort, played a role in Moscow's intentions and decisions.

I believe that today we have most of the elements needed for a new, and more satisfactory, interpretive hypothesis, capable of taking into account both the general and complex Soviet picture and the undeniable relevance of the national question.[7] This hypothesis can be put together using the excellent works of Ukrainian, Russian, and Western scholars as building blocks, thus breaking the wall that still partially separates their efforts. It is grounded in the research of outstanding scholars such as Viktor Danilov, R. W. Davies and Stephen Wheatcroft, N. A. Ivnitskii, D'Ann Penner and Viktor Kondrashin, Stanislav Kul'chyts'kyi, James Mace, Terry Martin, France Meslé and Jacques Vallin, Iurii Shapoval and Valerii Vasyl'iev, and also Oleg Khlevniuk, whose works on Stalin and his circle, though not focusing directly on the Famine, allowed us to situate it in its proper political context.[8]

In the next pages I will try to sketch the outline of such an interpretation. I hope not only to push forward the interpretation of the "Great Famine" (a collective name for the 1931–1933 famines), but also to stimulate a debate that will contribute to the breaking of the even taller and stronger wall that isolates its students from their colleagues studying the European twentieth century, a century that is simply impossible to fully understand without considering those famines.

In order to formulate this new interpretation, we need first to define the object of our investigation. As should be clear by now, we are in fact dealing with what it would be more correct to call, on a pan-Soviet level, the *1931–1933 famines*, which had of course common causes and a common background, but included at least two very different and special phenomena: the Kazakhstan famine-*cum*-epidemics of 1931–1933 and the Ukrainian-Kuban (the latter area, though belonging to the Russian republic's province of Northern Caucasus, being mostly inhabited by Ukrainians) Holodomor of late 1932 to early 1933.

Many past misunderstandings have been caused by the confusion between these two *national* tragedies and the general phenomenon that provided their framework. In a way, it is as if students of Nazism would confuse Nazi repression in general with quite specific and crucial cases, such as the extermination of Soviet prisoners of war, or that of Poles and Gypsies—not to mention the Holocaust, an exceptional phenomenon that cannot be explained simply as an aspect or element of Nazi killings at large, and yet certainly was also a part of them. Both Nazi repression in general and such "specific" tragedies existed, and both must be studied, as in fact they are, in and of themselves as well as in their connections.

A very clear distinction between the general phenomenon and its republic-level or regional manifestations should therefore be introduced in the Soviet case. However, most "A" supporters are in fact speaking specifically of the Holodomor, while many of the "B" proponents think on a pan-Soviet scale. If we analytically distinguish what they are doing, we end up discovering that in many, albeit not all, ways they are correct in their respective domains.

The second step toward a new interpretation consists of yet another analytical distinction. We must separate the 1931–1932 "spontaneous" famines—they too, of course, were direct, if undesired, consequences of choices made in 1928–1929— from the post–September 1932 Famine, which took on such terrible features not least because of human decision. (Events in Kazakhstan followed an altogether different pattern and I will therefore only make some passing references to them.)[9] Finally, the third step we need to take is to gather and combine useful elements from both "A" and "B" and drop their unsatisfactory parts.

"A" people are right in drawing our attention to the national question. Anyone studying the Soviet Union should be acutely aware of its importance, as Lenin and Stalin themselves were (after all, the former decided not to call the new state Russia, and the latter, who initially opposed such a choice, never reversed the decision in later years). One should be equally aware of the Ukrainian primacy in this matter. In late 1919 Lenin started the shift towards indigenization (*koreni-zatsiia*),[10] until that time considered to be a request of "extreme nationalists," because of the Ukrainian Bolsheviks' defeat of 1919,[11] and Stalin gave a new spin to *korenizatsiia* in late 1932 because of the Ukrainian crisis. But in Ukraine, at least up to 1933, the national question *was* the peasant question. This is what both Lenin and Stalin thought, and rightly so. "A" people seem instead to be wrong in thinking that the "Famine" (meaning also the pan-Soviet one) was organized ("planned") to solve the Ukrainian national, or rather peasant, problem.

"B" people give us a detailed reconstruction of the causes and wider context of the Famine on a pan-Soviet scale, with all its complexity, and are thus able to criticize convincingly the simplistic views of the "A" camp. However, they seem unable to fully understand or accommodate the national factor; that is, to "descend" from the pan-Soviet to the republic level. "B" people also do not always seem capable of seeing that Stalin, even when he did not initiate something willfully, was always very quick to take advantage of "spontaneous" events, giving them a completely new turn. The obvious parallel here is with Kirov's murder, which Stalin most probably did not organize, but quite certainly "creatively" used. One can thus use good "B" data for the development of the pan-Soviet crisis, stressing however that at this level, too, Stalin at a certain moment decided to *use* hunger to break the peasants' opposition to collectivization. For a number of reasons, such opposition was stronger in non-Russian areas, where events soon started to follow their own course. By reconstructing this course we can crack the secret surrounding the 1932–1933 events from their inception—a secret which, as Raskol'nikov's letter seems to suggest, was known to the Bolshevik elite.

What can therefore be said? From 1931 to 1933 scores, perhaps hundreds, of thousands of people died of hunger throughout the USSR. In Kazakhstan, Ukraine, Northern Caucasus, and the Volga basin (Povolzh'e), however, the situation was completely different. But for Western Siberia, these were the country's most important grain-growing regions, where the post-1927 state-village conflict over the crop was strongest. Since 1918–1919, moreover, the war between the regime and peasants and nomads there had been particularly brutal because of the intensifying role of national and religious factors, and in the Volga because of both the Russian peasant movement's strong traditions and the presence of German colonists.

Except in Kazakhstan, the phenomenon's causes were *similar* across these areas: the devastating human toll, as well as the toll on the capacity for production, taken by dekulakization—a de facto nationwide, state-led pogrom against the peasant elite; forced collectivization, which pushed peasants to destroy a large part of their inventories;[12] the kolkhozes' inefficiency and misery; the repeated and extreme requisition waves originated by a crisis-ridden industrialization, an urbanization out of control, and a growing foreign debt that could be repaid only by exporting raw materials; the resistance of peasants, who would not accept the reimposition of what they called a "second serfdom" and worked less and less because of both their rejection of the new system and hunger-related debilitation; and the poor weather conditions in 1932. Famine, which had started to take hold sporadically already in 1931 (when Kazakhs were dying in mass), and had grown into solid pockets by the spring of 1932, thus appears to have been an undesired and unplanned outcome of ideology-inspired policies aimed at eliminating mercantile and private production. Based on the results of the 1920–1921 war communism policy, the Famine should not have been difficult to foresee.

Yet if one analyzes the Famine's origins and pre–autumn 1932 developments on a pan-Soviet level, it seems arduous to claim that famine was the conscious goal of those policies, as it is maintained by those who support the hypothesis that famine was willfully implemented to break the peasant resistance or to execute a Moscow- (sometimes meaning Russian-) planned Ukrainian genocide.

However, the intensity, course, and consequences of the phenomenon, which new studies and new documents allow us to analyze, were undeniably and substantially *different* in different regions and republics. Out of the six to seven million victims (demographers now impute to 1930–1931 part of the deaths previously imputed to 1932–1933), 3.5 to 3.8 million died in Ukraine; 1.3 to 1.5 million in Kazakhstan (where deaths reached their peak in relation to the population size, exterminating 33 to 38 percent of the Kazakhs and 8 to 9 percent of the Europeans); and several hundred thousand in Northern Caucasus and, on a lesser scale, in the Volga, where the most harshly hit area coincided with the German autonomous republic.[13]

If we consider annual mortality rates per thousand inhabitants *in the country-side*, and make 1926 equal to 100, we see them jump in 1933 to 188.1 in the entire USSR, 138.2 in the Russian republic (which then still included both Kazakhstan and Northern Caucasus), and 367.7—that is, *almost triple*—in Ukraine. Here life expectancy at birth dropped from 42.9 years for men and 46.3 for women registered in 1926 to, respectively, 7.3 and 10.9 in 1933 (it would be 13.6 and 36.3 in 1941). Also, in Ukraine there were 782,000 births in 1932 and 470,000 in 1933, compared with an average of 1.153 million per year in the period from 1926 to 1929.[14] The extreme figures for Ukraine are explained by the Famine's different course there, for which different Moscow policies were largely responsible.

In Ukraine, as elsewhere, in the spring of 1932 local officials, village teachers, and republican leaders noted the spreading of hunger and the beginning of a mass rural exodus.[15] Stalin, urged by the Ukrainian party, which asked for a reduction in procurements, acknowledged in early June that this was indeed necessary, at least in the most hard-hit areas, also out of a "sense of justice." Such reductions, however, had to be moderate and local, because, despite Viacheslav Molotov's report that "today we have to face, even in grain-producing areas, the specter of famine," the Politburo concluded that "procurement plans must be respected at all cost."[16] This conclusion was dictated by the need to avoid the repetition, on a larger scale, of that spring's urban food riots and strikes and to honor the German bills due between the end of the year and the beginning of 1933.

Already in June, however, Stalin was developing what Terry Martin has called a "national interpretation" of the Famine, well before Ukrainian nationalists outside the USSR even started to think about it.[17] At the beginning, he ranted in private against the republic leaders, whom he held responsible for failing to deal with the situation with the necessary firmness. Between July and August, however, after a Ukrainian party conference had implicitly disagreed with Moscow and on the basis of OGPU reports that accused local communists of being infected with nationalism, Stalin produced a new analysis of the situation and its causes.[18]

What was perhaps the last recorded disagreement with Stalin in a Politburo meeting also possibly played a role. On 2 August 1932 someone, probably Hryhorii Petrovs'kyi (then the Ukrainian Central Executive Committee [VUTsVK] chairman), objected to Stalin's draft of what was to become on 7 August the draconian law on the defense of state property against peasant theft.[19] A bit later, on 11 August, in spite of the recent signing of the Polish-Soviet non-aggression pact,[20] in a crucial letter to Lazar' Kaganovich, Stalin wrote that Ukraine was now the *main issue* (his emphasis), that the republic's party, state, and even political police organs teemed with nationalist agents and Polish spies, and that there was a real risk of "losing Ukraine," which should instead be transformed into a Bolshevik fortress.[21]

Such an interpretation, developed on the basis of the Ukrainian experience, was later extended by Stalin to the Cossacks (who had been singled out as enemies of the regime already in 1919 when they were hit by decossackization),[22] the Volga Germans, and, albeit in less stark terms, Belarusians. The crisis thus spurred Stalin to apply his by then well-developed model of preventive, category-based, and therefore collective repression (which had reached its first peak with dekulakization) to a number of national and social-national groups that in his judgment posed a threat to the regime. As events were to prove, however, Ukraine and Ukrainians remained foremost in his mind.

When, as it was to be expected, procurements proved unsatisfactory throughout the grain-producing lands, Molotov, Kaganovich, and Pavel Postyshev were sent to Ukraine, Northern Caucasus, and the Volga to redress the situation. The decision to *use the famine*, thus enormously and artificially strengthening it, in order to impart a lesson to peasants who refused the new serfdom[23] was thus taken in the fall of 1932, when the crisis caused by the first five-year plan peaked and Stalin's wife committed suicide. The punishment was tragically simple: he who does not work—that is, does not accept the kolkhoz system—will not eat. Stalin hinted at such a policy in his famous 1933 correspondence with Mikhail Sholokhov. The Don's "esteemed grain-growers," on whose behalf the writer pleaded, had waged—Stalin wrote—a "'secret' war against Soviet power, a war in which"—he added, reversing roles—"they used hunger as a weapon," and of which they were now bearing the consequences; that is, implicitly, famine.[24]

Most of the stricken areas were not extended any help until the spring of 1933 (Don peasants got something only in May). Moreover, while Commissar of Foreign Affairs Maxim Litvinov officially denied the Famine's existence in his answers to foreign officials' queries, the state "ferociously fought" (in Kaganovich's words) to fulfil these areas' procurement plans.

In those places where the "peasant question" was complicated—that is, strengthened and thus made more dangerous by the national one (let us remember that Stalin explicitly linked the two questions in his writings on nationalism, and that the Soviet leadership had seen this hypothesis confirmed by the Ukrainian countryside's great social and national revolts of 1919, repeated, albeit on a lesser scale, in early 1930)[25]—the resort to hunger was more ruthless and the lesson much harsher. According to demographic data, in Ukraine, too, mortality depended on residency, urban or rural, and not on nationality, meaning that people living in the countryside suffered independently of their ethnic background. Yet one cannot forget that, as everybody knew, in spite of the previous urbanization-*cum*-Ukrainization, villages remained overwhelmingly Ukrainian, while cities had largely preserved their "alien" (Russian, Jewish, Polish) character.[26] In Ukraine, therefore, the countryside was indeed targeted to break the peasants, but with the full awareness that the village represented the nation's spine.

The fact that, because of the "national interpretation," the decision to use the Famine took on very specific traits in Ukraine and Kuban is confirmed by measures that were, at least in part, very different from those taken on a pan-Soviet scale, with the partial exception of the Don Cossack lands. On 18 November 1932, the Ukrainian Central Committee, which Molotov and Kaganovich had crushed into submission, ordered peasants to return the meager grain advances over the new crop that they had received in recompense for their work. The decision (one may imagine what its implementation meant) opened the way for the repression of local officials who had helped out starving peasant families by distributing grain to them. Hundreds of such officials were shot and thousands arrested, often on the charge of "populism." Meanwhile, in Ukraine and Kuban the state resorted to fines in kind in order to also seize meat and potatoes from peasants, a measure which was not extended to the Volga, where—with the possible exception of the German autonomous republic—Postyshev dealt less harshly with local cadres (although less severe punishment did not prevent mass hunger-related deaths). Specific areas of Northern Caucasus and Ukraine, where the opposition to collectivization had been stronger, were punished even more cruelly: all goods, including non-agricultural, were removed from stores and all inhabitants were deported from certain localities.

Famine thus took on forms and dimensions much bigger than it would have if nature had followed its course. It was less intense, in terms of both drought and the area it affected, than the 1921–1922 Famine (the 1932 crop, though quite low, was still higher than the 1945 crop, when there were no comparable mass hunger-related deaths), yet it caused three to four times as many victims—essentially because of political decisions that aimed at saving the regime from the crisis to which its very policies had led and at assuring the victory of the "great offensive" launched four years previously.

The awareness that in Ukraine and Kuban the peasant question also was a national question determined the need to deal with and "solve" these questions together. In order to make sure that such a "solution" was there to stay, it was complemented by the decision to get rid of the national elites and their policies, which were suspected, as we know, of abetting peasants.

On 14 and 15 December 1932, the Politburo passed two secret decrees that reversed, but *only* in the Ukrainian case, the official nationality policies decided upon in 1923. According to these decrees *korenizatsiia*, as it had been implemented in Ukraine and Kuban, had spurred nationalistic feelings rather than checking them, and produced enemies with a party membership ticket in their pocket. Peasants were not the sole culprits of the crisis, but shared responsibility with the Ukrainian political and cultural classes.

On these premises, Ukrainization programs in the Russian republic were abolished. Several million Ukrainians who, following the pro-Russian border choices of the mid-1920s, were living in the RSFSR thus lost those education, press, and self-government rights that other nationalities continued to enjoy. The 1937 census would reveal that only 3 million RSFSR citizens defined themselves as Ukrainians versus the 7.8 million of 1926 (at least part of this decline was caused by the promotion of Kazakhstan, previously a RSFSR autonomous republic, into a Soviet one).

A few days later, on 19 December, similar though less harsh measures hit Belarus too, where—as in Ukraine—the peasant and the national questions largely coincided, a fact that had also caused problems during the civil war, albeit not on the Ukrainian scale. Here, too, in early March the party was accused of abetting nationalism, and party cadres and the national intelligentsiia were repressed for such crimes. The fundamental difference in Soviet nationality policies, which were much more tolerant in the east and the north of the USSR than in the west, was thus reaffirmed, although there was no reversal of "Belarusization."[27]

On the night of 20 December, at the urging of Kaganovich, the Ukrainian Politburo committed itself to new targets for grain requisitions. Nine days later it declared that the precondition to fulfilling the plan was the seizure of seed stock reserves.[28] On 22 January 1933, soon after Postyshev, Moscow's new plenipotentiary in Ukraine, arrived with hundreds of central cadres, Stalin and Molotov ordered the OGPU to stop peasants from fleeing Ukraine and Kuban in search of food. The Central Committee and the government, they wrote, "are convinced that this exodus, like that of the previous year, has been organized by enemies of Soviet power, Socialist Revolutionaries and Polish agents, in order to agitate by 'using peasants' against kolkhozes and, more generally, against Soviet power in the USSR's northern territories. Last year party, government, and police organs failed to uncover this counterrevolutionary plot . . . A repetition of such a mistake this year would be intolerable."[29] In the following month, the decree led to the arrest of 220,000 people, predominantly hungry peasants in search of food; 190,000 of them were sent back to their villages to starve.

Ukrainian cities too, which were far better, albeit still miserably, supplied, were surrounded by antipeasant roadblocks, while villages were left to starve.[30] What the Ukrainian party secretary, Stanislav Kosior, wrote Moscow on 15 March confirms that the hunger was used to teach peasants subservience to the state. "The unsatisfactory course of sowing in many areas," he lamented, "shows that famine hasn't still *taught reason* to many kolkhozniks" (emphasis mine).[31] These measures were accompanied, and followed, by a wave of anti-Ukrainian terror, which already presented some of the traits that were later to characterize the 1937–1938 "mass operations." Thus ended the national-communist experiment born of the civil war, with the suicide in 1933 of important leaders such as Mykola Skrypnyk and writers such as Mykola Khvyl'ovyi as well as the repression of thousands of its cadres.

The adoption of the term Holodomor seems therefore legitimate, as well as necessary, to mark a distinction between the pan-Soviet phenomenon of 1931–1933 and the Ukrainian Famine *after* the summer of 1932. In spite of their undeniable close relationship, the two are in fact profoundly different. The same applies to the Famines' consequences, which also were partially similar yet essentially different. Whereas throughout the USSR the use of hunger broke peasant resistance;[32] guaranteed the victory of a dictator whom people feared in a new way and around whom a new cult, based on fear, started to develop; opened the door to the 1937–1938 terror; marked a qualitative change in the lie that had accompanied the Soviet regime since its inception; allowed, by means of the subjugation of the most important republic, the de facto transformation of the Soviet federal state into a despotic empire; and left a dreadful legacy of grief in a multitude of families that were prevented from dealing with it (Gorbachev too lost three paternal uncles then) because of the Famine taboo and the dogma about life having become "more joyous"—in Ukraine and in Kazakhstan famine dug even deeper.

In Kazakhstan, the traditional society's very structures were seriously impaired. In Ukraine, both the body and the top of national society were badly damaged, slowing down and distorting nation building. I think, for instance, that only thus can we account for the much weaker presence, as compared to what happened in 1914–1922, of the Ukrainian national movement in the great crisis of 1941–1945 (Galicia, which in 1933 was not part of the USSR, was not surprisingly the rather extraordinary exception).

The number of victims makes the Soviet 1931–1933 famines into a set of phenomena that, in the framework of European history, can be compared only to later Nazi crimes. The course of events in Ukraine and Northern Caucasus, and the link this course had to both Stalin's interpretation of the crisis and the policies that originated from this interpretation, reintroduce, in a new way, the question of its nature. *Was there also* a Ukrainian genocide?

The answer seems to be *no* if one thinks of a famine conceived by the regime, or— this being even more untenable—by Russia, to destroy the Ukrainian people.

It is equally *no* if one adopts a restrictive definition of genocide as the planned will to exterminate *all* the members of a religious or ethnic group, in which case only the Holocaust would qualify.

In 1948, however, even the rather strict UN definition of genocide listed among possible genocidal acts, side by side with "killing members of the group, and causing serious bodily or mental harm to members of the group," *"deliberately inflicting on members of the group conditions of life calculated to bring about its physical destruction in whole or in part"* (emphasis mine). Not long before, Raphael Lemkin, the inventor of the term, had noted that, "generally speaking, genocide does not necessarily mean the immediate destruction of a nation . . . It is intended rather to signify a coordinated plan of different actions aiming at the destruction of essential foundations of the life of national groups."[33]

Based on Lemkin's definition—if one thinks of the substantial difference in mortality rates in different republics; adds to the millions of Ukrainian victims, including the ones from Kuban, the millions of Ukrainians forcibly Russified after December 1932, as well as the scores of thousands of peasants who met a similar fate after evading the police roadblocks and taking refuge in the Russian republic; keeps in mind that one is therefore dealing with the loss of approximately 20 to 30 percent of the Ukrainian ethnic population; remembers that such a loss was caused by the decision, unquestionably a subjective act, to use the Famine in an anti-Ukrainian sense on the basis of the "national interpretation" Stalin developed in the second half of 1932; reckons that without such a decision the death count would have been at the most in the hundreds of thousands (that is, less than in 1921–1922); and finally, if one adds to all of the above the destruction of large part of the republic's Ukrainian political and cultural elite, from village teachers to national leaders—I believe that the answer to our question, "Was the Holodomor a genocide?" cannot but be positive.

Between the end of 1932 and the summer of 1933:

1. Stalin and the regime he controlled and coerced (but certainly not Russia or the Russians, who suffered from famine too, even though on a lesser scale) consciously executed, as part of a drive directed at breaking the peasantry, an anti-Ukrainian policy aimed at mass extermination and causing a genocide in the above-mentioned interpretation of the term, a genocide whose physical and psychological scars are still visible today.[34]
2. This genocide was the product of a famine that was not willfully caused with such aim in mind, but was willfully maneuvered towards this end once it came about as the unanticipated result of the regime policies (it seems that the even more terrible Kazakh tragedy was "only" the undesired, if foreseeable, outcome of denomadization and colonial indifference towards the natives' fate).[35]
3. It took place within a context that saw Stalin punishing with hunger, and

applying terror to, a number of national and ethnosocial groups he felt to be actually or potentially dangerous.[36] As all the quantitative data indicate, however, the scale of both punishment and terror reached extreme dimensions in Ukraine for the reasons I listed, thus growing into a qualitatively different phenomenon.

4. From this perspective, the relationship between the Holodomor and the other tragic punishments by repression of 1932–1933 do in a way recall the already-mentioned relationship between Nazi repressions and the Holocaust. The Holodomor, however, was much different from the Holocaust. It did not aim at exterminating the *whole* nation, it did not kill people *directly*, and it was motivated and constructed theoretically and *politically*—might one say "rationally"?—rather than ethnically or racially. This different motivation at least partially accounts for the first two differences.[37]

5. From this perspective, the Holocaust is exceptional because it represents the purest, and therefore qualitatively different, genocide imaginable. It thus belongs in another category. Yet at the same time it represents the apex of a multilayered pyramid, whose steps are represented by other tragedies, and to whose top the Holodomor is close.

Were it true, as I believe it to be, this affirmative answer has great moral and intellectual consequences upon our image and interpretation of the European twentieth century. In an essay published in *Harvard Ukrainian Studies*, after discussing the problems related to the "Great Famine's" medium- and long-term impact on Soviet history, I tried to address some of these consequences and would now like to recall three of them.[38]

How does the awareness of the Famines' modalities, entity, and responsibilities affect the judgment we are called upon to pass, as human beings first but also as historians, on the Soviet system and its first generation of leaders, a group that must be extended to cover the functionaries who executed their decisions, without of course forgetting the many who bravely refused to participate in or boycotted the state's policies and were punished for it? In the light of 1932–1933, doesn't that system much more resemble, for at least a stage in its history, a violent and primitive state headed by a wicked despot than a modernizing "totalitarianism," ideologically aimed at conquering and recasting the consciousness of its subjects?

Is it possible to maintain that if at the root of the Soviet system, as recast by Stalin, there was such a crime, then its collapse is somehow related to this original sin, a sin covered for decades by lies because it could not be acknowledged? From this angle, the "Great Famine" assumes the features of a formidable obstacle to the survival by renewal of a system that could not speak the truth about its past and was thus swept away by the surfacing of this truth, often by virtue of people who wanted to reform it and make it more humane, and started to do so by settling accounts with the past, only to discover that such accounts could not be settled.[39]

We thus enter the extremely interesting question of the evolution of "totalitarianism," a category I do not like in part because it makes it difficult to account for such evolution, which in the Soviet case is nonetheless undeniable. Jacob Burckhardt wrote, "even a state founded at the beginning only upon the curses of the oppressed is forced with time to evolve some kind of law and civil life, because rightful and civil people slowly gain control over it."[40] Can it be that if peace prevails for a long enough period, at least the progress, if not the final triumph, of such evolution is indeed possible, even when that state's history is marked by genocide? Were it so, Soviet history would be not just the astonishing moral parable that indeed it is, but also the harbinger of hope in much more general terms.

NOTES

1.   Raskol'nikov, a famous civil war commander, served in Sofia from 1934 to 1938. His "open letter" to Stalin was published in *Novaia Rossiia* (Paris) on 1 October 1939, three weeks after his death in Nice. For the letter, with much new material, see A. Artizov et al., eds., *Reabilitatsiia—kak eto bylo: Dokumenty Prezidiuma TsK KPSS i drugie materialy*, vol. 2, *Fevral' 1956–nachalo 80-kh godov* (Moscow, 2003), 420–53. Emphasis mine. Unless otherwise noted, all translations are my own.

2.   Robert Conquest, *The Harvest of Sorrow: Soviet Collectivization and the Terror-Famine* (New York, 1986).

3.   Andrea Graziosi, "'Lettres de Kharkov': La famine en Ukraine et dans le Caucase du Nord à travers les rapports des diplomates italiens, 1932–1934," *Cahiers du monde russe et soviétique* 30, no. 1–2 (1989): 2–106; Graziosi, ed., *Lettere da Kharkov: La carestia in Ucraina e nel Caucaso del Nord nei rapporti dei diplomatici italiani, 1932–33* (Turin, 1991); United States Congress Commission on the Ukraine Famine, *Investigation of the Ukrainian Famine, 1932–1933: Report to Congress* (Washington, D.C., 1988), see esp. appendixes; Marco Carynnyk, Lubomyr Y. Luciuk, and Bohdan S. Kordan, eds., *The Foreign Office and the Famine: British Documents on Ukraine and the Great Famine of 1932–1933* (Kingston, Ont., 1988); D. Zlepko, *Der ukrainische Hunger-Holocaust* (Sonnenbühl, 1988) [a poor edition]; Victor Kravchenko, *I Chose Freedom: The Personal and Political Life of a Soviet Official* (New York, 1946); S. O. Pidhainy, ed., *The Black Deeds of the Kremlin: A White Book*, vol. 2, *The Great Famine in Ukraine in 1932–1933* (Detroit, 1955); Miron Dolot, *Execution by Hunger: The Hidden Holocaust* (New York, 1985), and others. In the mid-1960s Dana G. Dalrymple reviewed the available sources in "The Soviet Famine of 1932–1934," *Soviet Studies* 15, no. 3 (1964): 250–84; 16, no. 4 (1965): 471–74. There are now several online bibliographies on the Famine. See, for instance, the official site of the State Committee on Archives of Ukraine: "Genotsyd ukraïns'koho narodu: Holodomor 1932–1933 rr.," http://www.archives. gov.ua/Sections/Famine.

4.   This attitude was not limited to the 1932–1933 Famine. The profession was still dominated, and not without reason, by the authority of E. H. Carr, who in his multivolume opus on 1917–1929 devoted only a few pages—in which neither the peasants' behaviors and fate, nor the national implications of the disaster were analyzed—to the 1921–1922 Famine, which was central to the early Soviet experience and later developments. We also knew very little about the 1946–1947 Famine, in spite of the central role Khrushchev assigned it in his 1970 memoirs (see his *Vospominaniia—vremia, liudi, vlast'*, 4 vols. [Moscow, 1999]). See also V. F. Zima, *Golod v SSSR 1946–1947 godov: Proiskhozhdenie i posledstviia* (Moscow, 1996); O. M. Veselova, V. I. Marochko, and O. M. Movchan, *Holodomory v Ukraïni 1921–1923, 1932–1933, 1946–1947: Zlochyny proty narodu* (Kyiv, 2000). Recently Karel C. Berkhoff has also investigated the German-organized starvation of Kyiv in 1941–1942 in his *Harvest of Despair: Life and Death in Ukraine under Nazi Rule* (Cambridge, Mass., 2004).

5.   Naum Jasny, *The Socialized Agriculture of the USSR* (Stanford, 1949); Alec Nove,

An Economic History of the USSR (London, 1969; 3rd ed., London, 1992). See also Moshe Lewin's 1974 article "'Taking Grain': Soviet Policies of Agricultural Procurements before the War," reprinted in Lewin, *The Making of the Soviet System: Essays in the Social History of Interwar Russia* (New York, 1985), 142–77.

6. James E. Mace, *Communism and the Dilemmas of National Liberation: National Communism in Ukraine, 1918–1933* (Cambridge, Mass., 1983); Sergei Maksudov [Alexander Babyonyshev], *Poteri naseleniia SSSR* (Benson, Vt., 1989). Zhores A. Medvedev, in his book *Soviet Agriculture* (New York, 1987), devoted an excellent chapter to the Famine, where he correctly addressed its pan-Soviet features but overlooked its national aspects. See also Bohdan Krawchenko, *Social Change and National Consciousness in Twentieth-Century Ukraine* (New York, 1985).

7. In 1996, in *The Great Soviet Peasant War: Bolsheviks and Peasants, 1918–1933* (Cambridge, Mass., 1996), I tried to look for such a solution, but did it in a way that I now deem inadequate and partially incorrect.

8. V. Danilov, R. Manning, and L. Viola, eds., *Tragediia sovetskoi derevni: Kollektivizatsiia i raskulachivanie*, vol. 3, *Konets 1930–1933* (Moscow, 2001); R. W. Davies, Oleg V. Khlevniuk, and E. A. Rees, eds., *The Stalin-Kaganovich Correspondence, 1931–36* (New Haven, 2003; Russian ed., Moscow, 2001); R. W. Davies and Stephen G. Wheatcroft, *The Years of Hunger: Soviet Agriculture, 1931–1933* (New York, 2004); N. A. Ivnitskii, *Kollektivizatsiia i raskulachivanie* (Moscow, 1996); Ivnitskii, *Repressivnaia politika sovetskoi vlasti v derevne (1928–1933 gg.)* (Moscow, 2000); V. V. Kondrashin and Diana [D'Ann] Penner, *Golod: 1932–1933 gody v sovetskoi derevne (na materiale Povolzh'ia, Dona i Kubani)* (Samara, 2002); S. V. Kul'chyts'kyi, ed., *Holodomor 1932–1933 rr. v Ukraïni: Prychyny i naslidky* (Kyiv, 1995); Kul'chyts'kyi, ed., *Kolektyvizatsiia i holod na Ukraïni, 1929–1933* (Kyiv, 1992); Kul'chyts'kyi, *Ukraïna mizh dvoma viinamy (1921–1939 rr.)* (Kyiv, 1999); F. M. Rudych et al., eds., *Holod 1932–1933 rokiv na Ukraïni: Ochyma istorykiv, movoiu dokumentiv*, comp. R. Ia. Pyrih et al. (Kyiv, 1990); V. M. Lytvyn, ed., *Holod 1932–1933 rokiv v Ukraïni: Prychyny ta naslidky* (Kyiv, 2003); Terry Martin, *The Affirmative Action Empire: Nations and Nationalism in the Soviet Union, 1923–1939* (Ithaca, N.Y., 2001); France Meslé and Jacques Vallin, *Mortalité et causes de décès en Ukraine au XXe siècle* (Paris, 2003); Iurii Shapoval and Valerii Vasyl'iev, *Komandyry velykoho holodu: Poïzdky V. Molotova i L. Kahanovycha v Ukraïnu ta na Pivnichnyi Kavkaz, 1932–1933 rr.* (Kyiv, 2001). Timothy Snyder's work in progress on Polish-Ukrainian-Soviet relations is also very useful. See, for example, "A National Question Crosses a Systemic Border: The Polish-Soviet Context for Ukraine, 1926–1935" (paper presented at the congress of the Società Italiana per lo Studio della Storia Contemporanea, Bolzano-Bozen, September, 2004).

9. See M. K. Kozybaev et al., *Nasil'stvennaia kollektivizatsiia i golod v Kazakhstane v 1931–33 gg.: Sbornik dokumentov i materialov* (Almaty, 1998); Isabelle Ohayon, *La sédentarisation des Kazakhs dans l'URSS de Staline: Collectivisation et changement social (1928–1945)* (Paris, 2006); Niccolò Pianciola, "Famine in the Steppe: The Collectivization of Agriculture and the Kazak Herdsmen, 1928–1934," *Cahiers du monde russe* 45, no. 1–2 (2004): 137–92.

10. In 1923, after the USSR had been organized as a Federation of Republics based on titular nationalities, the party formally adopted a set of measures to promote the development of "backward" nationalities by granting them a number of privileges and rights. *Korenizatsiia* was the collective name of these measures. See Martin, *Affirmative Action Empire*.

11. In Richard Pipes, ed., *The Unknown Lenin: From the Secret Archive* (New Haven, 1996), 76–77, one can read the previously secret draft theses that Lenin wrote in November 1919, "Policy in the Ukraine." Among other things, he demanded "greatest caution regarding nationalist traditions, strictest observance of equality of the Ukrainian language and culture," as well as to "treat Jews and urban inhabitants [that is, largely non-Ukrainians] in the Ukraine with an iron rod."

12. Interestingly enough, an OGPU report on grain procurements of May 1929 already mentions peasant protests ignited by the authorities' withdrawal of bread and other necessities from villages that had not fulfilled the plan. As in the civil war, hunger was thus used by the regime in order to punish and tame peasants from the very beginning of the collectivization drive. See Nicolas Werth and Gaël Moullec, *Rapports secrets soviétiques* (Paris, 1994), 112.

13. The uncertainty in both the Ukrainian and especially the Kazakh figures is caused by the difficulty of accounting for the net result of the exodus the Famine caused. Many refugees died around railroad stations or along the way; others were able to take refuge in the Russian republic, Transcaucasia, or China.

14. Maksudov, *Poteri naseleniia SSSR*; Kul′chyts′kyi, *Holodomor 1932–1933 rr. v Ukraïni*; Davies and Wheatcroft, *Years of Hunger*; Meslé and Vallin, *Mortalité et causes de décès en Ukraine*; E. M. Andreev, L. E. Darskii, and T. L. Khar′kova, *Demograficheskaia istoriia Rossii, 1927–1959* (Moscow, 1998); Iu. A. Poliakov, ed., *Naselenie Rossii v XX veke: Istoricheskie ocherki*, vol. 1, *1900–1939 gg.* (Moscow, 2000).

15. The 1920–1922 tragedy also started with local famines in the spring of 1920. See A. Graziosi, "State and Peasants in the Reports of the Political Police, 1918–1922," in *A New, Peculiar State: Explorations in Soviet History, 1917–1937* (Westport, Conn., 2000), 95–107 (in which, however, I mistakenly quote the old, excessive estimates on that Famine's mortality); Bertrand M. Patenaude, *The Big Show in Bololand: The American Relief Expedition to Soviet Russia in the Famine of 1921* (Stanford, 2002).

16. Quoted in N. A. Ivnitskii, "Golod 1932–1933 godov: Kto vinovat," in *Golod 1932–1933 godov*, ed. Iu. N. Afanas′ev and N. A. Ivnitskii (Moscow, 1995), 59.

17. The best reconstruction of the origin of Stalin's "national interpretation" is in Martin, *Affirmative Action Empire*. Mace too, however, came to the conclusion that something crucial for subsequent developments happened in July 1932.

18. On 5 August, for instance, the OGPU reported that fractions within Ukrainian communism and national communists within Ukraine "carry out the orders of the

Second Department of the Polish General Staff." See Danilov, Manning, and Viola, *Tragediia sovetskoi derevni*, 3:420–22, 443.

19.   Kaganovich speaks of such opposition, without directly mentioning Petrovs'kyi, in a letter to Stalin that he perhaps didn't mail: "Только что собрались специально для беседы по вопросу о проекте декрета. В проекте декрета объединены три раздела в духе Ваших указаний. Против третьего раздела вчера возражал…, сегодня его не было, он уехал. Сомнения и даже возражения по 2-му i 3-му имелись также и у…, но в конце концов мы остановились на этом тексте в основном." The second point of the decree sentenced those responsible for stealing kolkhoz property (meaning grain) to death, or to five to ten years of forced labor if mitigating circumstances were present. The third punished those inciting peasants to leave the kolkhozy with five to ten years of forced labor. See O. V. Khlevniuk et al., eds. *Stalin i Kaganovich: Perepiska 1931–1936 gg.* (Moscow, 2001), 134, 256.

20.   The pact was signed on 25 July 1932. In his "A National Question Crosses a Systemic Border" (see note 8), Snyder convincingly maintains that even if Moscow, after Piłsudski's 1926 coup, perceived itself as open to attack, after 1930 Warsaw grew more and more willing to officially reconfirm the status quo. And it is indeed probable that—as Snyder suggests—Stalin, having resolved the Polish threat to his own satisfaction by the summer of 1932, felt free to exploit its remnants in order to remove potential internal foes and solidify his own position.

21.   Khlevniuk et al., *Stalin i Kaganovich*, 273–74.

22.   Peter Holquist, "'Conduct Merciless Mass Terror': Decossackization in the Don, 1919," *Cahiers du monde russe* 38, no. 1–2 (1997): 127–62.

23.   Sheila Fitzpatrick, *Stalin's Peasants: Resistance and Survival in the Russian Village after Collectivization* (New York, 1994); M. A. Beznin and T. M. Dimoni, "Povinnosti rossiiskikh kolkhoznikov v 1930–1960-e gody," *Otechestvennaia istoriia*, no. 2 (2002): 96–111.

24.   For the correspondence, revealed by Khrushchev in 1963, see Iurii Murin, comp., *Pisatel' i vozhd': Perepiska M. A. Sholokhova s I. V. Stalinym: Sbornik dokumentov iz lichnogo arkhiva I. V. Stalina* (Moscow, 1997), 59–69.

25.   Andrea Graziosi, *Bol'sheviki i krest'iane na Ukraine, 1918–1919 gody* (Moscow, 1997); Graziosi, "Collectivisation, révoltes paysannes et politiques gouvernementales à travers les rapports du GPU d'Ukraine de février–mars 1930," *Cahiers du monde russe* 35, no. 3 (1994): 437–632; Lynne Viola, *Peasant Rebels under Stalin: Collectivization and the Culture of Peasant Resistance* (New York, 1996); A. Berelowitch and V. Danilov, eds., *Sovetskaia derevnia glazami VChK-OGPU-NKVD*, vol. 3, *1930–1934*, bk. 1, *1930–1931* (Moscow, 2003).

26.   Stalin never worried about "splinters flying when wood is cut" (a favorite expression). And he was perhaps the foremost practitioner of the "statistical" school of repression, which destroyed entire categories to make sure specific, and even

foreseeable, problems were "solved." See A. Graziosi, O. Khlevniuk, and T. Martin, "Il grande terrore," *Storica* 6, no.18 (2000): 7–62.

27.   See Politburo decrees *O sel'sko-khoziaistvennykh zagotovkakh v Belorussii* (Russian State Archive of Sociopolitical History [hereafter RGASPI], fond 17, opis' 3, delo 912, listy 8, 42–43, Pb [politburo meeting] of 16 December 1932, protocol no. 126, p. 1); and *Ob izvrashchenii natsional'noi politiki VKP(b) v Belorussii* (RGASPI, fond 17, opis' 3, delo 917, list 7). I am grateful to Oleg Khlevniuk for reminding me of them.

28.   Danilov, Manning, and Viola, *Tragediia sovetskoi derevni*, 3:603, 611.

29.   See "Direktiva TsK VKP(b) i SNK SSSR o predotvrashchenii massovogo vyezda golodaiushchikh krest'ian," in ibid., 3:635.

30.   Italian and Polish consuls in Kyiv wrote of cases of death by starvation on the streets and in the courtyards counted not in tens, but in hundreds daily. Most, however, were peasants who had somehow been able to reach the city. Their bodies were quickly removed.

31.   These are the original words: "То, что голодание не научило еще очень многих колхозников уму-разуму, показывает неудовлетворительная подготовка к севу как раз в наиболее неблагополучных районах," from a report note [*dopovidna zapyska*] from Kosior to Stalin and the VKP(b) Central Committee, 15 March 1933. See Ruslan Pyrih, ed., *Holodomor 1932–1933 rokiv v Ukraïni: Dokumenty i materialy* (Kyiv, 2007), 771.

32.   Already on 17 May 1933, after visiting the Don region, a VTsIK (All-Russian Central Executive Committee) instructor reported a slight increase in the number of kolkhozniks reporting for work, a fact he explained by their desire to receive the food that local authorities distributed on the basis of days actually worked. In most villages, he added, the "conspiracy of silence" had been broken: peasants who up to a few weeks before refused even to talk to the authorities had started to speak at meetings, mainly to ask for bread in exchange for the promise to work properly. In the same way and even more than in 1921–1922, therefore, the Famine served government policy by breaking the peasants' backs (see Werth and Moullec, *Rapports secrets soviétiques*, 155). On 11 July an Italian diplomat argued precisely the same point on the basis of the opinions of some German agricultural specialists returning from Ukraine and Kuban (see Graziosi, *Lettere da Kharkov*, 152ff.).

33.   *Yearbook of the United Nations* (New York, 1948–1949), 959; Raphael Lemkin, *Axis Rule in Occupied Europe* (Washington, D.C., 1944), 82. See J. Otto Pohl, "Stalin's Genocide against the 'Repressed Peoples,'" *Journal of Genocide Research* 2, no. 2 (2000): 267–93.

34.   N. Valentinov [Vol'skii], "Tout est permis," *Le contrat social* 10 (1966): 19–28 and 77–84. As the author noted in this short but insightful article, Stalin and Hitler belonged to the very small group of a peculiar and terrible kind of twentieth-century European revolutionary, those for whom "everything is permitted."

35.   The case for genocide has been argued, for instance by Kul'chyts'kyi, from yet another point of view, that is, by presenting the Famine both at the pan-Soviet and the Ukrainian level as an ideologically motivated genocide, in view of its being the outcome of choices inspired in 1929 by what was the then current understanding of communist ideology and tenets among the Soviet leadership. The fact that there were communist ideals, however primitively conceived, behind Stalin's revolution from above and thus behind the policies that provoked the 1931–1932 crisis is difficult to contest. It is certainly difficult to maintain that Stalin was ignorant of what such policies could provoke. The experience of 1921–1922 had already shown this, and before 1927 Stalin himself had told Trotsky more than once that to abandon NEP in favor of accelerated industrialization and collectivization would cause a crisis in the relations with peasants and result in famine (a word he did use). A hypothesis such as Kul'chyts'kyi's thus contains at least a kernel of truth, but I believe that Stalin, though knowing that the 1929 offensive would cause a crisis, did not anticipate its seriousness, and in fact at the end of 1930 believed he had won the battle with the countryside. Therefore, this argument, though in part correct and rightly pointing to the role of communist ideology and erroneous economic beliefs, ends up in my opinion rather weak.

36.   In a letter to the author, Oleg Khlevniuk rightly points to the fact that many of Stalin's policies had what could be called "genocidal" features. He writes, "No matter what problem arose in the country, it was solved through the application of violence directed at specific and well-defined sociocultural or national groups of the population." These groups and the treatment inflicted on them, from preventive measures to liquidation, varied over time according to the internal and international situation and the despot's own beliefs. They included Cossacks, peasants, the old and the various national intelligentsiias, religious figures, and "enemy nations"—from Poles and Germans to Jews and Chechens, etc. The Holodomor must be understood against this background.

37.   Some may maintain that a racially or plot-theory motivated genocide, based on the convinction that a nation's or a "race's" future requires the extermination of another people is just as "rational." After all, the decision to exterminate originates from what might pass for logical reasoning. Yet I believe that an important difference lies in the kind of rationality involved. Stalin's was fairly sophisticated, implying as it did the use of a refined theory of the process of nation and state building, peasant behavior, the possibility of influencing them, and so on.

38.   A. Graziosi, "The Great Famine of 1932–1933: Consequences and Implications," *Harvard Ukrainian Studies* 25, no. 3–4 (2001): 157–65.

39.   Needless to say, I am not claiming this was the reason for the Soviet collapse. However, the unredeemable nature of its past certainly complicated the life of a system that was slowly strangled by its economic, demographic, and national contradictions and that was finally killed by the attempts to reform it.

40.   Jacob Burckhardt, *Meditazioni sulla storia universale*, 2nd ed. (Florence, 1985), 35ff.

Sources and Resources on the Famine in Ukraine's State Archival System[*]

HENNADII BORIAK

During the last few years the State Committee on Archives of Ukraine has developed and posted on the web a comprehensive database of documentary resources on the 1932–1933 Famine-Genocide in Ukraine. The site includes the pilot version of the "Electronic Archive of the Holodomor" with full texts of 1,500 documents from state archives of Ukraine and Russia; the most comprehensive available set of photo and film documents on the Holodomor; related party leaders' speeches; a full list of documentary online exhibitions posted on the web by state archival institutions; an online bibliography of source publications and surveys of sources; announcements on the latest source publications; documentary Internet resources; and other reference materials.[1]

Today archivists and scholars are approaching the end of the second decade of intensive efforts to seek out, declassify, and make available these materials. The time has come to draw conclusions and at least pose, if not fully answer, the following questions: What is the documentary base for studying the Famine-Genocide? Is the information potential of this documentary base sufficient? What is the ratio between published and unpublished documents? Are there any as yet unstudied groups of documents? Should we expect sensational new archival

[*] This article is based on a paper delivered at the symposium "Breaking the Great Silence on Ukraine's Terror-Famine on the 75th Commemoration of the Famine and the 25th Anniversary of the HURI Famine Project," Harvard Ukrainian Research Institute, Cambridge, Mass., 30 November–1 December 2007. A video recording of the event is available at http://video.google.com/videoplay?docid=-4651663665332904756&hl=en (accessed 16 April 2008). A shortened Ukrainian-language version of this article was published as "Arkhivy Holodomoru 1932–1933 rr. v Ukraïni: Suchasnyi stan ta perspektyvy doslidzhen'," Konstanty (Kherson), no. 1 (13) (2007): 3–13.

discoveries? In other words, what is the state of the art of Holodomor archives and sources?

The next question is what should be done further. Which sources should be put on the agenda as priority items for researchers?

First of all, let us recall that in Ukraine *not a single archival document* about the Famine was published until the end of the 1980s. For over half a century, all Western historiography relied solely on oral evidence, episodic documents from diplomatic archives, materials from journalists, and sporadic photographs. Generally, this was the period of what can be called the "pre-archival" historiography of the Holodomor.

During the almost two decades of "archival" historiography, we have learned that a great mass of written information, both secret and open, about the preconditions, causes, scale, and consequences of the Famine had been produced at all levels of state power. Even though they were aware of the dangerous nature and content of these documents, central authorities were unable to establish total control over or prohibit the flow of papers "born of" the Holodomor, much less destroy them all. Party committees, governmental institutions, and newspaper editorial boards were deluged with letters, complaints, appeals, and statements about the real situation in rural regions.

The most precarious time for these documents was the initial period of their existence. It may safely be assumed that a significant part, mainly those related to the registration of illnesses and deaths in hospitals and village councils, was destroyed immediately, "while still hot." Today we have in our possession documented, direct instructions issued by governing bodies ordering the destruction of such records,[2] and also evidence confirming the falsification of causes of death in civil registry and medical records of that time.[3]

Paradoxically, in the post–World War II period the preservation of republic- and all-Union-level documents in secret, controlled-access archival collections (*spetsfondy*) secured their conservation and integrity exceptionally well. In this instance the regime itself rendered a service to future historians. By contrast, the documents of local authorities and regional institutions and organizations were regarded as inconsequential and thus "neglected," never to be put into closed secret collections.

After the collapse of the communist regime, the archival administration of Ukraine undertook a disclosure of documents unrivaled in any other territory of the former USSR. This process has continued, and today the proportion of classified documents in the state archives of Ukraine (which stood at 0.55 percent at the end of 2006 and 0.47 percent at the end of 2007) is one of the lowest in Europe.[4] Naturally, among the declassified materials the documents related to the history of the 1932–1933 Holodomor were in greatest demand. They have become the principal source base for scholarly research into this painful topic and have helped to destroy numerous false myths of the twentieth century.

Unfortunately, in the maelstrom of political battles in present-day Ukraine, the source base for researching the Holodomor has become the object of numerous attempts to manipulate the facts. I would like to mention just a few.

One of them, recently advanced by the Ukrainian communists, is very curious. Their leader, Petro Symonenko, cynically misconstruing documents of the higher party leadership, has included Stalin's henchmen of the 1930s as being among the first to publish historical sources related to the Holodomor: "Communists were the first to provide information about the Famine in Ukraine. It was as early as 1933 that the Politburo of the Communist Party of Ukraine published all of the most significant materials about the situation of 1932–33, not hiding the truth about these events." Furthermore, the "archives expert" assuredly declares, "Today one cannot find a single document that proves that the Famine was an intentional policy to eradicate the peasantry," and draws the conclusion, "Therefore, the position of the Communist Party today is the following: famine and tragedy did occur, but this was a tragedy not just of the Ukrainian nation, but of all the peoples of the Soviet Union and Ukraine."[5] His thesis is thus quite simple: there indeed was a famine, the communists were the first to recognize the starvation, and they published all the relevant documents themselves. We can therefore close the books on the Holodomor archives.

Fittingly, the position of the Ukrainian communist leader fully coincides with the conception of another document—the guidelines proposed by the Russian Federal Archival Agency (Rosarkhiv) for a collaborative project titled "Famine in the USSR: 1932–33." I would like to cite some of the cynical instructions contained in that document: "Considering the 'Ukrainian factor,' we should select the documents in such a way that they prove the universal character of the grain-requisitioning agricultural procurement process in 1932 . . . in the crisis regions"; and "at the same time, document selection should be conducted in such a way as to portray a tragedy of the Soviet peasantry as a whole, without emphasizing Ukraine . . . To this end, one can publish a selection of civil registry offices' certificates from the Volga region [Povolzh'e], with specific records of starvation deaths in the Lower and Middle Volga territories in 1933." In other words, by selecting several examples of deaths by starvation in Ukraine, the Volga region, and the Northern Caucasus, the project could conclude that the entire USSR suffered from the Famine equally.[6] Of course, there is no denying that famine struck other parts of the Soviet Union. However, this should in no way diminish the fact that Soviet authorities deliberately targeted ethnically Ukrainian rural areas with measures to ensure the starvation of the peasantry there, and that the devastation wreaked by this action was massive.

Moreover, in keeping with the best traditions of communist propaganda, the above document recommends emphasizing that "anti-Soviet organizations . . . used the existence of the Holodomor in the USSR to achieve their propaganda aims." It was obviously in this way that the document's authors expect us to interpret the efforts of the Ukrainian public in Western Ukraine in 1933 to provide the world with information about the Holodomor. The author of this concept is Viktor Kondrashin, a professor at Penza University and director of the project. In a recent interview he characterized the Ukrainian law acknowledging the Holodomor as an act of genocide (adopted in November 2006) as "dancing on the bones of victims" and an attempt by "certain political forces" to "line their pockets" using the history of the Famine.[7]

Ukrainian historians and archivists categorically rejected this approach and proposed instead to prepare a number of individual volumes of documents devoted to specific regions of the USSR, with relevant comments and conclusions in each volume. We insisted on distinguishing between famine resulting from state grain procurements, and *artificial* famine resulting from *grain procurements coupled with a total non-grain food requisition*. Our proposals were met with displeasure and labeled as an attempt to "blur the overall picture of this phenomenon [starvation] in the common history of the state that existed at that time." "The differentiation between 'famine' [*holod*] and 'famine-genocide' [*Holodomor*] would not withstand scholarly criticism," we were told, and then presented with the initial results of our Russian colleagues' manipulation of source material: "Analysis of documents discovered in the Russian State Archive of the Economy that deal with vital statistics for 1933 has already shown that the correlation of mortality and birthrates in Ukraine and Russia in the epicenter of the Famine was roughly the same. *No unique distinction of these processes in Ukraine was observed when compared to Russia* [my emphasis]."[8] This dreadful conclusion, which has the sound of a judge passing sentence, was reached *before any* serious study and comparative analysis of the vital statistic registers from affected territories in Ukraine and Russia had begun.

Let these statements lie on the conscience of those who make them.

ARCHIVAL SOURCES

To give an idea of the large and diverse complex of archival sources on the Holodomor of which we are aware today, we refer to the classification scheme proposed by Ruslan Pyrih, the well-known Ukrainian historian of the Famine-Genocide and former director of the State Archives of Ukraine.[9] Table 1 at right, based on our very preliminary estimates, shows how each group of documents figures in the overall representation of source materials for studies of the Holodomor.

The first group consists of documents of the Soviet Union's highest organs of power: the Central Committee of the Communist Party of the Soviet Union (CPSU), the Council of People's Commissars of the USSR, the People's Commissariat of Land Resources, the Committee for Procurement, the Unified State Political

Table 1. Approximate proportion of the principal groups
of documents on the 1932–33 Famine-Genocide in Ukraine.

Source of documents	percentage of total
All-Union organs of power and administration	12
Republic-level organs	23
Local party and government organs	49
Foreign diplomatic legations, political and public organizations, and materials of foreign press media	1
Letters, claims, complaints, petitions	8
Oral testimonies (published)	7

Administration (OGPU), the All-Union Committee for Migration, and many others. The documents in this group are of crucial importance for studying the main issues of the Famine-Genocide. They are kept in Moscow at the Archive of the President of the Russian Federation, the Russian State Archive of Social and Political History (RGASPI), the State Archive of the Russian Federation (GARF), and the Russian State Archive of the Economy (RGAE).

The documents of the Politburo of the Central Committee of the CPSU, the supreme state and party authority, reflect the true policy followed in all areas of societal life. Some 270 matters directly related to Ukraine were discussed during the 69 meetings of the Politburo held in 1932–1933. The reason for such careful and consistent attention to the republic was, according to Stalin, "the danger of losing Ukraine," a strategic region for the Soviet empire in which the rural population retained its spirit of patriotism and aspirations to independence and resisted collectivization, grain and food procurements, and sovietization.

A mass of Chekist documents from the OGPU, preserved at the Central Archive of the Federal Security Service of Russia (FSB), also belongs in this group. Here one finds dispatches, reports, circulars, and instructions regarding the social and political situation in rural regions of Ukraine—discontent, resistance to grain confiscation, group protests, the intent to emigrate, a mass exodus out of Ukraine, and measures in response, including the repression of participants in protests, the hunting down and arrest of kulaks and people in nationalistic organizations, more confiscations of grain and bread, and the organization of blockades at railroads.

The statistics generated by the higher levels of the OGPU should be treated with considerable caution, since they were subjected to an almost incredible downward revision. For example, one report from April 1932 contains information about "eighty-three cases of swelling and six cases of death because of starvation in Ukraine."[10] One can only imagine what sort of manipulation such data had experienced.

The first category should also include a group of NKVD archival fonds held at the State Archive of the Russian Federation. These concern specially displaced persons—the so-called "kulak deportation" to the Ural region and the other parts of the GULAG. There are also 32,000 personal files of Ukrainian "special settlers" held at the State Archive of Sverdlovsk Oblast.[11]

Key documents from the archives of higher party and government agencies were published extensively in the early 1990s, usually with financial support from Western institutions. This was the decade of "skimming off the cream" from declassified Russian archives. More recently, thanks to the efforts of leading Russian historians, some landmark titles have appeared, including *Stalin i Kaganovich: Perepiska* (2001; 2003), *"Sovershenno Sekretno": Lubianka Stalinu o polozhenii v strane* (2001–), and the distinguished five-volume edition, *Tragediia sovetskoi derevni*, prepared by the prominent historian Viktor Danilov and his colleagues (the third volume [pub. 2001] contains documents from 1930 to 1933). Also notable is a volume edited by the Ukrainian historians Iurii Shapoval and Valerii Vasyl'iev, which contains the travel diaries of Viacheslav Molotov and Lazar' Kaganovich during their visit to Ukraine and the Northern Caucasus in 1932–1933, along with Politburo minutes from that period and other documents from the Russian State Archive of Social and Political History (2001). Many documents of this first group were later republished in Ukrainian editions.[12]

The second group includes documents of republic-level (i.e., Ukrainian) governmental and administrative bodies: the Central Committee of the Communist Party (Bolshevik) of Ukraine (KP[b]U), the Council of People's Commissars of the Ukrainian SSR (RNK), the All-Ukrainian Central Executive Committee (VUTsVK), the People's Commissariat of Land Resources, the Ukrainian Collective Farms Center, the State Political Administration (GPU), the People's Commissariat of Justice, the General Prosecutor's Office, the Supreme Court, and various other people's commissariats (i.e., Health Care, Education, and others). These documents are preserved in Ukrainian central and departmental (*haluzevi*) state archives: the Central State Archives of Public Organizations (TsDAHO), the Central State Archives of Supreme Bodies of Power and Government (TsDAVO), the State Archives of the Security Service of Ukraine (DA SBU), and the State Archives of the Ministry for Internal Affairs (DA MVS). Almost all of the documents of the Communist Party and a part of the key documents of Soviet governmental agencies have already been published.

This group is notable for its high informative level as to the immediate causes, conditions, mechanics, technologies, and executors of the man-made Famine.

There is extensive factual material regarding the total confiscation of foods, extensive food shortages, widespread bloating from starvation, mortality, and cannibalism. The absolute subordination of these republic-level authorities to instructions from Moscow is quite striking in the documents here. They are similar in nature to the first group, as they were produced by the republican counterparts to all-Union structures.

The documents of the Central Committee of the KP(b)U are the most informative because of the party's key place among governing bodies. It should be noted, however, that the amount of information in a document is almost always inversely proportional to the level of its origin: the higher the level, the less information about the Famine it contains.

Documents of republic-level executive authorities (mainly the People's Commissariat of Land Resources, Ukrainian Collective Farms Center, All-Ukrainian Union of Agricultural Collectives, and the People's Commissariat of Workers' and Peasants' Inspection) contain extensive factual material about the Famine according to the sector of administration involved. As for the archives of the People's Commissariat of Health Care, at least 12,000 files from the early 1930s were destroyed in Kyiv in 1941 as Soviet troops retreated.[13]

The documents of law enforcement bodies—the GPU, People's Commissariat of Justice, and the General Prosecutor's Office—are of specific importance, as these institutions participated intensively in the mass repression of the peasantry and carefully documented their activities.

The archives of the GPU—the most powerful branch of the republic's repressive punitive-justice system—were the last major collection related to the Holodomor to be declassified in Ukraine.[14] In 2006 over 150 documents (more than 1,000 pages) were made public in digital form through posting on the Internet; subsequently, they went on display for over a year in a large-scale touring exhibition titled "Declassified Memory." During this time, the exhibit was shown in every oblast capital city (usually supplemented with local documents from the state oblast archives) and arguably has become the most influential instrument for raising awareness in Ukraine about this tragedy. The process of making these documents public reached its culmination in August 2007 with the publication of a documentary collection bearing the same name (and comparable content) as the exhibit.

GPU papers of day-to-day operations document the extent of Chekist and militia involvement in the mass confiscation of foods through intensive repressions. The GPU's statistics, as mentioned earlier, include falsified data about the scale of starvation and mortality; even the Chekists themselves recognized this fact. One can cite the chief of the Kyiv oblast branch of the GPU, from March 1933, to appreciate just how much the agency's figures deviate from the real situation in Ukraine and complicate the process of drawing up a register of victims' names:

"The GPU *raion* [district] offices do not keep a tally, and sometimes even a village council does not know the true number of those who died from starvation."[15] In a similar vein, the chief of the Kharkiv city branch department of the GPU stated in June 1933 that "the mortality rate has become so high that a host of village councils have stopped registering those who died."[16] We have no reason to believe that the situation in other regions was any different.

The documents of the People's Commissariat of Justice and the Prosecutor's Office of the Supreme Court of the Ukrainian SSR provide evidence of government-led terror against the peasantry through the judicial system.

The key documents of the State Archives of the Ministry of Internal Affairs are concentrated in the collections titled "Protocols of Special Proceedings and Tribunals [*troiky*]" and "Criminal Cases in Trial Courts and Extrajudicial Organs." The criminal files reveal the shocking truth about the total social collapse in rural regions and the mental aberrations that led to the eating of cadavers and cannibalism. Of the 83,000 such cases launched by the NKVD in 1932–1933, we have a record of no more than 3,000 today (the rest were destroyed in 1956). More than 2,500 people were convicted of cannibalism. Documents for 1,000 of these cases have survived. In my opinion, the public is still not ready today to accept these grisly photo and text records. However, the Kherson Oblast State Administration has posted a documentary piece titled "The Famine of 1932–33 in Kherson Oblast" on the Internet and published eleven photographs without any reference to their origin. Three of them appear to be photos from the criminal cases of those convicted of cannibalism.

A separate block of documents of the Ministry of Internal Affairs archive contains the approximately 426,000 criminal cases of so-called special settlers and deportees—persons interned in 1932–1933 in the Krasnoiarsk territory, the Irkutsk, Kemerovo, Tomsk, and other oblasts, and the Komi Republic.[17]

The third group is the largest. It includes the documents of local party and government organs: oblast, city, and raion committees of the Communist Party; oblast and raion executive committees; and the local organs of the GPU, the militia, the judiciary, the prosecutor's office, health care bodies, educational institutions, workers' and peasants' inspections, village councils, and the like. The orders issued by these agencies provide little information, as they essentially applied the political estimations and directives coming from above to local conditions. In contrast, the reports and correspondence of regional offices with Ukrainian central authorities provide highly detailed and personalized accounts of the events involved. They present a vivid picture of starvation and death, local political attitudes, and manifestations of mass protest and resistance.

The documents of this group are concentrated primarily at the state archives of those seventeen (present-day) oblasts on whose territories the Holodomor raged and in the network of corresponding oblast archives of the SBU and the Ministry of Internal Affairs. Only a tiny part of these documents have been published, naturally in local editions.

The fourth group of documents includes materials from foreign diplomatic legations, political and public organizations, and the foreign press.[18] This is the smallest and least studied group of documents in Ukraine. Included in this category are reports of the German and Italian general consulates in Kharkiv, Kyiv, and Odesa; information from British diplomats and economic experts; and analyses by the Polish police. The authors of these reports were unanimously convinced of the undeniably man-made nature of the Famine, a deliberate measure taken by the regime to suppress the Ukrainian peasantry.

The fifth group includes letters, affidavits, complaints, petitions, and diaries. These are vivid, deeply psychological depictions of the personal experience when confronted by the reality of this tragic event.

Letters were typically sent to republic-level institutions in Kharkiv (VUTsVK, RNK, and the Central Committee of the KP[b]U), or addressed personally to highly placed officials (such as Hryhorii Petrovs'kyi or Vlas Chubar), or to local government, land-management, and law-enforcement bodies. The letters of peasants addressed to Stalin, Molotov, and Kaganovich and sent to the editorial boards of central newspapers constitute a significant block of documents. Mikhail Kalinin's office alone received approximately 30,000 letters. The higher party and governmental leaders were quite aware of the damning nature of these letters, which reflected the slaughter that had become the reality of life in the village. It is hardly accidental that five million letters from the 1930s disappeared from the Russian State Archive of the Economy without a trace.[19] Only a small number of items from this group has been published. No special editions with such documents have yet appeared in Ukraine.

Recently the State Archives of the SBU made public excerpts from two unique diaries from the Famine era, one by Oleksandra Radchenko, a teacher, and another by Dmytro Zavoloka, a party investigator and official with the Kyiv Oblast Auditing Commission. Both reveal a profound comprehension of the situation and attempts to come to grips with the tragedy emotionally. Both the diaries and their authors were suppressed.[20]

In sum, according to our preliminary estimates, the entire archival legacy of the Holodomor consists of about 70,000 to 80,000 documents concentrated within about 2,000 archival fonds and collections. The overwhelming majority of them, being documents of local authorities, are found in the regional archives of Ukraine.

Published Sources

As for the body of published material that is out in the open and has gone into academic and public circulation, the general bibliography of scholarly works related to the Holodomor of 1932–1933 includes about 1,500 items. Of these, only about 250 are documentary publications: up to 35 book editions of documents (of which 26 are regional in scope) that appeared between 1990 and 2007, and the remainder—over 200 items—journal and newspaper publications. In total, documentary publications reproduce about 5,000 archival documents, representing some 6 to 7 percent of their total number.[21]

Is this a great or a small number? I think it is sufficient. Despite the relatively small number of items, the most important and crucial materials in terms of range and content have been published. They afford us the possibility of making conceptual and legal conclusions about the conditions, causes, and consequences of the man-made Famine. Moreover, today there is not much hope of making sensational new discoveries of related documents.

The continual republication of documents that have appeared in earlier editions is strong testimony to a certain exhaustion of the source base. The share of republished materials in documentary editions ranges from 30 to 70 percent, suggesting that their publishers are beginning "to go round in circles." The latest document collections confirm this thesis. I would like to mention several of them.

First and foremost is the comprehensive *Holodomor 1932–1933 rokiv v Ukraïni: Dokumenty i materialy*, compiled by Ruslan Pyrih and published in August 2007.[22] The author is not only a renowned researcher, but also a pioneer in the publication of documents from the former Archives of the Central Committee of the Communist Party of Ukraine. Let us remember that in 1990, on his own risk and responsibility, he personally untied the"archival sources bag" and published the first documentary collection on the Holodomor in Ukraine.[23]

Pyrih's 2007 publication, with approximately 700 documents from 20 Ukrainian and 5 Russian archives, is the largest known collection of Holodomor documents. Reprinted items constitute more than 60 percent of the total number. Thus, while *searching* for archival documents was the primary task for publishers of archival materials in the late 1980s, today's authors face the no less daunting problem of *selecting* documents for their compilations. Generally, this book may be considered the first documentary encyclopedia as well as the first scholarly anthology on the Holodomor. It truly represents a culmination of a succession of broadly based national documentary publications that appeared over the last two decades.

At about the same time, the volume *Rozsekrechena pamiat': Holodomor 1932–1933 rokiv v Ukraïni v dokumentakh GPU-NKVD* came out, containing declassified materials from the archives of the secret police.[24] The exceptional value of these documents lies in the fact that they reveal the lesser-known elements of the mechanics of creating the Famine and also the scale of the resistance coming from the Ukrainian village. First and foremost, they clearly document the confiscation of non-grain foodstuffs from villagers. This signals a specific operation that transformed the grain confiscation into a widespread famine. Second, these documents reconstruct the larger picture of the spread of anti-Soviet sentiment: the mass walkout of peasants from collective farms and their claims for the return of their horses and plots, the seizure of assets, and open acts of protest. This, naturally, spurred the authorities to an energetic fight against "counterrevolution." See, for example, the anti-Soviet leaflet from the Chernihiv region from the early 1930s (figure 1, below). The main idea of this "enemy propaganda" is, to quote, "Down with Soviet power, which oppresses people and forces them into slavery!" In fact, this is a counterrevolutionary appeal![25]

After the openly anti-Ukrainian signal from Stalin—his instruction not to "lose Ukraine" in his letter of 11 August 1932 to Kaganovich[26]—the agencies of the GPU were transformed into an instrument of terror against the peasantry. It is in the Chekists' documents that we find the (in my opinion) sensational definition used by the Chekists themselves for their operation in the villages—"*rural terror.*" This is the official terminology. The epithet "Petliurite," i.e., nationalist, is always used alongside the adjective "kulak" to mark not only the class enemy, but also the ethnic enemy at whom the genocide was aimed.[27]

A collection of documents of the GPU organization in Crimea includes clear instructions on establishing railroad blocks in order to prevent the shipping of grain northward, to the starving Ukrainian villages.[28]

The source base for yet another recent Kyiv publication, *Ukraïns'kyi khlib na eksport—1932–1933* (2006) by Volodymyr Serhiichuk, are the archives of the organizations responsible for removing grain from Ukraine both to meet the needs of the domestic market (i.e., the USSR) and to dump the grain aggressively onto the European market in the late 1920s to early 1930s. The lives of millions of Ukrainian peasants became the terrible price for this policy.[29]

As for recent regional publications, I would like to note the volumes prepared by Sumy, Vinnytsia, and Odesa archivists in 2005–2007, based primarily on local archives. The second edition of the Odesa volume, and also the Kharkiv, Cherkasy, Luhansk, and Donetsk volumes, should be mentioned as notable new contributions to the growing bibliography of regional documentary collections.[30]

NEW RESEARCH

In the context of our thesis that there has been a certain exhaustion of the archival source base for identifying the key moments and mechanisms in the creation of the Famine, I would like to draw your attention to several new, top-priority bod-

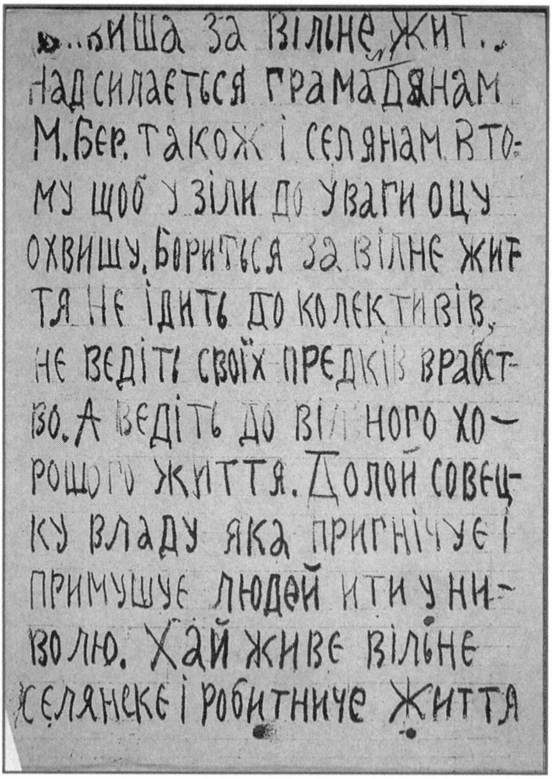

Figure 1. Anti-Soviet leaflet titled "For a Free Life!" (*Oxvisha za vil'ne zhyttia*) distributed in the city of Berezna in the Chernihiv region. Berezna Museum of Regional History, 2 copies.

Transcription: Охвиша за вільне життя надсилається грамадянам м. Бєр[езна] також і сєлянам втому щоб узіли до уваги оцу охвишу. Бориться за вілнє життя. Нє ідить до колєктивів, не вєдіть своїх прєдків врабство. А вєдіть до вільного хорошого життя. Долой совєцку владу яка пригнічує і примушує людей ити у ниволю. Хай живє вільнє сєлянскє і робитниче життя.

Translation: Leaflet for a Free Life, sent to the citizens of the city of Ber[ezna] and also to the villagers in order that they give this leaflet their consideration. Fight for a free life. Do not go to the collectives, do not lead your ancestors [*sic*] into slavery. Lead them, rather, to a free, good life. Down with Soviet power, which oppresses people and forces them into slavery. Long live a free peasants' and workers' life.

ies of material and the prospects for new investigative projects, especially for a careful reconstruction of the course of the tragedy of the Ukrainian village and an estimation of its consequences.

The first segment of the documentary base, almost completely unexamined and unavailable until recently, are the vital statistics registers kept by local civil registry offices. In accordance with enacted legislation, they have been held in the archives of the Ministry of Justice for seventy-five years and closed to researchers. The seventy-fifth anniversary of the Great Famine coincides with the termination of the confidentiality measures for personal information in the registers. At the request of the State Committee on Archives of Ukraine, oblast state archives have launched a large-scale project aimed at an early declassification and acquisition of the extant registers for 1932–1933 and subsequent years for preservation by the state. (In many cases, one volume of these registers will contain entries up to the end of the 1930s.)

In general, we can speak of about 4,000 vital statistics registers acquired by the state archives.[31] This amounts to at least one million pages of records for 1932–1933. According to very preliminary calculations, they contain information about no more than three million deaths. The extant mortality/birth registers for the years of 1932–1933 cover *a maximum of one-third* of the territory afflicted by the Famine, and mortality records *directly attributed* to the Famine constitute *no more than 1.5 percent* of the total mortality records of civil registry offices. The reason behind this was the strict prohibition on recording starvation as a death factor at that time. Thus, direct indications of death because of starvation ("starvation," "unbalanced diet," "exhaustion," "emaciation," "atrophy," "dystrophy," and "avitaminosis") are rare. At the same time there are certain regularities in identifying euphemistic diagnoses ("dropsy [edema]," "heart dropsy," "dysentery," "pneumonia," "intestinal tuberculosis," "swelling," etc.) and certain compound diagnoses (pneumonia-emaciation, myocarditis-emaciation, etc.). Figure 2, below, shows an example of one of these diagnoses.

In addition, medical and paramedics' documents were assigned names only for local residents, so that hundreds of thousands of unfortunate people fleeing starving villages remain anonymous in documents, which simply list them as nameless "beggars." Special methods will be needed to properly assess the demographic data as well as to reconstruct the instructions given to local physicians in making diagnoses. As noted earlier, the Chekists themselves acknowledged that local authorities produced falsified data about the scale of starvation and mortality.

Thus, this unique group of documents must be studied not only by historians, but also by professional physicians and demographers. The concentration of the registers in twenty-five state archives today (whereas previously they had been dispersed among hundreds of raion and local depositories) will open up this pos-

...нська с/рада Ставищанського району „21" червня міс. 1932 р. № 24

86

1. Прізвище померлого Коробій його ім'я Хросина по-батькові Олексія

2. Де постійно жив (назва району та села або міста, вул., буд. №) Є. Антонівка

3. Помер(ла) „21" червня міс. 1932 р. 4. Чоловік, жінка (підкреслити).

5. Вік „8" (скільки повних років мав)

6. Для дітей, що померли, не доживши до 1 р., точно зазначити: а) народилося „1" міс. 193 р.

б) якою у матері була померла дитина: перша, друга, або 5 в) батьки дитини живуть укупі, чи може розійшлися, батько помер, покинув родину, розлучилися тощо вкупі г) вік матері 45 років.

7. Громадянство померлого УСРР 8. Національність Українець

9. Родинний стан померлого: парубок, дівчина, удівець (а), одружений (а), розлучений (а)—підкреслити.

10. Чи здобував прожиток сам, а як не сам, то хто утримував На утриманні батьків

11. а) Ремество, промисел, посада і спеціяльність у них б) Якщо жив коштом держави чи громадських організацій, зазначити на які саме (пенсія, стипендія тощо) в) Якщо жив з інших джерел, точно зазначити з яких саме — Хліборобство

12. Становище в зайнятті: робітник, службовець, реміснник, кустар-кооперований (чл. артілі) чи ні, торговець, помічний у зайнятті член родини тощо—зазначити які саме. Для сільських господарів: одноосібник чи член колгоспу (комуни, с.-г. артілі, СОЗ'у) — Чл. С/г. арт. „Надія"

13. Назва підприємства, установи чи закладу, зазначаючи яке виробництво, де працює, служить або господарює. — в С/г. арт. „Надія"

14. Де помер (удома, в лікарні, дит. будинку тощо) в дома Якщо вдома, то чи користувався з лікарської допомоги померлий (так, ні) Ні

15. Причина смерти—зазначити докладно ~~з голоду~~ Не відомо

Додано лікарську довідку № — Чи може запис складено на оголошеного від суду за померлого —

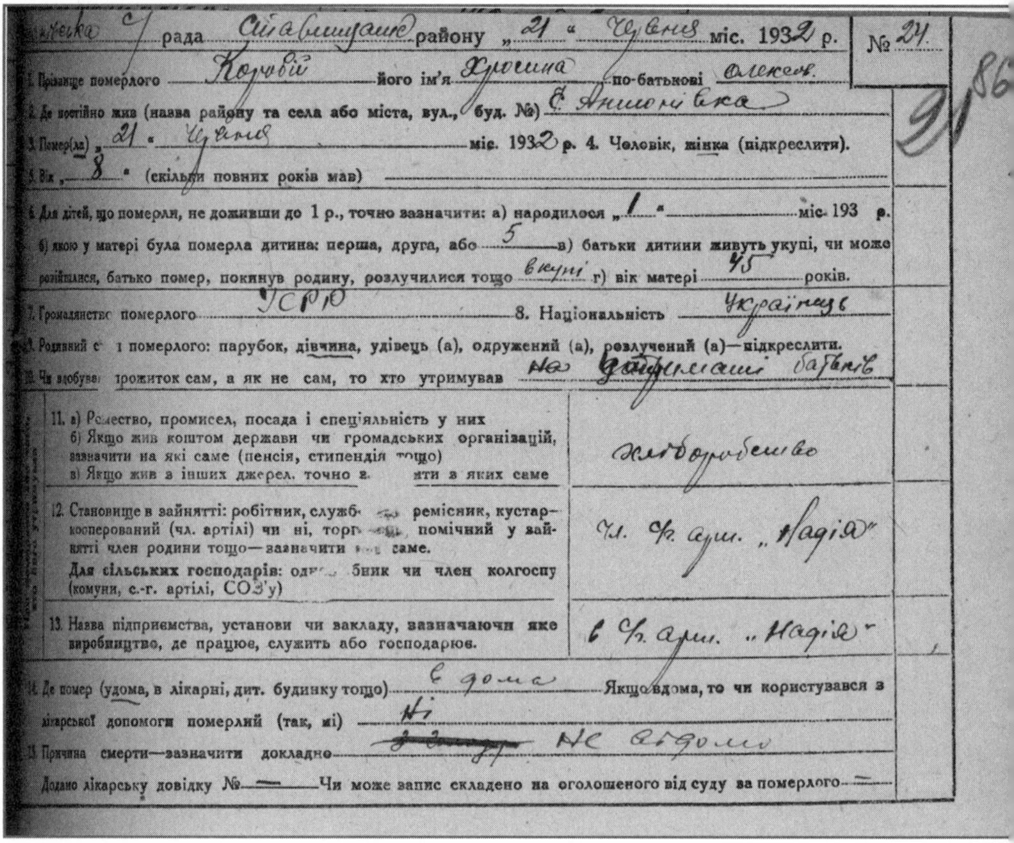

Figure 2a. Falsified diagnosis: Death record for eight-year-old Iefrosyniia (Khrosyna) Korobii, from the death record book for Antonivka village, Stavyshche raion, Kyiv oblast, 21 June 1932.
State Archives of Kyiv Oblast, fond 5634, op. 1, spr. 969, ark. 86.

14. Де помер (удома, в лікарні, дит. будинку тощо) в дома Якщо вдома, то чи користував... лікарської допомоги померлий (так, ні) Ні
15. Причина смерти—зазначити докладно ~~з голоду~~ Не відомо
Додано лікарську довідку № — Чи може запис складено на оголошеного від суду за померлого

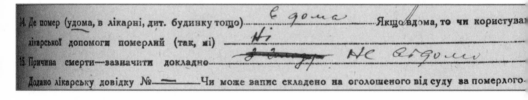

Figure 2b. Close-up of line showing crossed-out cause of death (“*z holodu*”).

sibility, although clearly it will be a complicated undertaking and one that may raise more questions than it answers. Certainly, the low number of documented names of Famine victims could itself become a factor for new insinuations on the part of those denying the Famine as genocide.

Another source that researchers and publishers of documents generally overlook is local press materials; namely, newspapers and nonperiodical publications from 1932–1933. Until recent times local press publications were more likely to be used as illustrations to the written documentation rather than as historical sources.[32]

These materials have an extraordinary informative potential. They contain numerous references about the harvesting process, reports on sessions of itinerant raion courts with their verdicts (including the death sentence), as well as dozens of names of persons condemned and lists of the villages posted on the "black list." The publications of local press media make it possible to reconstruct the personal aspect of this tragedy on a microlevel in each village. They contain invaluable data for compiling a chronicle and martyrology of those repressed during the Holodomor as well as a very accurate geographical map of the Great Famine.

Utilizing this resource requires considerable effort, a special methodology, and a carefully organized work plan, mainly because it is dispersed throughout a number of libraries, and also because of its great size. According to the Ukrainian Book Chamber, more than 1,000 newspaper titles were published in the 486 raion centers of the Ukrainian SSR in 1932–1933 with varying periodicity. The total number of the available press materials may be estimated at about 150,000 items.

A third group of documents, problematic in nature, are photos from the time of the Holodomor. Documentary photographs provide fertile ground for manipulation of public opinion, especially by those who deny the Famine-Genocide. For obvious reasons, one cannot find significant photographic evidence about the regime's crimes in the state archives. Only a tiny group—something in the range of one hundred or so items—may be considered authentic. I refer to thirty photos of victims of the Famine in Kharkiv taken by the engineer Alexander Wienerberger (preserved in the collection of the Viennese Cardinal Theodore Innitzer); the collection of about eighty photos by Marko Zhelezniak from the village of Udachne in Donetsk oblast; several unique photos by Mykola Bokan', the persecuted rural amateur photographer from Chernihiv oblast; and some photos made illegally by foreign correspondents.[33]

Understandably, the very limited quantity of Famine photos has led to the unfortunate practice of substituting photographs from other historical periods and regions as depictions of the 1932–1933 Famine in Ukraine. As a rule, these are photos from the period of the first Soviet Famine in 1921–1922, mostly from the

Volga Region.[34] On the other hand, some Russian authors use authentic Ukrainian Famine pictures to depict the famine in the Middle Volga region.[35]

This negligent practice, which sometimes is even a conscious decision on the part of some authors to use striking but non-authentic photos as the symbols of the awful tragedy, allows critics to claim falsifications (and not just of the photos). The latest publication by Ruslan Pyrih,[36] the documentary exhibitions from the archives of the SBU entitled "Declassified Memory,"[37] as well as many online exhibitions posted on the web by Ukraine's oblast state administrations have already become targets for such charges, particularly on the part of the communists. They regularly use arguments about falsified photos to discredit legitimate works.

On the other hand, it is a great mistake, in my opinion, to underestimate the value of the huge collection of official photo and film documents from the period of collectivization and the Holodomor. There are no dead bodies or emaciated corpses in these staged propaganda photos. However, they reproduce the frightening ambience in which the tragedy of the Ukrainian village took place: children gather frozen potatoes while smiling for a reporter; kulaks (in Ukrainian: *kurkuli*) are "dekulakized" and denounced in dramatic fashion; so-called "enemies of the people" are unanimously condemned; there are meetings of collective farmers, meetings of committees of poor peasants; columns of Chekists on the march; and there is harvesting with modern agricultural equipment and the issuance of rations to collective farmers.

Official photo-documents of 1932–1933 can be a powerful instrument in shaping public awareness. This was well understood by Andrei Marchukov, the author of a recent publication of documents titled "Operatsiia 'Golodomor'" in the popular Russian historical magazine *Rodina*.[38] Besides providing generally uninformative textual documents, he shows a sequence of eleven photographs that evoke the peaceful, cheerful, almost pastoral atmosphere of harvesting without a hint of the catastrophe. Photos from Ukraine are shown alongside photos from the Volga region, effectively "leveling out" any differences in the situation between Ukraine and other regions of the USSR. The one and only photo showing famine, titled "Starving People in Ukraine," looks unconvincing and somehow mythological. To add to this, the singular Famine shot is—seemingly "accidentally"—missing any reference to an archival source, while all the others, without exception, have specific references to archival collections. The reader thus receives the message that the provenance of the photograph is unknown and likely suspect. It cannot be attributed to a reputable archival source; otherwise the author would have mentioned it.

In my opinion, it is high time to make a definitive identification of the existing and widely used photos, possibly with the participation of scholars internationally via a special Internet forum, in order to dot the i's in the ongoing discussions regarding the quantity and authenticity of the documents of this group. I would especially like to stress the necessity for the creation of a centralized memorial register and the publication of all photo documents, without exception, that contain scenes from everyday life in the Ukrainian village during the early 1930s. They are presently dispersed throughout various archival and museum repositories. According to preliminary calculations, there are *no more than ten thousand* such items. The publication of these documents will make possible a reconstruction of the landscape of the tragedy in the widest sense.

The fourth segment of the documentary base that I would like to mention when speaking about potential avenues of investigation is regional archival materials. They constitute the largest group in terms of their quantity, but the least utilized to date in terms of research and publication. These documents allow us to study the question on the microhistorical level and to create the most accurate possible chronicle of the Great Famine in its regional manifestations.

By the order of the president of Ukraine, since the end of 2006 all state archives have been working on a nationwide register of archival fonds bearing a memorial character, in order to give due recognition to the many victims of famines and other political repressions of Soviet times. Documents related to the Great Famine have became the core of this "National Register of Memorial Collections." All of the materials are being professionally catalogued by collection (*fond*), file (*sprava*), and document group or individual document. At present some two thousand descriptions of these fonds have been sent to Kyiv to be posted on the website of the State Committee on Archives.[39]

One more group of unstudied documents consists of the over 400,000 criminal files of so-called special deportees—persons interned in 1932–1933 in different parts of the GULAG, and also 1,000 criminal files of persons convicted of cannibalism. They are kept at the State Archives of the Ministry of Internal Affairs of Ukraine. To this group should be added the archival fonds of the NKVD at the State Archive of the Russian Federation that concern specially displaced persons—the so-called kulak deportation.

The documents for the 1,000 cases of those convicted of cannibalism include photographs of the material evidence and of those who committed these crimes. This unique indictment of the communist regime remains a still unpublished body of documents related to the Famine.

Let me add a few words regarding the project titled "Electronic Archive of the Holodomor: A Consolidated Register of Archival Documents Online."[40] This project aims to provide open access to sources by publishing (electronically) *all* the documents related to the Famine-Genocide on the Web. Texts would appear in the database either transcribed from their published versions, or as scans of original documents (in PDF or other graphic formats). Each document would be accompanied by all requisite information—date, caption, location, bibliographic information (if need be), and so on. The pilot version of the database includes up to 2,000 documents. Consequently, it is the largest electronic documentary resource and most comprehensive chronicle dealing with the day-to-day life of the Ukrainian village at that time. We consider this project to be the final step in making available the broadest possible selection of Holodomor sources and the culmination of considerable work on documents and their publication over an almost twenty-year period. It should be noted that this large-scale project was made possible due to the generous support of the Ukrainian Studies Fund, Inc.

To conclude, let me present not a sensational but a unique, long-anticipated document (and the only one of its kind discovered to date). It is, in the full sense of the word, a "last minute find," which confirms the need to further process the regional documentary mass, in particular, death records at local civil registry offices. This document, recently found at the State Archives of Odesa Oblast and shown in figure 3 below, is the first *direct documentary* evidence testifying to large-scale actions by state authorities in 1934 to eliminate any traces of crime against the Ukrainian peasantry.

On 13 April 1934, the Odesa Oblast Executive Committee sent a "top secret" instruction to all local councils and raion executive committees of Odesa oblast (with copies to all party raion committees and inspectors of the National Economic Survey Administration [*Upravlinnia narodnohospodars'koho obliku*], later—the Central Statistical Board).[41] According to this instruction, in March 1934 the National Economic Survey Administration carried out an inspection of civil registry offices in village councils throughout Ukraine. It was found that "this work is actually in the hands of class enemies—kulaks, Petliura henchmen, special deportees, etc." This supposedly resulted in "*fraudulent overestimation* of death rates and *underestimation* of birth rates [my emphasis]" as well as the loss of records at civil registry offices' archives: "At village councils the records are kept in such a way that anyone can have free access to them. It was discovered that in some village councils the records have been simply stolen, possibly, for counterrevolutionary purposes."

With regard to supervising death and birth records at local archives and establishing "order" within vital statistics, certain measures were taken. Among them one can find the following instruction: "To withdraw death registration books from village councils: for 1933 from all village councils without exception and for 1932 according to the list provided by the National Economic Survey Administration. To transfer the withdrawn village council registration books to the raion executive committees for safekeeping as classified material."

From here the fate of the records remains unknown. No traces of the withdrawal or destruction of death records have been found in the archives of the central office of the National Economic Survey Administration kept in Kyiv.[42] Most likely, they were destroyed even before World War II. Paradoxically, in this case the lack of documents within a well-preserved and integral archival fond is much more revealing and significant than would be in the case of their availability. Those documents represented a fatal danger for the authorities; thus, they were destroyed "at the top," but hundreds of instructions, forgotten or neglected, were disseminated throughout Ukraine, with dozens of copies accumulated as classified documents in the fonds of Ukrainian local authorities and institutions.

I do hope that new, similar findings will soon appear to testify to the measures taken by the authorities to get rid of dangerous documents, so devastating to the reputation of the Soviet state. This will enable us to better understand the present-day circumstances of the remarkable phenomenon known as the "Holodomor archives."

НГ/ПК.
У.С.С.Р.

ОБЛИСПОЛКОМ.   ВСЕМ ГОРСОВЕТАМ и РАЙ ИСПОЛКОМАМ ОД. ОБЛАСТИ.

18.IV. 34 г.   Копия: - РАЙ ПАРКОМАМ, ИНСПЕКТОРАМ УНГО.-
№ 184/тс

УНХУ Украины в конце Марта этого года произвело обследование состояния работы ЗАГС"а в ряде сельсоветов всех областей Украины. Это обследование дало ряд фактов, свидетельствующих о преступно-безобразно поставленном учета рождаемости и смертности в сельсоветах.

В ряде сельсоветов эта работа находится фактически в руках классово-враждебных элементов - кулаков, петлюровцев, административно высланных и т.д.

Так, обследованием установлено, что в Одесской области в с.Дриново I - Джашевского района ведение книг ЗАГС"а было поручено некоему ЖЕРУЛЮ, дважды судившемуся и работавшему в сельсовете в порядке отбывания принудительных работ. После того, как этот вор-рецидивист сбежал с деньгами сельсовета, ведение книг ЗАГС"а было поручено сыну кулака Веськи. Нет сомнения, что в значительной части сельсоветов области дело учета населения находится в чуждых руках, классово-враждебных, прямо заинтересованных в запутывании учета населения, в искажении истинного положения вещей, в кулаческом преувеличивании смертности и преуменьшении рождаемости.

Как результат работы чуждых элементов, обследованием установлено, что на одних и тех-же умерших лиц выписывалось по две, три карточки, одни и теже лица регистрировались дважды на территории двух сельсоветов, или учет населения мышленно вовсе не производился. Даже в лучших по постановке дела сельсоветах актовые книги ведутся небрежно, нет подписей заявителей и смерти, подписей должностных лиц, нумерация перепутана, есть пропуски в книгах, что создает почву для всяких злоупотреблений и вредительских махинаций.

Хранение книг в сельсоветах такое, что к ним имеет доступ всякий". В некоторых сельсоветах оказалось, что книги просто похищены, возможно для контр-революционных целей.

Такое положение дальше не может быть терпимо и потому Облисполком ПРЕДЛАГАЕТ:

I. Немедленно организовать проверку сельских ЗАГС"ов, поставив задачу такого обследования - очистку аппарата ЗАГС"а от классово-враждебных элементов, упорядочение делопроизводства ЗАГС"а и хранения книг, как текущей регистрации, так и архив. Для проведения проверки выделить Инспектора УНГО и 2-х работников, особо доверенных, из состава районного актива.

2. Для обеспечения сплошного и постоянного контроля над ведением книг и предотвращения случаев повторных регистраций вменить в обязанность председателям сельсоветов не позже каждого 2-го числа посылать вторые экземпляры записей в Инспектуры Н.Х.У. Остающиеся в сельсоветах записи актов и пересылаемые в УНХУ вторые экземпляры должны иметь подписи заявителей и скреплены печатью сельсовета и подписями председателя и

Нач. спец-бюро
I Класса

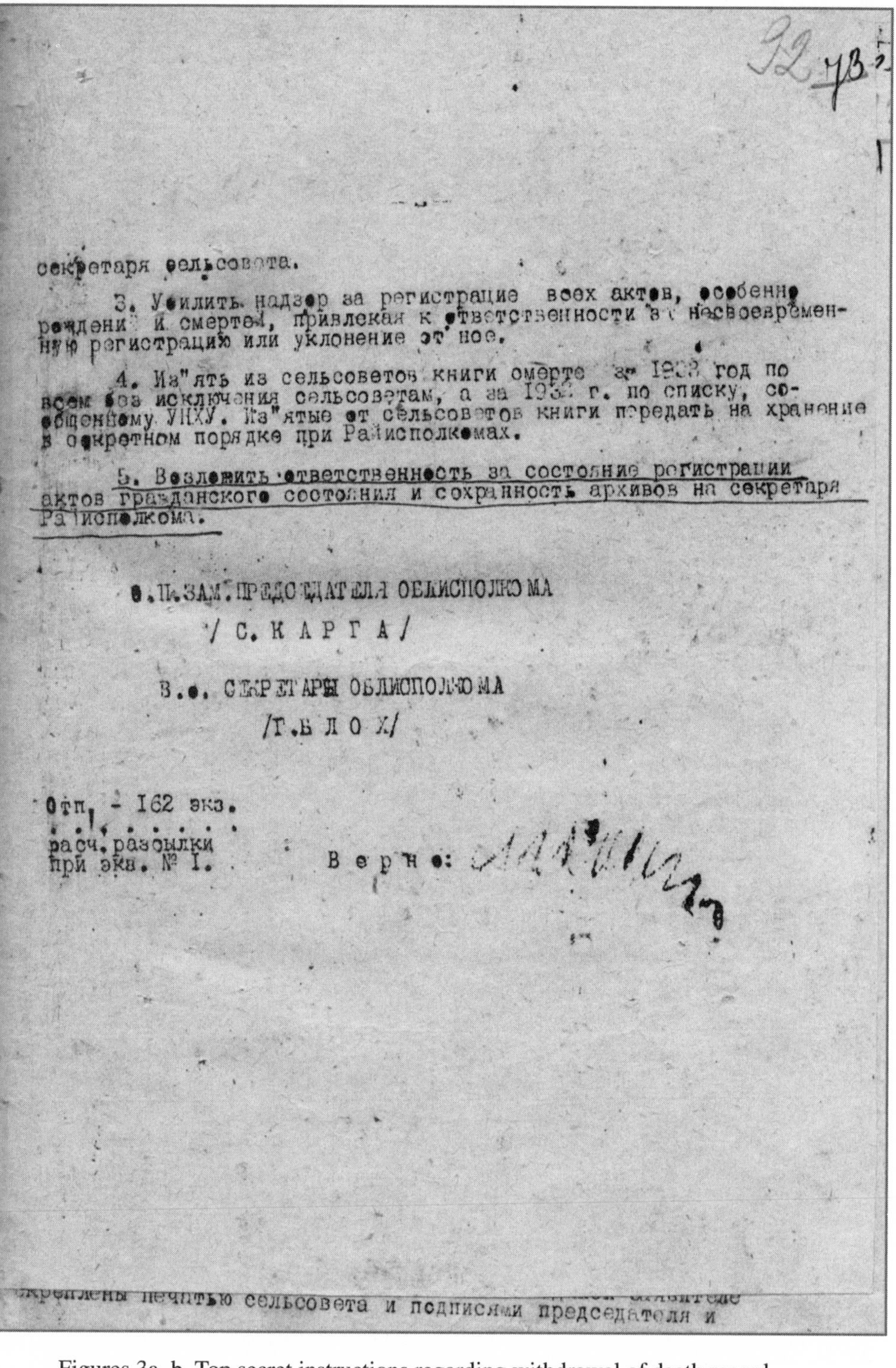

секретаря сельсовета.

3. Усилить надзор за регистрацией всех актов, особенно рождений и смертей, привлекая к ответственности за несвоевременную регистрацию или уклонение от нее.

4. Из"ять из сельсоветов книги о смерти за 1933 год по всем без исключения сельсоветам, а за 1932 г. по списку, сообщенному УНХУ. Из"ятые от сельсоветов книги передать на хранение в секретном порядке при Райисполкомах.

5. Возложить ответственность за состояние регистрации актов гражданского состояния и сохранность архивов на секретаря Райисполкома.

В.П.ЗАМ.ПРЕДСЕДАТЕЛЯ ОБЛИСПОЛКОМА

/С.КАРГА/

В.о. СЕКРЕТАРЫ ОБЛИСПОЛКОМА

/Т.БЛОХ/

Отп. - 162 экз.
расч. разсылки
при экз. № 1.   Верно:

закреплены печатью сельсовета и подписями председателя и

Figures 3a–b. Top secret instructions regarding withdrawal of death record books for the years of 1932–1933 from the local civil registry (ZAGS) archives of Odesa oblast into classified storage at the raion executive committees, April 1934. State Archives of Odesa Oblast, fond R-2009, op. 1, spr. 4, ark. 91–92.

НГ/П.К.   Экз. №   Сов. Секретно.
У.С.С.Р.   . . . .

– – –

ОБЛИСПОЛКОМ.   ВСЕМ ГОРСОВЕТАМ И РАЙИСПОЛКОМАМ
                          ОД[ЕССКОЙ] ОБЛАСТИ.

– – –

13.IV.34 г.   Копия: - РАЙПАРКОМАМ, ИНСПЕКТОРАМ УНГО.
№ 478 о.с[екретно]
overwritten by hand: 184 т[аємно]

УНХУ Украины в конце Марта этого года произвело обследование состояния работы ЗАГС"а в ряде сельсоветов всех областей Украины. Это обследование дало ряд фактов, свидетельствующих о преступно-безобразной постановке учета рождаемости и смертности в сельсоветах.

В ряде сельсоветов эта работа находится фактически в руках классово-враждебных элементов—кулаков, петлюровцев, административно высланных и т. д.

Так, обследованием установлено, что в Одесской области в с. Ясиново I— Любашевского района ведение книг ЗАГС"а было поручено некоему ЖЕРУЛЮ, дважды судившемуся и работавшему в сельсовете в порядке отбывания принудительных работ. После того, как этот вор-рецидивист сбежал с деньгами сельсовета, ведение книг ЗАГС"а было поручено сыну кулака Ваське. Нет сомнения, что в значительной части сельсоветов области дело учета населения находится в чуждых руках, классово-враждебных, прямо заинтересованных в запутывании учета населения, в искажении истинного положения вещей, в жульническом преувеличивании смертности и преуменьшении рождаемости. Как результат работы чуждых элементов, обследованием установлено, что на одних и тех-же умерших лиц выписывалось по две, три карточки, одни и теже лица регистрировались дважды на территории двух сельсоветов, или учет населения умышленно вовсе не производился. Даже в лучших по постановке дела сельсоветах актовые книги ведутся небрежно, нет подписей заявителей и смерти, подписей должностных лиц, нумерация перепутана, есть пропуски в книгах, что создает почву для всяких злоупотреблений и вредительских махинаций.

Хранение книг в сельсоветах такое, что к ним имеет доступ всякий. В некоторых сельсоветах оказалось, что книги просто похищены, возможно для контр-революционных целей.

Такое положение дальше не может быть терпимо и потому облисполком
П Р Е Д Л А Г А Е Т:

1. Немедленно организовать проверку сельских ЗАГС"ов, поставив задачу такого обследования—очистку аппарата ЗАГС"а от классово- враждебных элементов, упорядочение делопроизводства ЗАГС"а и хранения книг, как текущей регистрации, так и архив. Для проведения проверки выделить Инспектора НГО и

2-х работников, особо доверенных, из состава районного актива.

2. Для обеспечения сплошного и постоянного контроля над ведением книг и предотвращения случаев повторных регистраций вменить в обязанность председателям сельсоветов не позже кадждого 2-го числа посылать вторые экземпляры записей в Инстпектуры Н. Х. У. Остающиеся в сельсоветах записи актов и пересылаемые в УНХУ вторые экземпляры должны иметь подписи заявителей и скреплены печатью сельсовета и подписями председателя и секретаря сельсовета.

3. Усилить надзор за регистрацией всех актов, особенно рождений и смертей, привлекая к ответственности за несвоевременную регистрацию или уклонение от нее.

4. Из"ять из сельсоветов книги смертей за 1933 год по всем без исключения сельсоветам, а за 1932 г. по списку, сообщенному УНХУ. Из"ятые от сельсоветов книги передать на хранение в секретном порядке при Райисполкомах.

5. Возложить ответственность за состояие регистрации актов гражданского состояния и сохранность архивов на секрктаря Райисполкома.

      О. П. ЗАМ. ПРЕДСЕДАТЕЛЯ ОБЛИСПОЛКОМА
      /С. КАРГА/

      В. о. СЕКРЕТАРЯ ОБЛИСПОЛКОМА
      / Г. БЛОХ/

Отп. – 162 экз.

. . . .

расч. разсылки

при экз. № 1.   Верно:

Figure 3c. Transcription of figures 3a–3b.

NG/PK.   Copy No.

Ukr.S.S.R.

– – –

OBLAST

EXECUTIVE

COMMITTEE   TO ALL CITY AND RAION EXECUTIVE

COMMITTEES OF OD[esa] OBLAST

– – –

13.IV.34

No. 478 – t[op] s[ecret]

overwritten by hand 184-s[ecret]

Copy: — RAION PARTY COMMITTEES, UNHO* [NATIONAL ECONOMIC

SURVEY ADMINISTATION] INSPECTORS

At the end of March this year UNKhU* [National Economic Survey Administra-tion] of Ukraine carried out an inspection of the work of ZAGS [Civil Registry of Vital Statistics] offices in a number of village councils in every region of Ukraine. This inspection revealed a series of facts testifying to the criminally outrageous manner in which birth and death registration is conducted in the village councils.

In a number of village councils this work is actually in the hands of class enemies—kulaks, Petliura henchmen, special deportees, etc.

Thus, the inspection established that in Odesa oblast, in the village of Iasinovo I [Iasenove Pershe], Liubashivka raion, the entire recording process of the Civil Registry of Vital Statistics was entrusted to a certain ZHERUL′, a twice convicted criminal, who was sentenced to compulsory labor at the village council. After this repeat-offender thief ran off with the village council monies, the management of ZAGS books was entrusted to Vas′ka, the son of a local kulak. There is no doubt that in a great number of village councils the job of registering the population is in alien hands, the hands of the class enemy, directly interested in muddling the registration [process], in distorting the true state of things, in fraudulently inflating mortality and underestimating birthrates.

The inspection also revealed that as a result of the activity of class enemies, there were numerous cases when two or three cards were issued to one and the same deceased person, or the same person was registered twice in two village councils, or that vital statistics were maliciously not registered at all. Even in the best-managed village councils, registration books are handled carelessly, entries for deaths lack testifying signatures, [or] the signatures of council officials, the numerical order is jumbled, there are omissions in the [registration] books, all of which is conducive to all sorts of abuses and harmful machinations.

At village councils [registration] books are kept in such a way, that anyone can have free access to them. It was discovered that in some village councils the [registration] books were simply stolen, possibly for counterrevolutionary purposes.

This situation can no longer be tolerated and for this reason the Oblast Executive Committee P R O P O S E S:

1. To immediately organize an inspection of village ZAGS offices, with the aim of purging class enemies from the apparatus, [and] regularizing office routines and custody of [registration] books, including current registrations as well as archived material. To dispatch an UNHO [National Economic Survey Administration] inspector and two especially trustworthy workers from among the raion [party] activists to conduct the inspection.

2. To impose on the chairmen of village councils responsibility for mandatory forwarding of a second copy of [all] registrations to the Inspectorate of the National Economic Survey Administration no later than on the 2nd day [of each month] to ensure complete and continuous control over [registration] bookkeeping and to prevent occurrences of double registration. Both the copy of registrations remaining in the village council and the copy sent to the National Economic Survey Administration must be signed by those who reported the event and authenticated with the seal of the village council and signatures of the village council chairman and secretary.

3. To increase supervision over all document registration, especially birth and death [records] by holding [individuals] accountable for untimely registrations or for failure to register.

4. To withdraw death registration books from village councils: for 1933 from all village councils without exception and for 1932 according to the list** provided by the National Economic Survey Administration. To transfer the withdrawn village council registration books to the raion executive committees for safekeeping as classified material.

5. To make the secretary of the raion executive committee personally responsible for the proper conduct of civil registrations and the security of the archives.

> A[cting] F[irst] Dep[uty] Chairman of the Oblast Executive Committee
> /S. Karga/

> A[cting] Secretary of the Oblast Executive Committee
> /G. Blokh/

Number of copies typed — 162 copies
Recipients listed on copy no. 1
Verified [with the original]: *signature*

---

* The text uses both Russian and Ukrainian terminology interchangeably, e.g., *Upravlinnia Narodnohospodars'koho obliku* (UNHO) and *Upravlenie narodnokhoziaistvennogo ucheta* (UNKhU); see also "V. o." (*vykonuiuchyi obov'iazky*) in the second signature.
** No such list has been found in the archives to date.

Figure 3d. Translation of figures 3a–3b.

NOTES

1. See the special section of the official web portal of the State Committee on Archives of Ukraine, "Genotsyd ukraïns'koho narodu: Holodomor 1932–1933 rr.," http://www. archives.gov.ua/Sections/Famine/index.php (also in English as "Genocide of the Ukrainian People: The 1932–1933 Famine," http://www.archives.gov.ua/Sections/ Famine/index-eng.php). The "Electronic Archive of the Holodomor" comprises the core of this section; see http://www.archives.gov.ua/Sections/Famine/Publicat/.

2. Central State Archives of Supreme Bodies of Power and Government of Ukraine (hereafter TsDAVO), fond 318 (National Economic Survey Administration [*Upravlinnia narodnohospodars'koho obliku*], Kharkiv and Kyiv, 1923–1941), 1596 files (*spravy*).

3. See, for example, the death record from Antonivka village, Stavyshche raion, Kyiv oblast (21 June 1932), with cause of the death "died of starvation" crossed out and "unknown" added in its place (State Archives of Kyiv Oblast, fond 5634, opys 1, sprava 969, arkushi 86r–86v [hereafter op., spr., ark.]). See figures 2a and 2b.

4. Regarding the declassification of archives, see the web portal of the State Committee on Archives of Ukraine, "Rozsekrechuvannia arkhiviv," http://www.archives.gov. ua/Archives/Rozsekr-arch.php.

5. See interview with the leader of the Ukrainian Communist Party conducted by Anton Zikora, "Symonenko vyznaie til'ky odyn henotsyd—'Turechchyny proty Virmeniï,'" *UNIAN*, 24 November 2006, http://unian.net/news/print.php?id=174464 (accessed 28 April 2008). Unless otherwise noted, all translations are my own.

6. The cited document is preserved in the author's archives. See also facsimile publication of the guidelines for the above-mentioned project with comments: O. Palii, "Moskva nakazala Ianukovychu," *Ekspres* (Lviv), 5–6 May, 2007.

7. "Russian Federal Security Service (FSB) Archives to Offer Real Picture of the 1929–1932 Famine, Says University Rector," *Action Ukraine Report (AUR)*, no. 832, 22 April 2007, http://action-ukraine-report.blogspot.com/2007/04/aur832-apr-22-stalins-great-terror-70.html#a6; "Rassekrechennye arkhivy FSB prol'iut svet na golodomor," *Izvestiia*, 17 April 2007, http://www.izvestia.ru/news/news132448/. For other statements by Mr. Kondrashin, see "Istoriki nazyvaiut mifom genotsid ukrainskogo naroda v 1932–1933 godakh," *news.mail.ru*, 19 December 2007, http://news.mail.ru/politics/1532494; "Unikal'nye dokumenty iz arkhivov FSB o zhertvakh golodomora 1930-kh gg.," *www.directory.com.ua*, http://directory.com. ua/news101429.html. On the latter site Kondrashin states, "It would be absolute stupidity if the Famine were to be recognized as a genocide of the Ukrainian people." All sites accessed 29 April 2008.

8. Source document from the author's archives.

9. The first general professional survey and classification of sources on the Holodomor

was offered by Ruslan Pyrih in 2003 in a special chapter of a foundational work published by the Institute of History of Ukraine, National Academy of Science of Ukraine; see R. Ia. Pyrih, "Dokumenty z istoriï holodu u fondakh arkhivoskhovyshch Ukraïny," in *Holod 1932–1933 rokiv v Ukraïni: Prychyny ta naslidky*, ed. V. M. Lytvyn, 8–26 (Kyiv, 2003); http://www.archives.gov.ua/Sections/Famine/ Documents/Famine_32-33.php. An updated version of this survey is published as an introduction to a more recent publication; see Ruslan Pyrih, ed., *Holodomor 1932–1933 rokiv v Ukraïni: Dokumenty i materialy* (Kyiv, 2007), 5–33.

The 2003 volume also includes several other surveys of sources on the Holodomor: by N. V. Platonova and T. V. Vrons'ka on the State Archives of Ministry of Internal Affairs of Ukraine (pp. 26–41); by V. I. Marochko on materials in the Russian archives (pp. 41–50); by Vas. M. Danylenko and V. I. Prystaiko on the State Archives of the Security Service of Ukraine (SBU) (pp. 81–98); and an analysis of published documents by O. M. Veselova and Marochko (pp. 50–81).

10.   Pyrih, *Holodomor 1932–1933 rokiv v Ukraïni*, 12.

11.   V. I. Marochko, "Rosiis'ki arkhivni dzherela ta zbirnyky dokumentiv pro prychyny ta obstavyny holodomoru," in Lytvyn, *Holod 1932–1933 rokiv v Ukraïni*, 45–46.

12.   O. V. Khlevniuk et al., eds., *Stalin i Kaganovich: Perepiska 1931–1936 gg.* (Moscow, 2001; English ed., New Haven, 2003)); G. N. Sevost'ianov et al., eds., *"Sovershenno Sekretno": Lubianka—Stalinu o polozhenii v strane (1922–1934 gg.)*, 10 vols. (Moscow, 2001–); V. Danilov, R. Manning, and L. Viola, eds., *Tragediia sovetskoi derevni: Kollektivizatsiia i raskulachivanie*, vol. 3, *Konets 1930–1933* (Moscow, 2001); Iurii Shapoval and Valerii Vasyl'iev, *Komandyry velykoho holodu: Poïzdky V. Molotova i L. Kahanovycha v Ukraïnu ta na Pivnichnyi Kavkaz, 1932–1933 rr.* (Kyiv, 2001).

13.   Vadim Kogan, "Search and Findings: Primary Sources concerning the Famine in Ukraine in 1932–1933 (Medical Aspects [of] the Problem), *Agapit* (Kyiv), no. 13 (2002), http://histomed.kiev.ua/agapit/ag1/ag01-15e.html; republished on the the the website *ArtUkraine.com*, http://www.artukraine.com/famineart/medasp.htm.

14.   For the most recent survey of the SBU archives, see Vasyl' Danylenko, "Dokumenty Haluzevoho derzhavnoho arkhivu Sluzhby bezpeky Ukraïny iak dzherelo vyvchennia Holodomoru 1932–1933 rr. v Ukraïni," in *Rozsekrechena pam'iat': Holodomor 1932–1933 rokiv v Ukraïni v dokumentakh GPU-NKVD*, comp. V. Borysenko et al., 20–44 (Kyiv, 2007).

15.   Cited in Pyrih, *Holodomor 1932–1933 rokiv v Ukraïni*, 22.

16.   Ibid.

17.   See N. V. Platonova and T. V. Vrons'ka, "Arkhivni materialy NKVS i DPU u fondakh Derzhavnoho arkhivu MVS Ukraïny," in Lytvyn, *Holod 1932–1933 rokiv v Ukraïni*, 26–41.

18. For a survey of this group, see Pyrih, *Holodomor 1932–1933 rokiv v Ukraïni*, 28–31.

19. Marochko, "Rosiiśki arkhivni dzherela ta zbirnyky dokumentiv pro prychyny ta obstavyny holodomoru," 47–48.

20. See these diaries in Borysenko et al., *Rozsekrechena pam'iat'*, 539–72.

21. See my survey of published documents: Hennadii Boriak, "The Publication of Sources on the History of the 1932–1933 Famine-Genocide," *Harvard Ukrainian Studies* 25, no. 3–4 (2001): 167–86; http://www.archives.gov.ua/Sections/Famine/BoryakHarvard.pdf. An online bibliography of related source materials is published by the State Committee on Archives of Ukraine; see "Holodomor 1932–1923: Publikatstiï ofitsiinykh dokumentiv, inshykh arkhivnykh materialiv, spohadiv, svidchen'; Materialy do bibliohrafiï," http://www.archives.gov.ua/Sections/Famine/Documents/Bibliogr.php. It is based on a more comprehensive work published in 2001 by the M. Gorkii Odesa State Research Library and the Institute of History of Ukraine, National Academy of Science of Ukraine; see L. M. Bur'ian and I. E. Rykun, comps., *Holodomor v Ukraïni, 1932–1933 rr.: Bibliohrafichnyi pokazhchyk* (Odesa, 2001), 656 pp. See also a recent bibliography of selected documentary publications, L. P. Odynoka, L. F. Prykhoďko, and R. V. Romanovsʹkyi, comps., *Holodomory v Ukraïni 1921–1923, 1932–1933, 1946–1947: Materialy do bibliohrafiï dokumental'nykh publikatsii* (Kyiv, 2005), 55 pp.; http://www.archives.gov.ua/Publicat/Golodomori.pdf.

22. Ruslan Pyrih, ed., *Holodomor 1932–1933 rokiv v Ukraïni: Dokumenty i materialy* (Kyiv, 2007), 1128 pp.

23. Ruslan Pyrih et al., comps., *Holod 1932–1933 rokiv na Ukraïni: Ochyma istorykiv, movoiu dokumentiv* (Kyiv, 1990).

24. V. Borysenko et al., comps., *Rozsekrechena pam'iat': Holodomor 1932–1933 rokiv v Ukraïni v dokumentakh GPU-NKVD* (Kyiv, 2007), 604 pp.; full text online version, http://ssu.kmu.gov.ua/sbu/control/uk/publish/article?art_id=69643&cat_id=69642 (accessed 3 July 2008).

25. Two copies of the original leaflet under the title "Oxvisha za vil'ne zhyttia" are kept at the Berezna Museum of Regional History (Chernihiv oblast); online publication, http://www.archives.gov.ua/Sections/Avtografy/R-14.php?22. See figure 1.

26. Khlevniuk et al., *Stalin i Kaganovich*, 273–74.

27. See Vas. M. Danylenko and V. I. Prystaiko, "Dokumenty Derzhavnoho arkhivu Sluzhby bezpeky Ukraïny iak dzherelo vyvchennia holodomoru 1932–1933 rr. v Ukraïni," in Lytvyn, *Holod 1932–1933 rokiv v Ukraïni*, 81–98.

28. Borysenko et al., *Rozsekrechena pam'iat'*, 28, 57–58.

29. Volodymyr Serhijchuk, comp., *Ukraïns'kyi khlib na eksport—1932–1933* (Kyiv, 2006), 432 pp.

30. L. A. Pokydchenko, comp. *Holodomor 1932–1933 rokiv na Sumshchyni* (Sumy, 2006), 356 pp.; R. Iu. Podkur et al., comps., *Holod ta holodomor na Podilli 1920–1940 rr.*, (Vinnytsia, 2007), 704 pp.; L. H. Bilousova et al., comps., *Holodomor v Ukraïni: Odes'ka oblast' (1921–1923, 1932–1933, 1946–1947 rr.): Spohady, dokumenty, doslidzhennia* (Odesa, 2005), 152 pp.; Bilousova et al., comps., *Holodomory v Ukraïni: Odes'ka oblast' (1921–1923, 1932–1933, 1946–1947): Doslidzhennia, spohady, dokumenty* (Odesa, 2007), 460 pp.; Kharkiv Oblast State Archives and the Media Technology Research Center, "Holodomor 1932–1933 rr., Kharkivs'ka oblast': Svidchennia, dokumenty," http://www.golodomor.kharkov.ua/docs.php?lang=ua (full text database, includes 329 documents, accessed 15 May 2008); B. F. Parseniuk et al., *Nevhamovnyj bil', 1932–1933: Istorychni doslidzhennnia, narysy, svidchennia, spohady, dokumenty*, ed. S. F. Bliednov (Donetsk, 2007), 198 pp.; P. Zhuk et al., *Holodomor 1932–1933 na Cherkashchyni: Knyha pam'iati v dokumentakh ta spohadakh* (Cherkasy, 2007), 484 pp.; M. M. Starovoitov and V. V. Mykhailychenko, *Holodomor na Luhanshchyni 1932–1933 rr.: Naukovo-dokumental'ne vydannia* (Kyiv, 2008), 288 pp.

31. See public reports on the transfer of registers in November 2007: "U Lavrynovycha vyrishyly dostrokovo zaarkhivuvaty roky Holodomoru," *Ukraïns'ka pravda*, 23 November 2007, http://www.pravda.com.ua/news/2007/11/23/67313.htm; "Miniust Ukrainy peredaet v arkhivy sviditeľstva o gibeli ukraintsev ot Holodomora, *Obkom*, 23 November 2007, http://www.obkom.net.ua/news/2007-11-23/1710.shtml.

32. See for example, facsimiles of newspaper publications in the collections of documents from the Sumy, Odesa, and Luhansk regions: Pokydchenko, *Holodomor 1932–1933 rokiv na Sumshchyni*; Bilousova et al., *Holodomory v Ukraïni: Odes'ka oblast'*; Starovoitov and Mykhailychenko, *Holodomor na Luhanshchyni 1932–1933 rr.*

33. The most extensive collection of authentic photos is kept at the H. Pshenychnyi Central State FilmPhotoPhono Archives of Ukraine and presented online; see State Committee on Archives of Ukraine, "Genocide of the Ukrainian People: The 1932–1933 Famine," http://www.archives.gov.ua/Sections/Famine/photos.php.

34. Misattribution of the 1921–1923 photodocuments (mostly without any captions or references to sources) to depict the tragedy of 1932–1933 is becoming increasingly widespread. See, for example, "Holodomor u Kyievi (foto)," *Internet reporter*, 9 December 2006, http://rep-ua.com/56415.html; Raïsa Mykhailenko, "Holodomor na Chernihivshchyni: Slidy zlochynu, *Vysokyi val*, 24 January 2008, http://sian-ua.info/index.php?module=pages&act=print_page&pid=13090; Cherkasy Regional State Administration, "Holodomor 1932–33 na Cherkashchyni: Obzhynky smerty," http://www.oda.ck.ua/index.php?article=254; Kherson Regional State Administration, "Nad pam'iattiu ne vladnyi chas," http://www.oda.kherson.ua/cgi-bin/control.pl?lang=uk&type=body&id=../control/uk/data/politics/gniva.html (revealed are eleven photos, mostly from the times of the first Soviet Famine, including photos from criminal cases of those condemned for cannibalism); and

"V Berlins'komu muzeï vidkrylas' vystavka pro Holodomor," *INTV*, 15 October 2007, http://www.intv-inter.net/news/article/?id=57709269. Recently, a picture taken by the news service UNIAN was republished in the news report "Viktor Iushchenko: 'Holodomor—naibil'sha u sviti trahediia,'" *Svoboda* (New Jersey), no. 43, 26 October 2007. It shows President Yushchenko displaying a photo of victims from Samara gubernia during the first Soviet Famine as an illustration of the 1932–1933 Famine in Ukraine. The original photograph was taken by the Nansen mission and published in 1925 (see Antoni Starodworski, *Sowiecka reforma rolna: Przyczynek do zagadnen socjologicznych* [Warsaw, 1925], 49). I am grateful to Dr. Roman Procyk for alerting me to this example. The same photo, with the caption "Kladovyshche v Kharkovi. Zamerzli trupy ukraïns'kykh selian pomerlykh z holodu. 1933 rik," can be found in the discussion forum on the *Korrespondent.net* website, see http://forum.korrespondent.net/read.php?2,298227,page=1. The government newspaper *Uriadovyj kurier*, no. 191, 17 October 2007, contains a report on the official opening ceremony of the exhibition "Exterminated by Hunger: Unknown Genocide of Ukrainians" that features a photograph from Kazan gubernia, 1921. A discussion of many such misattributions can be found in the article, "Golod na Ukraine 1932–1933: Istoricheskie manipuliatsii," http://www.geocities.com/holod3233/index.html; and www.geocities.com/holod3233/false-h3.html.

35.   See the publication of the *Izvestiia* editorial office illustrated by documents from the State Committee on Archives of Ukraine web portal: Elena Loriia, "Unikal'nyie dokumenty iz arkhivov FSB o zhertvakh Golodomora 1930-kh gg.," *Izvestiia nauka*, 24 November 2006, http://www.inauka.ru/history/article69901.html.

36.   Pyrih, *Holodomor 1932–1933 rokiv v Ukraïni*. See especially the spine of the book, the dedication page, and the back endpaper (photos from the period of the 1921–1923 Famine).

37.   The exhibition is based mostly on a collection of declassified documents from the SBU archives; a facsimile of the entire documentary collection is published online, http://www.sbu.gov.ua/sbu/control/uk/publish/article?art_id=49757&cat_id=53076. Most of the documents are included in the recently published book, Borysenko et al., *Rozsekrechena pam'iat'* (see note 24).

38.   Andrei Marchukov, "Operatsiia 'Golodomor,'" *Rodina*, no. 1 (2007): 60–67; addendum, "Kogda bezumstvuiet mechta," 68–76. Online version (of introduction only), http://istrodina.com/rodina_articul.php3?id=2100&n=107.

39.   See selected materials submitted for the National Register of Memorial Collections, http://www.archives.gov.ua/Archives/Reestr/. To date, fonds from TsDAVO and the state archives of Dnipropetrovsk, Luhansk, Mykolaïv, Odesa, Kherson, Khmelnytskyi, and Chernihiv oblasts are listed.

40.   State Committee on Archives of Ukraine, "Elektronnyi arkhiv Holodomoru: Zvedenyi reiestr arkhivnykh documentiv," http://www.archives.gov.ua/Sections/Famine/Publicat/.

41. See Illustrations 3a and 3b, State Archives of Odesa Oblast, fond R-2009, op. 1, spr. 4, ark. 91, 92; published in Bilousova et al., *Holodomory v Ukraïni: Odes'ka oblast'* (facsimile); document online, http://www.archives.gov.ua/Sections/Famine?Citates. php#citate01.

In 1993 similar records from the State Archives of Vinnytsia Oblast were first referred to and quoted by Illia Shul'ha. At the time, Shul'ha had concluded that all death records for 1932–1933 were destroyed, save for a few rare exceptions (e.g., only four village councils in the entire Podillia region had preserved lists of dead for that period, accounting for 1,193 deaths). In 2003 Stanislav Kul'chyts'kyi and Hennadii Efimenko repeated the same flat conclusion about the destruction of all Civil Registry of Vital Statistics (ZAGS) records. The Russian historian Nikolai Ivnitskii (2000, 2003) followed his Ukrainian colleagues' conclusion (with no reference to archival documents) about the withdrawal and total destruction in 1934 of the ZAGS office register books from 1932–1933, noting that only few of them were preserved. In fact, at that time they could not have known that about 4,000 death register books had survived in Ukraine in local archives. See Shul'ha, "Holod 1932–1933 rr. na Podilli," in *Holodomor 1932–1933 rr. v Ukraïni: Prychyny i naslidky; Mizhnarodna naukova konferentsiia; Kyiv, 9–10 veresnia 1993 r.; Materialy*, ed. S. Kul'chyts'kyi (Kyiv, 1995), 141; Kulchytskyi and Efimenko, *Demohrafichni naslidky holodomoru 1933 r. v Ukraïni; Vsesoiuznyj perepys naselennia 1937 r. v Ukraïni: Dokumenty ta materialy* (Kyiv, 2003), 189n73 (online: http://www.history. org.ua/kul/contents.htm); N. A. Ivnitskii, *Repressivnaia politika sovetskoi vlasti v derevne (1928–1933 gg.)* (Moscow, 2000), 293; Ivnitskii, "Il ruolo di Stalin nella caresia degli anni 1932–33 in Ucraina (dai materiali documentari dell'archivio del Cremlino del Comitato centrale del Partito comunista dell'Unione Sovietica e dell'OGPU," in *La morte della terra: La grande "carestia" in Ucraina nel 1932–33; Atti del Convegno Vicenza, 16–18 ottobre 2003*, ed. Gabriele De Rosa and Francesca Lomastro (Rome, 2004), 90.

42. TsDAVO, fond 318 (National Economic Survey Administration, Kharkiv and Kyiv, 1923–1941), 1596 files.

Victory over the Peasantry[*]

SERGEI MAKSUDOV

> For you know, nuncle,
> "The hedge-sparrow fed the cuckoo so long,
> That it had it head bit off by it young."
> —*King Lear*, 1.4.214–16

These words of the Fool in Shakespeare's *King Lear* convey quite precisely what happened in the 1930s in the USSR. The peasant, feeding the country, was faced with the cruel alternatives of death by starvation or absolute submission to the state's authority. In a second civil war—a war of the poor against the prosperous, of the city against the village, of the state against the residents of rural areas—millions perished. The Soviet press called this cultural upheaval the collectivization of agriculture. Official propaganda declared that the campaign aimed to increase agricultural productivity through newly created socialist farms operating at peak efficiency. In actuality, the state sought to gain total control over the production and distribution of agricultural products. To achieve this end, the state had to control the life and death of the peasant. This battle culminated in the tragic Famine of 1931–1933. Facing starvation, peasants capitulated, surrendering themselves to the mercy of the authoritarian state. No mercy, however, was shown.

The events leading up to and following the Famine, particularly the human losses from the collectivization in Ukraine, became the focus of my research, which I completed in 1983. With generous grants from the Ukrainian Research Institute at Harvard University and from the Canadian Institute of Ukrainian Studies in Edmonton, Alberta, I prepared a lengthy manuscript, which is currently available at the libraries of these two institutes.[1] The present article draws on various parts of this longer work, emphasizing four important topics: the legislative actions that helped bring on the Famine; the diet of Ukrainian villagers during the collectivization; the dehumanizing effects of the Famine as it was seen by survivors; and the demographic assessment of the Famine, including estimates of population losses of that period.

THE REDEFINITION OF LEGAL NORMS

The kolkhoz system created in 1930–1931 enabled the state to procure a noticeably larger amount of grain. As Joseph Stalin said in 1931, "The party's achievement is that, instead of 500–600 million poods of marketable grain procured in the period when the individual peasant farm prevailed, it is now possible to procure 1,200–1,400 million poods of grain."[2] The high marketability of agricultural products, however, inevitably led to the decrease of farm products. A peasant, who had been promised a good life, became aware that he was getting less and less for his labor; accordingly, he lost interest in hard work. In 1932, the harvest was bad, but even worse was the job of harvesting. Basing their decisions on procurement laws of 1932, the authorities planned even bigger procurements than in preceding years, without taking into consideration how peasants were supposed to feed themselves during the remainder of the year. Moreover, the authorities enacted a number of severe laws aimed at preventing the theft of grain and punishing poor work habits.

The 1932 procurement laws encouraged state officials in Ukraine to engage in wide abuses, including the following provisions:

- Collective farm workers (kolkhozniks) and independent farmers had to surrender grain and renounce the right to retain any portion of the harvest for themselves.
- The homes of kolkhozniks and independent farmers could be searched at will and any grain found therein could be declared stolen or illegally issued.
- Kolkhozes and entire districts could be placed on a "black list," thereby allowing authorities to restrict commerce, seize goods, and repress the district administrators.
- Meat procurements could be required fifteen months in advance in regions that did not meet previous grain procurements, thereby removing domestic cattle and depriving village inhabitants of their only insurance against hunger.
- Commerce in food could be completely curtailed in cities through police cordons and restricted movement on railroads.
- Officials at all levels could be cruelly repressed.
- Seed and other funds could be removed from villages, or the shipment of such products severely restricted.

- Provisions of food and advance payment for workdays could be withheld from people in need.

The result of these actions was mass starvation and a huge loss of population.

With collectivization, Stalin began to realize his dream of a high market surplus. State grain procurements—which in the 1920s had achieved a level of about 110 million centners annually and represented approximately 14 percent of the gross yield of grain—rose to 161 million centners in the 1929 harvest; 221 million in 1930; and 228 million, or 33 percent of the gross yield of grain, in the 1931 harvest.[3] The seizure of grain from the villages was cunningly carried out. Authorities hid their intentions or lied about them, constantly striving to acquire an even higher portion. For example, in 1932, Molotov and Stalin signed into law a provision for grain procurement that contained not a word about the fact that a worse harvest was expected that year (1932) than in the preceding year (1931). Instead, the law stated that difficulties following a drought had been overcome even more successfully than previously, that in the villages the production of grain had increased, that in the cities goods were abundant, and that as a result authorities had decided to lower the state's grain procurement. To adjust the figures accordingly, the state employed a simple device: a comparison of the incomplete target quota for 1932 of 208.9 million centners (omitting the "mill" tax [*garntsevyi sbor:* a feudal-type tax in kind collected in grain by private and state enterprises from individual peasants for services such as milling]) with data from the preceding year, when procurements *together with* mill tax equaled 241.7 million. In reality, the state grain procurements proper in 1931 came to only 199.2 million. In other words, in 1932 it had been decided to take more than in 1931, and even more than had been taken in 1930, when that harvest had been unusually high. To add insult, the period of time allotted for delivering the procurements was decreased by almost a half a year. The reward for anyone who met this deadline and also produced the necessary seed fund was permission to freely sell any surplus grain at bazaars and markets.[4]

In the past there had been no formal prohibition against such sales. Various farmers, kolkhozniks, and even some artels resorted to these practices, to the displeasure of the authorities. Therefore, the state's granting such permission indicated, under the circumstances, the direct opposite of what was stated: by saying that trading could be undertaken only after complete fulfillment of the state quotas, the government had in fact introduced a type of prohibition, as it was entirely impossible to fulfill the plan in terms of the specified volume. Even orthodox Soviet historian Sergei Trapeznikov had to admit that "this was impossible and free trade did not come about."[5]

The state collected not only grain. It took increased shares of meat, milk, and eggs, and like Balzac's shagreen leather, production of these items shrank. In 1928, for example, meat production was 4.9 million tons, but by 1933–1936 it had decreased to an average of 2.6 million per year. Likewise, milk levels fell from 31 million tons to 21 million; eggs, from 10.8 billion to 5.2 billion. This drop in production was a heavy blow to the villages, which had roughly half the amount of grain, eggs, and milk—not to mention a third of the meat—that they had before collectivization.[6]

By 1932, many people had become accustomed to the state's procurement campaigns. It all seemed inevitable—the thousands of authorized agents, the searches of the property of the more prosperous villagers—such that many perceived it as a natural calamity. In Ukraine, the Party Central Committee, under a special resolution, mobilized brigades of three to four communist workers from various industrial centers to carry out the procurements. In addition, on 1 December 1932, party members in the villages were ordered to organize brigades of kolkhozniks to perform searches and to confiscate property of independent farmers.[7] According to some sources, as many as 112,000 people were enlisted in these brigades, called "tugboats" [boksirnye brigady], which were sent to districts other than their own in the belief that peasants would find participation in the plundering less offensive or awkward if performed outside their own villages.[8]

Near the end of fall 1932, the state's policy grew more cruel as it became clear that its measures had been insufficient. The Central Committee of the Communist Party (bolshevik) of Ukraine (KP[b]U) resorted to devastating methods never before used in order to fulfill the state's plan for grain procurement. As of 20 November 1932, all kolkhozes that had not fulfilled the plan were forbidden to create any reserve grain funds, whether seed, forage, or foodstuffs, or give out grain advances to the kolkhozniks. All existing funds were confiscated and credited toward procurement. Orders were issued to return so-called stolen grain, which had already been distributed to kolkhozniks as advances or funds intended for feeding people.[9]

In order to increase the pressure, a special commission was created in each oblast, which included the secretary of the party committee and the prosecutor. In many districts, between 15 percent and 20 percent of the kolkhoz administrations became subject to repressions. Special courts traveled about, examining cases of nonfulfillment of planned deliveries to the state. Hoping to punish and intimidate independent farmers, the KP(b)U Central Committee proposed to the Dnipropetrovsk and Kharkiv oblast committees that 1,500 peasants be selected in each oblast for maliciously failing to fulfill their procurement obligations according to contract. Their belongings, lands, and buildings were to be seized and sold. Political repression continued in the form of purges of party organizations and trials for the heads of sovkhozes deemed unproductive or inefficient. In December 1932 as many as 86 entire districts—over four million people—were listed on "black lists" [chernye doski],[10] with the result that fewer goods were delivered to those areas and the goods they did possess were removed. Additionally, commerce was banned, institutions closed down, and immediate repayment of credits and loans—in particular, with meat requisitions— was demanded. Furthermore, party and komsomol organizations were dissolved, and in some cases portions of the population were deported.[11]

Among the punishments for those who did not fulfill required grain deliveries was the penalty of having to surrender a fifteen months' supply of *meat* in advance.[12] In other words, the state officials knew there was no grain to be seized in payment. The peasants, of course, considered their livestock as insurance against a famine, either slaughtering the animals for food or selling them in order to buy grain. State confiscation of this livestock was a particularly malicious act. If a peasant sold his livestock on the open market, he could easily have paid his tax, but the authorities did not want it, preferring instead to take the livestock on a low fixed price as a form of punishment for the peasant's nonpayment of taxes. Such penalties in meat did not exempt the peasant from fulfilling his original grain procurement quota, which remained in effect.

The 1932 campaign featured widespread searches of homes and farms for grain that was to be surrendered to the state. Neither kolkhozniks nor independent farmers were immune. When people asked, "What will we eat?" the inevitable answer was: "You should have worked harder."

In his report the administrative head of the municipal police of the city of Kam'ianske [now Dniprodzherzhynsk] wrote as follows:

> Concealment: Soroka, Ivan Oleksiiovych, a worker living in the city of Kam'ianske, hid at his home grain brought there from the village by his sister. As a result of a search, 119 kg of wheat and 50 kg of millet were removed, and a case opened against him.
> Concealment: Shmet'ko, Mykola, a worker at the Dnipro State [Metallurgical] Plant (DDZ) hid grain at his place. As a result of a search, 48 kg of wheat were seized, and a case opened against him.
> Eighty-seven kg of various grains had been voluntarily surrendered by six people . . . .[13]

Altogether, on 23 February 1933, the Kam'ianske municipal police collected 4,438 kg of grain from kolkhozniks, farmers, peasants, and both communists and nonparty members.[14]

Frequently on the day following such a search, it was reported that officials would tour the area to catch offenders. "Well, children," they would ask those playing around a courtyard, "what have you eaten today?" If the children had eaten something or a piece of bread or some kasha were found for them at their homes, another search would be authorized. Peasants avoided using their stoves for fear of alerting police by the smoke coming from their chimneys.

Ironically, the state's income from such searches was not great, as nearly all proceeds went for the upkeep of the plunderers. The effect on the population, however, was enormous. From the peasants' point of view, the state authorities were all-powerful and ruthless. Clearly the state operated on the basis of taking its portion first and seizing grain without regard for the well-being of villagers. Under these conditions the onset of a famine was inevitable.

In his speech to the KP(b)U Central Committee plenum held in February 1933, First Party Secretary Stanislav Kosior points out that in the Dnipropetrovsk oblast it was forbidden to divulge data on the 1932 harvest, which would have shown that the state's plan for grain procurement was impossible to fulfill. What the oblast authorities ought to have done, according to Kosior, was to expose such data to be "kulak arithmetic," the machinations of the class enemy.[15] He chose to ignore the fact that these data included the state's calculations and projections as well as statistics from the kolzhozes themselves.

Notwithstanding all of the above harsh measures, the state's plan for 1932 was not fulfilled. Rather than the projected 208.9 million, it received only 188 million centners, a third of which was collected in Ukraine.[16] Nonetheless, for the population the results were devastating.

In Ukraine and the North Caucasus, the situation was much worse as well as more restrictive than elsewhere. The state prohibited the sale of railway tickets to peasants who could not prove they were moving about on official state business. Cordons around cities and at train stations and borders effectively stopped the sale of foodstuffs.[17] Whatever food did get in was out of the reach of most residents because of its high price. The state's actions placed the villagers in a desperate situation, dooming them to death by starvation.

Past experience showed that in years of bad harvests, the affected population had received a state loan for seed. No such loan was forthcoming in 1932, however. Indeed, on 23 September Stalin and Molotov drafted a memorandum to local party officials, warning that residents should not expect help from the state:

On Seed Advances

A number of local [party] organizations have turned to the Soviet of People's Commissars and to the Party Central Committee requesting seed advances for sovkhozes and kolkhozes.

In view of the fact that the present year's harvest is satisfactory and that a decreased plan [quota] for state grain procurement has been established by the government for the kolkhozes which must be completely fulfilled, the Soviet of People's Commissars [SNK] of the USSR and the Central Committee of the All-Union Communist Party (bolshevik) [VKP(b)] hereby resolve:

1. To turn down all proposals for giving out seed advances.
2. To warn that during the current year neither sovkhozes nor kolkhozes will be given seed advances for the winter or spring sowing.

3. To hold the kolkhoz chairmen, directors of machine tractor stations (MTS), and sovkhoz directors responsible for the full apportioning of seed funds for spring sowing within the period established by the Soviet of People's Commissars of the USSR and the Central Committee of the VKP(b) (no later than 15 January, 1933) and also for the complete security and integrity of those funds.

[Signed:]

Chairman of the SNK of the USSR, V. Molotov (Skriabin)

Secretary of the Central Committee of the VKP(b), J. Stalin

Moscow, Kremlin[18]

The contents of this memorandum were emphatically repeated in February 1933 by the KP(b)U Second Party Secretary Pavel Postyshev, writing in *Pravda:*

It must be explained to party and nonparty workers of kolkhozes that there cannot be any question of state aid in delivering seed stock. Grain must be found and sown by the kolkhozes, the kolkhozniks, and independent farmers themselves.[19]

A few months later, in mid-June 1933, Stalin explained the policy once again, in language even the most naïve and dull-witted could understand:

Central Committee of the VKP(b)   Top Secret

17.6.1933   Series K

No. 79/K-10

To the Secretary of the Central Committee of the KP[b]U, S. V. Kosior

Copy: To the secretaries of oblast, city, and district [*raion*] party committees

Expecting that we will continue to allow the squandering of our grain funds, several naïve comrades from among the lower party and soviet workers have mistakenly turned their gaze to the State Grain Procurement Agency [Zagotzerno] storehouses. We must finally make these comrades of ours understand that the Party Central Committee has already done everything possible that could be done on this question.[20]

Severe punishment awaited anyone who interfered with the distribution of grain. That task was now in the hands of those in the highest positions of authority, who then issued instructions to those in regional and provincial offices, asking them to prosecute anyone who compels the release of bread, grain or larger volumes of forage for purposes other than those designated. "Designated purposes" evidently did not include the feeding of kolkhozniks and independent farmers. Indeed, state leaders were deeply concerned that the population at large would seize and consume food slated for other needs, such as the feeding of livestock. This fear is the context for the following memorandum from January 1933:

> Moscow, Kremlin   Top Secret
> Central Committee of the VKP(b)   Series A
> 20.1.1933
> No. __ : A-10
> To the Secretary of the Central Committee of the KP(b)U, Comrade Kosior
> Copy: To the secretaries of the oblast, city, and district party committees
>   To the People's Commissar of the OGPU and the Prosecutor of the
>   republic
> The State Grain Procurement Agency [Zagotzerno] has been given instructions regarding the release, on a cash-payment basis, of forage grain for horses on the kolkhozes of Ukraine. Take urgent measures for receiving, transporting, and safeguarding this grain forage on the kolkhozes. The above-mentioned forage may only be used during the period of the spring sowing campaign of the current year.
>   Pay particular attention to the safeguarding of this grain forage on kolkhozes. Do not allow it to be used for other needs. Those guilty of theft, squandering and misuse must be mercilessly prosecuted under the law of 7 August 1932. Implementation to be reported to the Party Central Committee by 20 February of this year.
> [Signed: J. Stalin][21]

Eyewitnesses describe the distribution of grain for horses' consumption. In the presence of a brigade leader, a groom, and an authorized party representative, the horses ate their fill. Then the three men signed a special document in the stable, attesting that they with their own eyes had seen the grain eaten by the animals but not by any people.[22] Such an event seems too absurd and horrific to invent; it could only have happened in real life. But not even the most malicious enemies of socialism and the Soviet system could have imagined anything like this.

The law of 7 August 1932 and other such regulations were the state's basic weapons in preventing people from stealing food in the face of hunger. An unprecedented regulation in human history, the law stated that such theft was punishable by death. The law [*postanovlenie*] was published on 8 August 1932, and signed by Kalinin, Molotov, and Enukidze, and it included the following:

> The Central Executive Committee [TsIK] and the Soviet of People's Commissars [SNK] of the USSR consider public property (state, kolkhoz, cooperative) the basis of the Soviet system; it is sacred and inviolable, and those attempting to steal public property must be considered enemies of the people, in view

of which the decisive struggle against plunderers of public property is the foremost obligation of every organ of Soviet administration.

Based on these considerations and in response to the demands of workers and kolkhozniks, the Central Executive Committee and Soviet of People's Commissars of the USSR hereby resolve: . . .

1) To regard the property of kolkhozes and cooperatives (harvest in the fields, public reserves, livestock, cooperative storehouses, and stores, etc.) tantamount to state property and safeguard this property from theft in every way possible.

2) To apply as a punitive measure for plundering (thievery) of kolkhoz and cooperative property the highest measure of social defense— [namely,] execution with the confiscation of all property, which may be substituted, in cases where there are extenuating circumstances, by the deprivation of freedom for a period of no fewer than ten years with confiscation of all property.

3) To apply no amnesty to offenders convicted in cases concerning the plunder of kolkhoz and cooperative property . . .

[Signed:]
Chairman of the TsIK of the USSR, M. Kalinin
Chairman of the SNK of the USSR, V. Molotov (Skriabin)
Secretary of the TsIK of the USSR, A. Enukidze
Moscow—Kremlin
7 August 1932[23]

The reference in this document to the loss of freedom—given extenuating circumstances—for no fewer than ten years is strikingly ironic because sentences of more than ten years did not exist. The maximum period of incarceration in labor camps was precisely ten years, while the maximum period of incarceration in prison was only three years.

For Soviet legislation of that time this regulation was incongruously harsh. Six months before, the Supreme Court of the RSFSR had instructed that the theft of wheat from the kolkhoz fields was punishable by up to one year of forced labor or by the deprivation of freedom for up to five years. Counterrevolutionary acts such as sabotage, the willful damaging of tractors, and the slaughter of horses by kulaks were punishable by imprisonment for no more than three years. Capital punishment in the legislation was recognized only "temporarily, as a measure of the highest form of defense of the society . . . for struggle against the most grievous forms of crime threatening the foundations of Soviet power and the Soviet system."[24] In other words, stealing potatoes or a piece of bread was in the USSR now tantamount to counterfeiting or surrendering a military fortress, always viewed as especially dangerous crimes in various countries. Furthermore, the prohibition on amnesty made kolkhozniks even more dangerous and more incorrigible criminals than officers who had betrayed their country or the most malicious repeat offenders.

Gradually the law of 7 August took on an increasingly broad interpretation. It was applied to those who collected ears of wheat or beets in the fields, as well as to those who damaged farm implements through their own carelessness, and to those who lowered the quotas for sowing. Now the standard measure of punishment for villagers, the law condemned people to death or to ten years of confinement for acts that only a few years earlier would have brought a sentence of a small fine. Some of the rulings read as follows:

> For the illegal disbursement of grain collected as tax in kind [*garntsevyi sbor*] the owners and leasers of private enterprises and also officials of state, cooperative, and other public enterprises are subject to criminal responsibility in keeping with the law of the Central Executive Committee and the Soviet of People's Commissars of the USSR of 7 August 1932. . . . [25]
>
> Those caught stealing seed from storehouses and sowing machines or of sabotage by lowering quotas of sowing and sabotage during plowing and sowing, with the aim of spoiling fields and disrupting harvests, are to be viewed as looters [*raskhistiteli*] of kolkhoz and state property, and the law of 7 August 1932 is to be applied to them. . . . [26]
>
> The Central Committee of the Communist Party and the Soviet of People's Commissars of the USSR obligates all punitive and judicial organs to apply the law of 7 August 1932 on the preservation of public property very strictly to all thieves and looters of the kolkhoz and sovkhoz harvests. . . . [27]

From the moment this law was enacted, village laborers recognized they were subject to capital punishment for the least offense—stealing grain or beets, breaking a tractor, bad plowing, or being responsible for a horse that died. Unprecedented in the history of crime and punishment, the 7 August law was supplemented by a regulation, ostensibly harmless but most horrible in its consequences.

In obfuscation typical of the times, the regulation granted permission for the unrestricted sale of bread in Moscow oblast and the Tatar ASSR, but prohibited it elsewhere:

> The Soviet of People's Commissars of the USSR and the Central Committee of the All-Union Communist Party resolve:
> 1) In connection with the fact that the Tatar ASSR and the Moscow oblast have fulfilled, ahead of schedule, the state grain procurement plan established for them by the SNK of the USSR and the Central Committee of the VKP(b) for this year, both as a whole and by

individual grain cultures, and have assured for themselves seed for the spring sowing, effective immediately permission is given to kolkhozniks and independent farmers in the Tatar ASSR and the Moscow oblast to carry on the unimpeded sale of their grain (flour, grain, baked bread) to both state and cooperative organizations as well as at bazaars and rail stations of the Tatar republic and the Moscow oblast.

2) To give advance notice to kolkhozes, kolkhozniks, and independent farmers of the remaining oblasts, regions [*krai*], and republics that . . . in accordance with the decree law of the SNK of the USSR and the Central Committee of the VKP(b) of 6 May 1932, it is proposed that they, too, be given the right of unimpeded trading of their own bread earlier than the date established by the SNK of the USSR and the Central Committee of the VKP(b)—i.e., before 15 January 1933—if in these oblasts, regions, and republics the annual state grain procurement plan will be fulfilled ahead of schedule with grain ensured for the spring sowing.

3) To give advance notice to kolkhozes, kolkhozniks, and independent farmers in oblasts, regions, and republics not fulfilling the annual state grain procurement plan and not ensuring themselves with seed for spring sowing, that kolkhoz trading of bread will not be permitted, and also to warn them that selling grain in these oblasts, regions, and republics will be prosecuted as speculation [profiteering] according to the decree law of the Central Executive Committee and the Soviet of People's Commissars of the USSR of 22 August 1932.

[Signed:]
Chairman of the SNK of the USSR, V. Molotov (Skriabin)
Secretary of the Central Committee of the VKP(b), J. Stalin
2 December 1932[28]

On 23 January 1933, permission to trade as a reward for fulfilling the plan's quotas was bestowed on Belarus, Uzbekistan, Turkmenistan, the Northern territory [Severnyi krai] and the West-Siberian territory [Zapadno-sibirskii krai]. On 18 February, these privileges were extended to the Tadzhik and Georgian SSRs, as well as the Western, Central-Black Soil, Kyiv, and Vinnytsia oblasts (the Uzbek and Turkmen SSR were mentioned once again in the new regulation).[29] Thus, trading was forbidden and rendered equivalent to "speculation" in much of Ukraine, the North Caucasus, the Volga area, and Kazakhstan.

Prohibition against trading in grain meant starvation for many small producers who did not keep back enough for themselves, preferring to buy grain on the open market. The Soviet economist Vasilii Nemchinov estimated that in

1926–1927, some 140 million tons—nearly one fifth of the harvest—was traded in the internal domestic "intra-village" market.[30] Because of the bad harvest and the new circumstances in the countryside, some decrease in grain circulation should no doubt have taken place; however the number of people needing to buy grain and finding themselves without seed until the next harvest increased markedly. The decision prohibiting the sale of grain was sufficient in itself to cause a famine, even at a time of a good harvest. The 1931 and 1932 harvests, however, had been disastrous and for over a year many regions had suffered from insufficient provisions.

Thus the autumn of 1932 marked a new stage in collectivization and the lives of villagers. The state ceased to identify its own interest with that of the kolkhoz, and the kolkhozniks (like the kulaks and independent farmers before them) fell into the category of saboteurs who did not obey orders from above. The slightest infringements became subject to the most merciless punishments.

Many local party leaders and administrators, who were unable to put the state's interests above such considerations as economic expediency and the human toll, were seen as guilty of having committed offenses against the state. Officials deemed more obedient were selected to fill the ranks of the party. The authorities' mainstay was the OGPU (the Unified State Political Administration, or the state political police), whereas every peasant faced a clear choice: absolute submission, or prison—and, ultimately, death.

The poor harvest of 1931 led to an acute worsening in the standard of living, as well as loss of livestock and famine in many parts of the country. In 1932, the situation became even more menacing as the state policies for grain procurement were carried out mercilessly, in complete disregard for supplying the villagers with seed, feeding the livestock, and providing the people with something to eat. Rural residents were simply expected to surrender all grain without discussion. When a village or an entire region could not fulfill its grain quotas, it was placed on a black list, and further punished by having to surrender meat a year or more in advance of procurement. In the autumn of 1932, the state removed all limits on slaughtering domestic livestock in recognition of the fact that it was better to receive meat now than corpses of animals later.

Diet in Rural Areas

The consumption of food in the pre-Revolutionary and pre-kolkhoz periods has received much attention and has been studied with the aid of budgetary surveys among different social classes. Averages do not differ much between the two periods; however, in 1926–1927, consumption was probably more evenly distributed: the gap between the prosperous and the poor had decreased, just as that between the cities and the villages had grown more equal.

On average, food consumption in those years was quite high. In terms of calories, consumption exceeded the norm, largely because people traditionally overate in certain periods of the year. After the autumn harvest, for example, consumption typically increased, while it decreased during periods of religious fasting and during the warm periods when food preservation was more difficult. Social differences were also apparent. White-collar workers ate better than their blue-collar counterparts; peasants with large cultivations received food that was as much as 15 percent higher in calories than those with little cultivated land.[31]

In various regions food consumption differed dramatically. In the northern areas, where consumerism was higher, people ate more meat, milk, potatoes, and vegetables, whereas in the southern areas, known for their production, demand for grain cultures, pigs, and fowl ran higher. In the sparsely populated regions of Siberia, people had recourse to hunting and fishing, whereas the nomadic people of Kazakhstan, Buriatia, and Kyrgyzia relied on diets heavy in livestock products. In Central Asia and the Transcaucasus, fruit production from orchards and cattle products from farms provided different diets. People in the cities ate better than those in the villages, consuming more meat, eggs, and butter, as they gradually reduced their reliance on grains. In contrast, villagers ate more milk, farmer's cheese, and sour cream.

Table 1 shows food consumption of farmers in two different regions of Ukraine—the steppe and the forest zones—in contrast to farmers and nonfarmers in the entire USSR. The steppe is a typical grain-producing region, similar (in terms of people's diets) to the Volga region, the North Caucasus, and the agricultural areas of Siberia and Kazakhstan. That is, the staple of most villagers' diets was grain, primarily wheat, with potatoes and other grains such as buckwheat and millet playing a secondary role. Meat consumption was insignificant, whereas the annual consumption of oils and fats was relatively high—in addition to pork fat [*salo*] and butter, about 3–4 kg of vegetable oil was consumed per person. Villagers also consumed large quantities of milk and milk products, as more than two-thirds of them owned cows. And the typical diet included approximately 100 kg of fruit and vegetables, chiefly of the melon family, and several kilograms of sugar and fish.[32]

Consumption in the forest areas (Polissia) was typical for the central regions of the European part of the USSR (and partially for its northern territories), and it is not accidental that the majority of average indices for the USSR and other regions of Ukraine fall between the figures for the steppe and Polissia, where there is an increase in the consumption of potatoes and cereals such as buckwheat and millet, but a decrease in the use of bread grains, especially wheat. People in Polissia also consumed more meat, but less fats and in some places there was an increase in the consumption of fish. Vegetables most prevalent in diets were cabbages and cucumbers, both of which could be pickled for winter use. As indicated in table

1, the average city dweller in the USSR, in contrast, consumed almost twice the meat and fats, more fish and sugar, but much less grain and potatoes than did the agricultural residents of Polissia.

As a result of collectivization and the redistribution of products, the quality of diet for people dropped to levels not seen since the Civil War period. In the cities meat and other livestock products became luxuries, whereas fish provided the primary source of protein. Village populations, in contrast, were forced to lower their consumption not only of meat, fats, and milk, but also of bread. In

Table 1. Annual food consumption (in kilograms) per capita
in Ukraine (1927–1928) and the USSR (1928).

	Ukraine Farmers in Forest Areas	**Ukraine** Farmers in Steppe Regions	**USSR** Agricultural Communities	**USSR** Non-agricultural Communities
Bread (in grain)	205[a]	232[a]		
Cereals other than bread grains	25	8.7		
Total grains	**230[a]**	**240.7[a]**	**250.4**	**174.4**
Potatoes	189	93	141.1	87.6
Meat	17.6	12.6		
Pork fat	10.6	5.6		
Poultry	1.7[b]	6.0[b]		
Total meat products	**29.9**	**24.2**	**24.8**	**51.7**
Butter	1.0	1.8	1.55	2.97
Eggs (actual count)	45	65	58[c]	100[c]

a. Calculated on the basis of the amount of flour. Coefficient of grinding is 0.87.
b. Calculated on the basis of 1 unit = 1 kg.
c. Calculated on the basis of production and procurement data.

Sources: *Narodnoe khoziaistvo SSSR: Statisticheskii spravochnik 1932* (Moscow, Leningrad, 1932), 343–50; *Statystychna khronika* (Kharkiv), no. 147 (1929): 68–70; Iurii A. Moskhov, *Zernovaia problema v gody sploshnoi kollektivizatsii sel'skogo khoziaistva SSSR (1929–1932 gg.)* (Moscow, 1966), 136; *Strana sovetov za 50 let* (Moscow, 1967), 122–23.

the 1930s the villagers' diets grew worse than they had been during the Famine of 1921. Except for potatoes, villagers received less and less of the staples for life. According to Moshkov, in 1932, a peasant, on average, took in only 214.6 kg of grain, 125 kg of potatoes, 11.2 kg of meat, and 0.7 kg of oil.[33] This meager level, however, was only a harbinger of much worse things to come. In 1932, the typical kolkhoz family received only six centners of grain as payment for a whole year of work. In simple terms, if most of this grain were used for food—and some of it had to be assigned to forage—only 130 kg became available per person per year in 1933.[34] The gross yield of grain and the portion of state grain procurements of subsequent years show that this level of consumption became the norm. Not once, except for the good harvest of 1937, did the villager have a sufficient quantity of grain. In 1936, the state procured 277 million centners out of a harvest of 560 million. As a result each peasant received approximately 60–70 kg of grain for that year, nearly four times less than what he had received under normal conditions.[35]

Diets poor in meat, fats, and frequently bread and potatoes had been the norm for villagers for twenty years or more, as has been shown in particular by budget research on the Ukrainian kolkhozes in 1935. Most villagers filled up on potatoes, with a negligible amount of animal products. Table 2 reveals a surprising picture drawn from a comparison of new kolkhoz consumption with that of rural populations during the terrible Famine of 1921–1922. In the fall of 1921, provinces suffering from starvation had almost the same quantity of flour and non-bread cereals (e.g. buckwheat, millet) as the kolkhozniks of Dnipropetrovsk, Odesa, and Kharkiv had in 1935, and five times as much meat, farmer's cheese, oil, and sour cream as the kolkhozniks. Only potatoes figured less prominently in the diets of those enduring the earlier Famine, and only in the most difficult period—namely, the spring of 1922—were the living conditions in the famine-stricken provinces comparable to the kolkhozniks' standard of living. Whereas the inhabitants of provinces suffering from the Famine endured their poor diets for merely a few months, the kolkhozniks were doomed to their losses for many years.

Even the unusually low level of village consumption established after 1932 seems large in comparison with that in certain areas of Ukraine during the subsequent famine years. As early as 1931, approximately 45 million centners of grain, from a harvest of 160 million, remained in the villages for the population's use and for forage: a total of 28 million was reserved for seed; 76 million for the state; and 10 million were sustained in losses. In contrast, in 1925–1926 there were 47–50 million centners for forage; 60–63 million for food; 25 million for seed, and 10 million in losses. Only 30 million centners had been designated for the state's procurement.[36] These figures indicate that in 1931 the rural population of Ukraine received half its usual supply of grain. On an annual basis, each villager received 100–120 kg of grain; the daily supply of bread was a mere 300–400 grams per person. In 1932, the situation was even worse, as the grain consumption per capita decreased by almost twice the amounts of the previous year.

The "mill" tax [*garntsevyi sbor*], which required consumers to provide grain directly to the state for milling services, gives a general sense of the level of consumption in 1932 in the USSR. In previous years, the mill tax showed relatively significant but stable contributions: in 1929, for example, it amounted to 23 million centners, whereas in 1930, it came to 22 million, and in 1931, only 15 million. Officials planned to collect 21 million centners in 1932, but the mill tax fell far short: on 25 November, only 29 percent of the annual plan had been collected, as opposed to 45 percent on that date of the previous year. The shortfall was reported in a secret telegram from Stalin and Molotov to the oblast and district [*raion*] party committees, ordering them to collect more of the mill tax and report to the government every five days. In the final accounting, only 12 million centners were collected Union-wide, somewhat less than the amount in 1931. In Ukraine, however, only half as much grain was collected in mill tax in 1932 than in the previous year, suggesting a sharp decline in the amount of flour consumed.[37]

Given that the available grain was not distributed equally, we can assume that if in the course of 1932, half the peasants of Ukraine—some 12 million people—received paltry rations of 400–500 grams, then the other half had nothing at all, not even a crust of bread. A villager's mainstay in a time of bad harvest—for example, the Famine of 1921—was domestic cattle and surrogates, the by-products of agricultural production usually reserved for the feeding of cattle. It was thus no accident in the fall of 1921 the proportion of meat consumed in Ukrainian provinces experiencing crop failure was higher than that in other parts of the country and in many villages (see tables 1 and 2). Surrogates—which included oilcakes, poppy seed cakes, grain husks and chaff, acorns, and the like—represented 10–15 kg or 5 percent of Ukrainian villagers' consumption during the Famine of 1921–1922. For those living in provinces where crop failure was high, the proportion of surrogates in the diet was greater. For peasants without sown land the amount approached 60 percent of the typical diet.[38]

A distinctive feature of the 1932–1933 Famine was that the village inhabitant, having lost most of the land, also lost access to surrogates. Straw, chaff, and grain or beets left in the fields now belonged to the kolkhozes and any attempt to make use of such partially edible items was punishable by death or ten years' imprisonment according to the law of 7 August 1932.

Livestock, too, had been necessary to the peasant family's survival, providing not only food products (meat, milk, eggs, and so forth), but also a significant part of the family's income. So widespread was this dependence that only 5 to 10 percent of village inhabitants, those who were not connected with agricultural work, did not have domestic cattle in earlier times. Without livestock the peasants now

Table 2. Annual food consumption (in kilograms) per capita by rural populations of Ukraine, based on budget surveys.

Region	Period	Flour	Cereals (other than bread) and legumes	Potatoes	Meat, pork fat, fish, poultry	Vegetable oils	Animal fats	Farmer's cheese and sour cream	Eggs
Bad harvest areas of Ukraine[a]	Fall 1921	118[b]	22.3	79	36.7	3.7	4.7	50.8	no data
All Ukraine[a]	Fall 1921	170[b]	36.1	174	33.6	2.9	6.4	43.7	no data
Bad harvest areas of Ukraine[a]	Spring 1922	87[b]	20.4	53	19.7	2.6	2.6	58.0	no data
All Ukraine[a]	Spring 1922	131[b]	30.0	141	25.0	1.7	6.5	38.6	no data
Left Bank Ukraine	1927–1928	262	16.0	129	23.3[c]	no data	1.1	no data	60
Kolkhozes of Dnipropetrovsk, Odesa, Kharkiv oblasts	1935	125[b]	31.2	210	7.9[d]	0.8	0.6	13.8[e]	11

a. Per capita calculation based on a coefficient of 1.00 per man and 0.75 per woman.
b. The amount of flour was derived from the amount of bread based on a coefficient of 1.3.
c. Without fish.
d. Includes 2.2 kg of fish.
e. Milk is included with a coefficient of 0.1.

Sources: Narodnoe khoziaistvo Ukrainy v 1921–1922 godu (Kharkiv, 1923), viii, 1–12; Pitanie naseleniia Ukrainy zimoi 1921–1922 (Kharkiv, 1923); Statystychna khronika (Kharkiv), no. 147 (1929): 68–70; K. Kononenko, Ukraïna i Rosiia: Sotsiial'no-ekonomichni pidstavy ukraïns'koï natsional'noï ideï, 1917–1960 (Munich, 1965), 322.

faced semistarvation. For example, livestock provided insurance against famine: a slaughtered cow could provide some 350 kg of meat, whereas a pig brought 100 kg and a sheep around 35 kg. The cow alone could supply a family with food for several months. During the 1921 Famine, in those provinces with high crop failures some 3.6 domestic animals were slaughtered per household. Moreover, 8 percent of households lost all their livestock. Undoubtedly these families faced difficult times, but those who had animals to slaughter had a great advantage. As indicated in table 3, only an insignificant proportion of the population—namely, some 6.3 percent of villagers in those provinces with high crop failures (i.e., the steppe)—had no such insurance in 1921.[39]

The situation for Ukrainian peasants in the 1930s was quite different, however. Livestock ownership per household was as much as three times lower than that in 1921. The crop failure of 1931, combined with extravagant state procurements, dealt a shattering blow to livestock breeding. More than a third of households had

Table 3. Households (in thousands) in Ukraine without livestock according to spring surveys conducted in 1921–1922.

Households	All of Ukraine: 4,339,400 Households (est.)			Steppe: 1,609,000 Households (est.)		
	1921	1922	Change (+/–)	1921	1922	Change (+/–)
Without cows	816	1102	+286	262	417	+155
Without swine	2651	3679	+1028	868	1542	+674
Without poultry	812	1085	+273	338	585	+247
Without any livestock	329	443	+114	101	234	+133
Number of animals per household with livestock	7.65	5.87	-1.78	8.89	5.29	-3.60
Percent from Total Number of Households						
Without cows	18.8	25.4	+6.6	16.3	25.9	+9.6
Without swine	61.1	84.8	+23.7	53.9	95.8	+41.9
Without poultry	18.7	25.0	+6.3	21.0	36.4	+15.4
Without any livestock	7.6	10.2	+2.6	6.3	14.6	+8.3

Sources: *Statistika Ukrainy* (Kharkiv), no. 7 (1921): 1–2; no. 8 (1922): 4–41; no. 20 (1922): 10–20, 50–58.

no livestock at all. By mid-1932, nearly half the villagers tried to manage without domestic animals; two-thirds had no cow's milk (see table 4). Coming into the winter of 1932–1933, 12 million Ukrainian villagers had a negligible supply of animal fodder and grain, or lacked these entirely. Another 1.5 million (or 320,000 families) were added to that number over the course of the winter. We cannot assume that they had slaughtered their livestock for food, as they had during the Famine of 1921, since the state had substantially taken away the rights of owner-ship. People could not slaughter animals without permission from authorities, and what meat might have been available went to the state, which extended its powers by seizing meat up to fifteen months in advance of quota dates.

The change in the number of livestock in individual oblasts shows that in the northwest (Kyiv, Volyn, and Chernihiv oblasts) the situation was relatively better. Forty-two percent of households in this region completely lacked livestock in 1933, whereas in the rest of Ukraine 65 percent of households were lacking. In the Chernihiv oblast there were fifteen domestic animals for every ten families, nine or ten for those in Kyiv and Vinnytsia oblasts, but fewer than six for the same proportion of families in the rest of Ukraine. Of the sheep and pigs in Ukraine, 80 percent were concentrated in those few provinces.[40]

Table 4. Households (in thousands) in Ukraine without livestock according to summer surveys conducted in 1931–1933.
(Total households in Ukraine on 1 January 1931: 4,948,500)

Households	1931	1932	Change from 1931 to 1932	1933	Change from 1932 to 1933
Without cows	2054	2937	+883	3202	+265
Without swine	4300	4689	+389	4722	+33
Without any livestock	595	2336	+1741	2658	+322
Number of animals per household with livestock	2.72	2.32	-0.4	2.12	-0.2
Percent from Total Number of Households					
Without cows	41.5	59.4	+17.9	64.7	+5.3
Without swine	86.9	94.8	+7.9	95.4	+0.7
Total without livestock	12.0	47.2	+35.2	53.7	+6.5

Source: *Narodne hospodarstvo USRR* (Kyiv, 1935), 251–63.

The relative prosperity of the northwest districts is attributable to several factors: grain agriculture had a diminished role in the general production there, and state grain procurements in the fall of 1932 were accordingly less; people in these districts ate a higher proportion of potatoes; families had more livestock to begin with; many residents worked on the side; in addition, the oblasts of Vinnytsia and Kyiv managed to fulfill the state mandates, and it is possible that the harvest in these areas was relatively higher than the rest of the country, as often occurred in years of overall low production.

Why was the decrease in livestock in Ukraine of 1932–1933 less than that in 1931–1932? In terms of small animals such as pigs and sheep, there was simply no room for them to decrease: the thousands of such animals that survived in the steppe regions after 1931 evidently were in privileged hands. Such residents were more secure presumably either because of their social position or because they were living just outside the cities or hiding on *khutors* [private estates incorporating farming communities]. The number of cows declined in 1931 because of a sharp decrease in fodder, as the bad harvest affected not only grain production but also straw and hay. The 1932 state grain procurement did not include hay, which after all was sufficient because of reductions in livestock the year before. The 30 percent of villagers who continued to keep cows were able to set aside enough food for themselves to prevent their dying from starvation. A meager rationing of food was awarded to villagers for their hard work, but none for poor work or in cases of a bad harvest. In the winter of 1932–1933, after state procurements, the average Ukrainian villager had some 200 grams of grain per day, less than the minimum to sustain human life. For many of these people, certain death awaited.

Food Supplies in Urban Areas

The reorganization of agriculture and the decrease in food production dealt a heavy blow to the cities as well, especially given their rapid growth and the ruin of private trade. Confiscating all the surpluses from the villages, the government assumed the responsibility of supplying bread and some other foodstuffs to city residents, but under a complex and centralized hierarchical system. Workers received ration cards, but their dependents and other nonworkers were rationed two or three times less. Ration cards were be taken to specific pre-assigned stores, which "redeemed" them at various unannounced times, causing city residents to expend energy and waste time standing in long lines, often without receiving anything at all. Most families assigned to one of their members the job of having to retrieve rationed goods.

Ration cards came in various categories, depending on the state's perception of each worker's contribution to the level of the general production. For instance, workers in large and important enterprises and institutions such as railroads and steel mills, the secret police (OGPU), and white-collar workers fared better than others in the society. Moreover, not all areas in the country were supplied in the same way: Moscow, Leningrad, and the Donbas fared much better than other regions and cities, whereas small towns fared quite poorly.

On 5 February 1931, a directive from the Ukrainian Party Central Committee cut the nation's foodstuff fund by 7,000 centners a month. Eighteen cities, including Chernihiv and Poltava, lost access to the centralized supply depot. Only railroad workers were able to get food. In eight other cities only those working in basic enterprises received bread.[41] Distribution of bread and other items came under the control of the troikas—the secretary of the district party committee, the secretary of the district executive committee, and an OGPU representative.[42]

The bread-supply system in Ukraine rested on absolute centralization. Local authorities received an insignificant portion—0.6 percent—of the state grain procurement for their own use. Only medical personnel and hospitals, village teachers, the police, and members of the OGPU were supplied from the state fund.[43] Although local authorities were allowed to make purchases in the villages, in practice this privilege produced no substantial results because of the enormous gap between market and state prices.

In some cities large enterprises set up private plots or "kitchen gardens" where workers grew potatoes and vegetables, raised pigs, and caught fish, mainly for those working at the plants. Both blue- and white-collar workers cultivated these gardens during their free time, insuring that some city dwellers had necessary provisions. Such self-sufficiency expanded on a large scale in 1932–1933. Workers of the North Caucasus Coal Trust harvested 14,700 tons of vegetables and potatoes in 1932, and another 26,900 tons in 1933. The agricultural machine-making plant Ros Sel Mash in Rostov reaped 4,600 tons and 6,500 tons in the same two-year period. Railroad workers of the North Caucasus gathered 13,000 tons and 25,400 tons, while the Grozny Oil Trust took in 4,300 tons and 10,400 tons respectively. In Rostov and Taganrog alone, fifteen enterprises caught 1,875 tons of fish. Meanwhile, mine workers in the North Caucasus raised 2,268 suckling pigs and 162 calves. Of the workers in this trust, 16,185 of them had individual private plots; moreover, in the three-year period 1931–1933, they put in 126,000, 476,000, and 1,995,000 workdays respectively on suburban farmsteads.[44] From this small sample we can appreciate the contribution that people made in supplying food for themselves. Possibly this form of food supply played a role in lowering the turnover in personnel in 1933, as well as in the overall decline in the number of workers, since each enterprise had a limited number of ration cards.

Bread was the one product that the state tried to supply to city dwellers. In 1931, for example, 33.2 million people received ration cards for bread, whereas in 1932 the number grew to 40.3 million. As economic conditions worsened, consumption of meat, butter, and milk fell in the cities whereas bread consumption increased. Many city residents, however, were not so fortunate to have ration cards. If we exclude those technically "outside" the city—for example, fishermen, lumberjacks, prisoners, and special settlers—we see that millions of urban residents managed without state provisions. Likewise the inhabitants of small towns, elderly people living alone, craftsmen, former "nepmen" (profiteers of the New Economic Policy) who had lost their jobs, professionals, and city residents who worked in the villages and frequently had land there until they lost it under collectivization.

All these residents suffered when market prices soared. In 1933, a shoemaker's usual monthly income might cover 2–3 kg of bread. Although a few city residents had personal valuables they could trade for food or had relatives abroad who could send them money, the vast majority of people in the early 1930s had no sources of food other than their private plots and livestock they raised themselves.

Eyeing even these relatively insignificant resources, the state began assessing residents for their food income. Taxes were levied on private plots; milk and meat from all domestic livestock had to be surrendered to the state. A resident of Velizh, Faddei Dodon, requested that his assessed quota of 15.7 tons of potatoes and 500 liters of milk be rescinded. He had paid eight rubles of tax in 1930. In 1931 he had contributed 3.9 tons of potatoes and 60 poods of hay to the state. His cow failed to supply much milk, since all winter long it had had only rye straw to eat. In a letter Dodon invited the city soviet to send inspectors to see for themselves, adding that he was 80 years old and was supported by a son who as "an unskilled worker" helped construct bridges. This letter prompted a response from the Workers and Peasants Control Commission and the Velizh city soviet: "Refused, as he has a surplus of potatoes."[45]

In another case a citizen named Voitsekhovskii appealed on 1 June 1931, to the Velizh district executive committee. Supporting a family of eight and owning only one cow, Voitsekhovskii was assessed a tax of 1,000 liters of milk, but when he asked that his tax be reduced to 300 liters or that his cow simply be taken away from him, the commission issued its decision: "It has been verified and established that the firm quota was correctly assigned to this person as a prosperous citizen, but that it is out of proportion, and therefore will be lowered to 600 liters, since there is one cow for eight people."[46]

Many city residents received no aid from the state and had to pay heavy duties in taxes. In the winter of 1932–1933, needy city dwellers found that the sale of food products at farmers' markets was practically nonexistent. The opening of special state retail outlets (*kommercheskie magaziny*) that carried a greater selection of goods eased their plight somewhat, although these goods came at very high prices and often in exchange for foreign currency or precious metals. As such, the state stores became a prime vehicle for extorting money from the population at large.

After 1 January 1935, the two systems of urban supply merged: ration cards were abolished, and new prices were established. These prices were lower than the ones in the state stores but markedly higher than the ration card prices. Thereafter, each family's level of consumption was determined by its income, and the nature of its diet gradually began to improve.

Supplies to city residents reached their lowest level in 1932. Meat disappeared almost entirely, as the typical resident had only 16.9 kg per year in contrast to the 51.7 kg he enjoyed in 1928; butter supplies were cut in half to 1.75 kg, down from 3.0 kg in 1928. Likewise there was less milk and cheese; there were fewer eggs and vegetables. Meanwhile, as a "compensation," the supply of bread increased: 211 kg of grain per person in 1932, in contrast to 174 kg in 1928.[47]

In the 1930s fish replaced meat throughout the country, as the supply to Ukrainian cities in 1932–1934 exceeded that of meat by a factor of two or three. Usually each city resident had the equivalent of about 25 kg of fish per year, except for the Donbas regions where the supplies were 30 kg. In all of Ukraine, only the workers in the Donbas received meat—15 kg per person in 1932; 28 kg in 1933–1934. Moreover, the Donbas received supplies of other products in markedly greater quantities than other regions did: vegetable oil (10 kg per person); potatoes (over 100 kg). Residents of Ukrainian cities outside the Donbas got much less: 5–6 kg of vegetable oil; 3 kg of lard and other animal fats; even less bread and fewer potatoes. The Dnipropetrovsk oblast, for example, received 25 percent less of these products in 1932 than it received in either 1933 or 1934.[48]

Never before had the residents of Ukrainian cities faced such dire conditions. Even in the Famine of 1921, their diets, on average, had fared better. In the fall of 1921 the average per capita annual consumption of meat stood at 39 kg; in the spring of 1922 it was 32kg. They likewise consumed 6–7 kg of vegetable oil and animal fats and 25–45 kg of certain milk products such as sour cream, cheese, and farmer's cheese. In addition, each resident ate, on average, 140 kg of grain and 25–30 kg of cereals such as buckwheat and millet.[49] Thus, even during the peak of the 1921 Famine, Ukrainian city residents ate better than they did in 1932–1934. The same can be said of the urban residents throughout the USSR. During the difficult years of the Civil War, each person consumed 200–210 kg of grain annually and 15–20 kg of meat, no less than in 1932.[50]

THE FAMINE OF 1932–1933 IN UKRAINE: TESTIMONIES OF WITNESSES

Numerous memoirs of eyewitnesses to the events of the Famine present a horrible picture of everyday life in 1933. In this section are described some of these events in various parts of the USSR. They are stories of misery, unbearable suffering, and the tragedy of the total degradation of humankind.

Famine takes horrible forms, and it is horrible and painful to write about them.

In 1932–1933, it was so widespread that almost no one received a satisfactory amount of food, apart from a handful of the highest-placed leaders and, at the far end of the scale, the cannibals. All together, they numbered hardly several thousand. Millions of other citizens went to bed thinking of food, remembering the luscious breads and hams of years past, now ready to do whatever it took to get their hands on a piece of bread. Regardless of whether they lived in the cities or the villages, they suffered from malnutrition and a lack of basic staples.

When bread was sold in the special state stores at "commercial" prices in 1933, thousands of people stood in line from morning until night, afraid to lose their places, afraid that the rabble would break up the line. Clasping each other, they rocked from side to side, shouting, wailing, and crying. If one had a ration card, one still had to stand in line, but not without a shred of hope that there would be bread at the end of the day. Those who had lost their jobs and consequently their ration cards—the "disenfranchised" and villagers—were among the ones who waited the longest and usually came away empty-handed. One man described his setting out on the earliest train from a suburb of Kharkiv in order to take his place in line at a special state store, but rarely with success.[51]

Divided by starvation, people lost their sense of compassion, holding on to what little they had. Extant photographs show people rushing by a child doubled up with hunger and lying in a ditch, or women with shopping bags conversing not far from corpses on the side of the road. Eyes pleading for help, hands outstretched for alms appear in other photographs, signs of hopelessness in a cruel time.

A child of six years old, Tania Pokyd'ko, picked a few heads of garlic from the garden belonging to her neighbor Havrylo Turko, who then beat the child so badly that she barely crawled back to her home and died. Tania's father Stepan, a former Red partisan, took four other children, all of whom were swollen with hunger, to the district committee to seek help. Rebuffed by the committee, Stepan left the children with the secretary of the district committee, exclaiming, "Better you eat them than I should watch them suffer." He then hanged himself in the district committee's courtyard. His wife Odarka, who had eaten a lot of frogs at one time, also died, as did two of the four children who had been placed in orphanages.

A female neighbor of the Fedorchenko family felt sorry for the two children, Mykola and Olia (six and two years old, respectively), and agreed to give each a mug of milk every day. The children, however, did not receive the milk. She inquired with their mother why this was so and discovered that their father, Omel'ko Fedorchenko, had said to his wife, "All the neighbors' children have died a long time ago, and now we are going to feed these two. We better save ourselves before it's too late." When the neighbor grew angry and refused to give milk unless the children drank it in her presence, Omel'ko informed on her to the authorities, alleging that she had hidden grain in her yard.[52]

Thousands upon thousands of peasants left their native parts, not counting on the railroad. They walked, fell down, got up again, and kept going. When they had no strength to walk any farther, they crawled.

Peasants came to the cities to barter goods for food. They spread far north, reaching Moscow—repeating in reverse the pattern of the Civil War when city residents went to the villages to barter their goods for food. Some found jobs in mining or in construction, occupations for which the authorities turned a blind eye to matters of social origin because they needed workers. Many of those suffering from starvation, however, were no longer fit to do such heavy physical labor and were reduced to begging and scavenging. The police took peasants from the train stations, marketplaces, and streets, loaded them on trucks, and drove them away, primarily just to get them out of sight. Some were taken to sovkhozes, whereas others labored at state-sponsored enterprises. Others froze to death huddled on the thresholds of houses.

Serhii Fursa describes the Iuzivka [now Donetsk] train station where police searched people and confiscated whatever they found. From one peasant they took five pounds of groats and two loaves of bread, even though he pleaded that he had a sick wife and children at home—all to no avail. Pleading for help from his fellow travelers and receiving none, he threw himself in the way of an oncoming train and was killed.[53]

Death greeted those who returned home to their families. Mass graves were dug to accommodate dozens of people, and no one doubted that in a matter of days they would be full. Wagons full of corpses rolled through the villages, as solicitous authorities sent their agents to the houses to inquire (not without reason) whether the heads of households or some other family member had died. If the response was affirmative, these agents helped throw the dead bodies into the public pit.[54]

In spring when the grass appeared, dysentery and diarrhea proved more deadly than starvation, as people were reduced to consuming acorns, bran, chaff, frozen beets, dried leaves, and sawdust. Cats, dogs, crows, earthworms, and frogs came to replace meat. A teacher from the Kharkiv Technical Institute who visited a kolkhoz with his students reported:

> When we went to eat our dinner, hungry children and even adults began to come running to beg for bread or *zatirka* [mash dumplings]. Struck by the horrible look of the hungry children, students began to give them pieces of bread and cooked *zatirka*. The children and adults hurled themselves greedily at the food . . . . Half an hour to an hour later, the children, who, after long starvation, had eagerly eaten their fill of bread, began to fall to the ground, shouting and crying, writhing in pain. Some of the female students began hysterically screaming . . . . Then the leaders ordered the students to go to the school building [where they were staying] and the children off to the village . . . . We went to the field to work, to weed. And again misfortune

struck. The kolkhoz had attached a villager to our brigade to sharpen the hoes. The kolkhoznik silently fulfilled his task until lunchtime. Then, out of generosity, the students gave him a goodly amount of bread and some cooked kasha, not foreseeing any problem. The hungry man ate well, and about half an hour later he died right before our eyes.[55]

People actually forgot how to eat. According to one witness, in the spring of 1933, each person in a village in Kyiv oblast received a kilogram of buckwheat. Some ate their portion unground, having no access to anyone who could grind it for them; others ate their portion raw. Although the food was quite nutritious, many died from consuming it in unhealthy ways.[56]

In the spring of 1933, a limited program of communal feeding was established in a few places for peasants working in the fields, although this program by no means received full acceptance. Threats from the previous year over unnecessary grain expenditures remained in most people's minds. When an official in the Chornukhy district, for instance, ordered that the potatoes which had been meant for planting but had spoiled be sold to the kolkhozniks, he was summarily dismissed. Similarly a director of the Machine Tractor Station (MTS) asked for grain to feed people on the kolkhozes serviced by the MTS. He too was expelled from the party for treasonous behavior.[57]

Everywhere in the fields authorities were on guard protecting the harvest. Birds and rodents no longer were the great pests; rather it was the people themselves who were forbidden to taken even an ear of wheat. Surveillance towers appeared across the countryside; mounted patrols hid in ambush; adults and even small children were employed to spy on their friends and relatives. Kosior estimated that 500,000 Pioneers guarded the fields from their own parents during the summer of 1933.[58] The law of 7 August that threatened execution or imprisonment for anyone caught stealing grain came to be called the "ears of wheat" law.

Other witnesses, however, present a less patriotic picture. One eyewitness recalled seeing:

> tired kolkhozniks coming back from the fields talking with one another. And, suddenly, what was this? At the edge of the village they overtook a strange mob of children, old women, and old men under the protection of the head of the village soviet, Zozula Samoilo, who was armed with a rifle and pistol, and on horseback. The crowd trudged along. Their children [wore] filthy pants and shirts patched a hundred times over; all were barefoot, and most had knapsacks containing ears of wheat—evidence of great crimes against the state. The head of the district police, Smirnov himself, coming out to meet the important criminals, said, "Herd them all into the shed, and tomorrow we'll figure out who goes where!" The next morning a funeral brigade took the corpses of several children to the cemetery.[59]

As with all lies, a lot of energy was spent on controlling rumors and concealing the truth about the Famine. TASS refuted such gruesome reports, calling them a slander against the wonders of the Soviet system.[60] In order to hide the facts of the Famine from the public, the state limited visits of foreign correspondents and issued directives such as the following:

> Kharkiv 22.5.1933   Top Secret
> No. 17/198/k.   Series K
> To all heads of the oblast divisions of the OGPU of the Ukrainian SSR and to the oblast prosecutors
> Copy: To district [*raion*] OGPU divisions and district prosecutors
> The department on the codification of laws under the People's Commissariat of Justice of the USSR in its letter No. 175-K of 15 May of this year has issued a clarification:
> In view of the fact that existing criminal legislation had not foreseen punishment for people guilty of cannibalism, all matters concerning accusations of cannibalism should therefore be quickly transferred to the local organs of the OGPU. If cannibalism was preceded by murder, as defined in Article 142 of the criminal code, these cases also should be removed from the courts and investigative organs of the People's Commissariat of Justice, and transferred for review by the OGPU board in Moscow.
> This order is to be put into effect at once.
> [Signed:]
> Dep. People's Commissar of the OGPU of the Ukrainian SSR   (Karlson)
> Prosecutor of the Republic   (Mykhailyk)[61]

Nikita Khrushchev, who even then was a major official in the Moscow Party Committee, wrote that he did not learn of what was actually occurring until several years after the fact. In his memoir, he recalls the following:

> Mikoyan told me that Comrade Demchenko, at the time the first secretary of the Kyiv oblast committee, saw him once in Moscow. And this is what Demchenko said to him: "Anastas Ivanovich, does Comrade Stalin or anyone in the Politburo know what is going on in Ukraine? Well, if not, I'll give you an example so you may have some idea. Recently a train arrived in Kyiv loaded with the corpses of people who had died from starvation. This was a train which picked up corpses along the rail line between Poltava and Kyiv. I think it might be a good thing if someone informed Comrade Stalin about this situation."[62]

From the secretaries of oblast committees to the simplest peasant, people looked to Stalin for wisdom, leadership, and help. One eighth-grader, the daughter of a Red partisan from a village in the Novi Sandzhary district in Poltava oblast, wrote: "I loved you and I still love you, Iosyp Visarionovych. And I don't believe that you will allow me to die tragically and senselessly in the bloom of youth from starvation."[63] This child tells Stalin that her family has had no bread for over a month, but whether Stalin was moved by her plight we have no way of knowing. What is known is that Stalin himself, the teacher of humanity, never missed a meal and was known as a connoisseur of Kremlin feasts.

THE GEOGRAPHY OF THE FAMINE AND DISTRIBUTION OF LOSSES BY REGION

If we analyze the demographic data reported in the 1959 USSR census on those born in the years 1929–1933, and make note of their regional distribution, we can estimate the population losses in various regions of the USSR, including those in Ukraine. Three age groups are discussed (as presented in five-year units in the census tables): those born 1924–1928, 1929–1933, and 1934–1938.

The demographer Frank Lorimer estimated the number of those born in the USSR in 1924–1928 at 31.7 million, in 1929–1933 at 29.2 million, and in 1934–1938 at 28.1 million.[64] As I have shown elsewhere, new information appearing after World War II has made it possible to refine this report; nonetheless, Lorimer's thesis about the overall tendency for a decreasing birth rate through the 1930s—a result of rapid urbanization and the spread of birth control—remains valid. This rate of reduction decreased at the end of the thirties after abortion was prohibited in 1936.

In the subsequent twenty years, the demographic fate of each of the three age groups varied. The annexation of the territories of eastern Poland and the Baltic states in 1939 increased the difference in population totals of the three age groups only slightly, as the tendency toward a declining birth rate in the 1930s affected these regions as well.[65] The normal mortality rate, on the other hand, somewhat reduced the divergence, since it affected mostly the oldest group (b. 1924–1928). Similarly, the two groups that suffered the greatest loss in numbers during the war years were the oldest, who went to the front lines, and the youngest (b. 1934–1938), who were most vulnerable to the vicissitudes of that conflict.

Twenty years later in the 1959 census we might have expected that the differences in numbers among the three age groups, in absolute and relative terms, would be reduced, while the correlation between the numbers of each age group remained the same, i.e., the number of 30–34 year olds would be greater than the number of 20–25 year olds, and the number of 20–25 year olds would be greater than the number of 20–24 year olds. It would be natural to expect this correlation to be maintained especially among women who did not endure losses at the front. The results, however, point to the opposite conclusion: there are more people in the age group 20–24 than in the 25–29 group. These results can be explained only by collectivization and famine in 1932–1933, which decimated the population of children born in these years.[66]

The results of the 1959 census[67] also provide evidence as to which territories and nationalities suffered the most from the Famine. In the three groups cited above, we can discount the effects of migration by analyzing only the results pertaining to women in rural areas. In addition, since abortion was the primary means of birth control, especially in the cities, a focus on the rural areas limits the effects on population from abortion. True, abortion gradually spread to the Russian and Ukrainian villages, and the prohibition of the practice led to a sharp increase in the birth rate in 1937–1938 here: the rate for that time period was roughly 25 percent higher than the level for 1933–1935. As can be seen from the total number of births in the USSR, however, the prohibition of abortions did not change the overall tendency of a declining birth rate and only somewhat slowed it down. In terms of the intensity with which people in outlying areas controlled childbirth through abortion, it was much less than, say, the degree in Moscow and Leningrad, which accounted for a third of all abortions performed between 1928 and 1936.[68] Table 5 shows that those born in 1928–1933 in Moscow suffered losses not nearly as great as in the cities and villages of Ukraine and the North Caucasus. It is apparent that the reduction of generations of women in the rural areas was not caused by abortion.

A note about migration is in order for this discussion. Among the groups of villagers migrating to the cities, young people were, not surprisingly, much more likely to move than older inhabitants. Migration affected the generations disproportionately, shifting the balance in the villages to the older age groups. The fact that in 1959 there were fewer people in the 25–29 age group than in the 20–24 group suggests that factors other than migration were in operation. Furthermore, we can assume that the dimensions of the migration of contiguous age groups have approximately the same character throughout all the territories of Ukraine.

Muslims, or those close to them in lifestyle and attitudes, did not experience a decline in birth rates in the early 1930s. On the contrary, as we would expect from the traditional population pyramid, each generation was more numerous than the one coming before it. Accordingly in this ethnic group, people in the 20–24 age group would be expected to be more numerous than those in the 25–29 group. A drop in numbers of the 25–29 age group as compared to both the older and younger contiguous groups can only speak of heightened population loss; a measure of the losses can be seen in the shortfall in numbers of people aged 25–29 in comparison to those in the 30–34 group. As table 5 shows, for European peoples the ratio of those in the 25–29 group to those aged 20–24 can serve as a measure of population losses, whereas for eastern (Muslim) peoples it is the ratio of those aged 25–29 in comparison to those in the 30–34 group.

These census results can be explained only by citing the Famine of 1932–1933, one of historical proportions, which decimated the population of children born in the early 1930s. For those born after 1934, the numbers in the 1959 census are more typical and predictable (see table 5). The areas of greatest loss are shaded in table 5: Ukraine, the North Caucasus, Kazakhstan, and to some extent the Volga area and the Far East. We should note too that for the European population of Kazakhstan and for the inhabitants of the Far East, the pre- and postwar migrations of the population had great significance. In Kazakhstan, for instance, the ethnic Germans who had been deported there, as well as settlers from Ukraine, the Volga area, and the European part of the USSR changed the population structure and distorted somewhat the proportions such that the size of the 20–24 age group and the losses it suffered may have been overestimated. Evidently the same applies to the groups in the Far East.

Table 6 shows the geographical distribution of the Famine within Ukraine and to some extent its intensity. The greatest population losses occurred in the Dnipropetrovsk, Cherkasy, Luhansk, Kharkiv, Kyiv, and Kirovohrad oblasts. A somewhat smaller loss (about 20 percent) can be noted in the Zaporizhzhia, Poltava, Mykolaïv, Kherson, and Crimea oblasts. A third group includes the oblasts of Donetsk, Odesa, Sumy, Zhytomyr, and Vinnytsia, where the losses constitute 5 percent to 15 percent. Two areas—Chernihiv and Khmelnytskyi—show a slight gain in population.

In contrast, none of the Ukrainian territories annexed in 1939 and none of the areas of Belarus and the Russian regions on the border with Ukraine shows a similar trend (table 7). It is difficult to advance any hypothesis such as increases in migration or abortions that can account for such differences. Indeed, there is no reason to suppose that in the villages of Belgorod oblast fewer abortions were performed than in the neighboring oblasts of Kharkiv and Poltava, given the almost identical lifestyles, values, and national compositions of their populations. The disparity is directly attributable to the conditions of famine in these areas in the mid-1930s (see tables 6, 7).

In Ukraine and the North Caucasus, the difference in population in 1959 between the 20–24 and 25–29 age groups was as great as 20 percent. The numbers were somewhat less in the Volga area (see tables 5, 6, and 8). In comparison with figures from the Transcaucasus and Central Asia, the number of Kazakhs who died was enormous. Out of the thirty-three nationalities inhabiting the USSR about whom we have reliable information by age groups, we note a marked population decline of four in the 25–29 group—namely, Ukrainians, Kazakhs, Mordvinians, and Russians. The obvious conclusion is that all these peoples suffered death from famine and its attendant illnesses (see table 9).

Hundreds of witnesses have told of the horrible human losses in individual families and villages. In some places as many as one in ten people died; in others it was one in two. Witnesses have also testified to the annihilation of villages.

While we cannot extrapolate from individual cases to the general population—the Famine was too diverse, and conditions too different—we can examine the testimonies that have come down to us.

Table 5. Number of women (in thousands) by generation according to the census of 1959.

	Age Year of Birth	20–24 1934–1938 I	25–29 1929–1933 II	30–34 1924–1928 III	Ratios II:I	II:III
	Region					
	Leningrad-Karelia	164	179	191	1.09	
	Central Industrial	393	412	470	1.05	
	Volga-Viatka	211	216	227	1.02	
	Central Black Soil	241	255	295	1.06	
	Urals	345	348	373	1.01	
	West Siberia	200	205	233	1.03	
Rural	East Siberia	145	145	145	1.00	
	Far East	60	57	61	0.95	
	Lower Volga	257	243	285	0.95	
	North Caucasus	322	256	308	0.79	
	Ukrainian SSR	665	546	753	0.82	
	Belarusian SSR	244	249	241	1.02	
	Baltic Region	116	118	116	1.02	
	Areas with Muslim Populations					
	Transcaucasus	270	233	195		1.19
	Central Asia	377	378	315		1.20
	Kazakh SSR	250	184	214		0.86
Urban	Moscow	253	239	286	0.94	
	North Caucasus	271	202	270	0.75	
	Ukrainian SSR	1109	856	1091	0.77	

Note: Data in columns I, II, and III are rounded off to the nearest whole.
Note: Shaded areas represent regions with population losses.

Source: *Itogi Vsesoiuznoi perepisi naseleniia 1959 goda: SSSR* (Moscow, 1962), 54–71, 211–25; *RSFSR* (Moscow, 1963), 62–97; *Ukrainskaia SSR* (Moscow, 1963), 32–43; *Kazakhskaia SSR* (Moscow, 1962), 30–41.

William Henry Chamberlain, one of the first Western correspondents to describe
the Famine, reported that the village soviet secretary of Cherkasy, a village near
Bila Tserkva, had told him that 634 out of 2,072 inhabitants had died in 1933. In
addition, only one marriage and six births had been registered.[69] Given that the
normal death rate for a village of this size would have been 40–50 people, the rate
for 1933 was nearly fifteen times higher. Similarly the village soviet secretary of
Stara Pryluka in the Vinnytsia region said that of the 5,000 inhabitants 867 had
died and 480 had simply disappeared.[70]

The village of Bilousivka, west of Poltava in the Chornukhy district, had 800

Table 6. Number of rural women (in thousands) by generation
in the oblasts of Ukraine according to the census of 1959.

Age Year of Birth	20–24 1934–1938 I	25–29 1929–1933 II	30–34 1924–1928 III	Ratio II:I
Oblast				
Dnipropetrovsk	34.5	24.3	36.5	0.70
Cherkasy	49.9	34.9	57.5	0.70
Luhansk	21.8	16.0	23.5	0.73
Kirovohrad	33.4	24.3	40.2	0.73
Kyiv	56.9	41.4	58.4	0.73
Kharkiv	39.3	28.9	47.0	0.74
Zaporizhzhia	27.9	21.5	29.9	0.77
Poltava	45.0	36.0	55.5	0.80
Kherson	22.9	18.3	23.1	0.80
Mykolaïv	26.0	21.0	28.3	0.81
Crimea	22.0	18.3	22.2	0.83
Donetsk	25.9	22.2	29.2	0.86
Odesa	46.8	41.2	49.3	0.88
Sumy	40.0	35.5	50.4	0.89
Zhytomyr	52.0	46.5	53.6	0.89
Vinnytsia	73.6	69.0	85.9	0.94
Chernihiv	46.7	47.0	62.3	1.01
Khmelnytskyi	51.0	55.1	59.4	1.08

Source: *Itogi Vsesoiuznoi perepisi naseleniia 1959 goda: Ukrainskaia SSR* (Moscow,
1963).

families, which lost approximately 500 people 1932–1933, according to a peasant who lived there. This represented a 12 percent decline rather than the normal 2 percent. In this entire district there were 52,672 inhabitants on 1 January 1932. Exactly two years later, there were only 45,714. Official registration data records that 7,113—approximately 13 percent of the population—had died. Of these, 3,549 were children and adolescents up the age of 18; adult males numbered 2,163, and 1,401 were adult women.[71] Such evidence is extremely valuable because it embraces the entire region and accords with official documentation. The annual natural loss of inhabitants of Left Bank Ukraine came to about 1.8 percent in 1929. Furthermore, the death rate of children under the age of 18 should not have exceeded 40 percent of the overall loss—that is, a total of 800. In fact, it was nearly five times higher than the norm, as was the death rate for adult men, whereas the loss of adult women was some 2.5 times higher.[72]

Losses were not evenly distributed within a given district. The estimates for the

Table 7. Number of rural women (in thousands) by generation in oblasts of Ukraine annexed after 1939 and in Russian oblasts neighboring Ukraine, according to the census of 1959.

Age Year of Birth	20–24 1934–1938 I	25–29 1929–1933 II	30–34 1924–1928 III	Ratio II:I
Oblast				
Volyn	31.3	34.6	31.2	1.11
Zakarpattia	30.3	30.5	28.5	1.01
Ivano-Frankivsk	42.2	43.3	35.8	1.03
Lviv	57.8	61.1	51.8	1.06
Rivne	39.6	40.0	33.3	1.01
Ternopil	41.3	44.3	39.3	1.07
Chernivtsi	27.8	27.5	25.5	0.99
Orel	27.6	29.7	33.4	1.08
Kursk	45.6	48.8	54.6	1.07
Voronezh	57.6	63.9	74.9	1.11
Lipetsk	30.5	31.7	35.9	1.04
Belgorod	38.7	39.5	48.2	1.02
Briansk	39.0	44.4	48.5	1.14

Source: *Itogi Vsesoiuznoi perepisi naseleniia 1959 goda: Ukrainskaia SSR* (Moscow, 1963); *RSFSR* (Moscow, 1963).

village of Bilousivka, for example, are approximately twice those for the Poltava oblast in general, but exactly why this should be so is difficult to explain. Judging by indirect evidence from the losses of livestock and the demographic correlation of generations in 1959, we note that Poltava occupied a somewhat intermediary position between the more prosperous northwest districts and the Dnipropetrovsk oblast, which suffered the effects of the Famine much more.

According to the secretary of the district executive committee, in the Novi Sandzhary district of Kharkiv oblast there were 11,680 deaths or 19.47 percent of all the district's inhabitants. This figure was confirmed when the remaining residents were questioned during the German occupation in the Second World War. Lists of those who had died in 1932–1934 were compiled by all twenty-five village soviets, showing that the total number of deaths in that period exceeded 10,000.[73]

Having compiled figures on several *khutors* in Sumy oblast, Hryts'ko Siryk describes 83 households, over 90 families, and the fates of 490 people (260 men and 230 women). He notes that 36 of these residents worked on the railroad or in industry, but even some of them were unable to avoid arrest and dekulakization. Fourteen farms were sold and, for some, their properties confiscated. Such dekulakization was carried out on northern *khutors* later than it was in the southern

Table 8. Number of rural women (in thousands) by generation in the North Caucasus, Lower Volga Basin, and several other RSFSR oblasts, according to the census of 1959.

Age Year of Birth	20–24 1934–1938 I	25–29 1929–1933 II	30–34 1924–1928 III	Ratio II:I
Oblast				
Krasnodar	103	74	111	0.72
Stavropol	62	50	63	0.81
Rostov-on-Don	62	52	68	0.84
Volgograd	34	30	38	0.88
Saratov	40	34	45	0.85
Orenburg	44	39	47	0.89
Cheliabinsk	32	29	34	0.91
Omsk	43	41	44	0.95
Amur	13	11	11.5	0.85

Source: *Itogi Vsesoiuznoi perepisi naseleniia 1959 goda: RSFSR* (Moscow, 1963).

regions of Ukraine, primarily in the years 1932–1933 and in 1934. Deportation to the north from this area was relatively rare, although Siryk mentions six individuals and six families who fled out of fear of being arrested and deported. Arrests, however, could be made for practically anything, including the failure to fulfill procurements. Eleven arrests occurred in this region in 1928–1932 and only ten in 1935 and in the following years.[74] Siryk also notes that seven *khutor* residents, including his own father, died of hunger in 1932–1933. From descriptions of the fates of individual families, however, it appears that the number was higher. Death from starvation was nearly always associated with the actions of authorities who seized or destroyed provisions. Siryk writes:

Table 9. Number of women (in thousands) of various nationalities living in rural areas.

Age	20–24	25–29	30–34	Ratios	
	I	II	III	II:I	II:III
Nationality					
Russian	1997	1972	2285	0.99	
Ukrainian[a]	988	879	1061	0.89	
Belarusian	240	241	234	1.00	
Kazakh	147	95	115		0.83
Georgian	81	75	70		1.07
Uzbek	193	200	155		1.29
Azerbaijani	103	84	56		1.5
Armenian	62	53	49		1.08
Kyrgyz	34	37	30		1.23
Tadzhik	53	49	37		1.32
Turkmen	27	27	23		1.17
Estonian	14	15	15	1.07	
Latvian	23.5	24	24.5	1.02	
Lithuanian	58	60	57	1.03	
Mordvinian	35	33	40	0.94	

a. Includes residents of territories annexed in 1939.

Note: The number for each nationality is given for the territories inhabited chiefly by the nationality in question—that is, within the borders of each Soviet national republic. The number of Russians, however, is given for the entire USSR.

Source: *Itogi Vsesoiuznoi perepisi naseleniia 1959 goda: SSSR* (Moscow, 1962), 54–71, 211–25.

Demyd Serdiuk, 65 years old, was arrested in 1931 for not paying his taxes, sentenced to forced labor, but soon released because of illness. His wife was nearly insane from grief. In 1932 the procurement brigade took all edible supplies from the house and arrested their son. In the winter of 1933, Demyd and his wife died on the same day and were buried in the same grave.

Trokhym Matviiovych Siryk, 55 years old, father of the author of the book. In 1930 he was dekulakized. In autumn 1932 the brigade took all his grain and, on the basis of a denunciation by a female neighbor, it found potatoes hidden in the yard. (The neighbor sought vengeance against Trokhym's wife, the author's stepmother, who had once made fun of her husband.) Trokhym died on 30 April 1933, having lived until the nettles and sorrel sprouted, but could not cope with diarrhea, and the local doctor could not help him at all. Three children were left orphans and in danger of starving to death, but the kolkhoz party worker gave orders that they each be issued 20 kg of buckwheat per month against possible future workdays on the kolkhoz.

The family of the rich kulak Iakym Rodionov. He died in 1927 from cancer. His wife Maria, son Sashko, and Hapka, the wife of his dead brother, lived with his nephew Vasyl', [who was a foreman] in a factory in the city. It is known only that all three died in 1933. Famine was not necessarily the direct cause for the death of two elderly women and a child. But undoubtedly the family experienced serious difficulties with food, since Maria and Sashko did not officially have the right to ration cards.[75]

In one form or another, the Famine hastened the death of these ten adults and two or three children described by Siryk. Comparatively speaking, these losses may not seem great when we consider the number of deaths in other parts of Ukraine. The elderly and the very young comprise the majority of those who died. Indications are that residents had a very poor diet but did not suffer the mass starvation described by other authors. Almost all cases of death by starvation in this district resulted from the searches and seizures of foodstuffs during the autumn of 1932 at the hands of the brigade of workers who had come merely for that purpose. A similar situation was to be observed in many parts of the Sumy oblast and other surrounding territories.

In contrast, the Book of Civil Records of Deaths of the Village of Romankove in Dnipropetrovsk oblast shows a catastrophic death rate.[76] Entries (documents 434–598) date from 1 August 1933, through 2 January 1934. The documents for 1 and 2 January (that is, nos. 597 and 598) have been crossed out, and to all appearances a new book was started to mark the beginning of 1934. For the preceding year, however, there must have been books containing documents numbered 1 through 433.

The number of deaths in the village for the year 1933 totaled 596, of whom 146 died in the last five months of the year. The total population of Romankove is not known, although we do know the total population of the Krynychky [formerly a part of the Kam'ianske] district in 1926: the 110 villages and 14 village soviets numbered 35,038 residents. Extrapolating from the demographic distribution in the district in 1959, we can estimate the population of Romankove in 1932 at between 4,500 and 5,000 people.[77] Indirect confirmation of the higher number is provided by the addresses of those who had died. That is, given that street addresses occur as high as 800, it is evident that there were hundreds of houses and presumably thousands of people.

The loss in one year of 12 percent of the population far exceeds the norm of 2 percent. In 1929, large cities such as Zaporizhzhia, Chernihiv, and Cherkasy numbered residents' deaths in the range 500–700.[78] In comparison with other villages, it should be pointed out, Romankove was in a rather good position, situated as it was near the town of Kam'ianske, now Dniprodzerzhynsk. As indicated in the registry of deaths, many of the residents worked in the Dnipro State [Metallurgical] Plant (Dniprovs'kyi derzhavnyi zavod im. Dzerzhyns'koho).

Between May and July 1933, twelve deaths are recorded (with incomplete information), but in August the number increases to 41. This is followed in September with 22 deaths, 28 in October, 27 in November, and 16 in December (again, with incomplete information). This death rate is higher than normal in all months, but in August it was four times the normal rate. Moreover, the average loss for the first half of 1933 was even higher, as more than 60 people per month died.

Of the 146 recorded deaths most (104) were registered immediately—that is, either on the day of the death or the day after. Eighteen other deaths were registered within three days, whereas nine deaths were entered anywhere from four to ten days after the fact. Another ten cases were registered 11–20 days after the death occurred, and five cases did not appear in the registry until several months later. In other words, the registration of 15 percent of the deaths was carried out after the funeral, although this was a prerequisite for the burial rite. This evidence suggests that at times deaths were never registered: if it were possible to register a death six months after the fact, then it was possible not to register it at all.

On 11 October 1933, four months after their deaths, the registrar M. Pletnev made the following entries regarding the fate of the Holenko family:

No. 536. Holenko Volodymyr. 2 years old, village of Romankove, Kam'ianske district, Ukrainian, boy, died 11/X. Mother, a domestic. Died at home. From bodily emaciation. 11/X. Signed: the registrar.

No. 537. Holenko, Hryhorii Maksymovich. 18 years old. Died 15/VI, 1933. Village of Romankove, 12th hundred (address), Ukrainian, male. Sister

an unskilled worker at the Dzerzhyns'kyi Plant. At home. From dysentery.
Signed: the registrar.

No. 538. Holenko, Kateryna Platonovna. 63 years old. Village Romankove,
Kam'ianske district, 12th hundred. Died 30/V in 1933. Woman, widow.
Daughter unskilled worker at the Dzerzhyns'kyi Plant. At home. From dys-
entery. Signed: the registrar.

No. 539. Holenko, Motria Maksymivna. Village Romankove, 12th hundred.
17 years old. Died 31/VI 33. Girl, Ukrainian. Sister unskilled worker, works at
the Dzerzhyns'kyi Plant. At home, from dysentery. Signed: the registrar.[79]

From these entries we can surmise that at the end of May 1933, the oldest
member of the family, Kateryna Platonovna, died. Fifteen days later, the son Hryhorii died, and fifteen days after that, a daughter, Motria, died. They all perished
at home from "dysentery," apparently without medical aid. There was no one to
report their deaths, perhaps no one even to bury them. Only a child, Volodymyr,
two years old, remained among the living for another three and a half months until
he too died. The cause cited is "bodily emaciation," apparently a euphemism for
starvation, although we have no direct evidence from the registry.

It is significant that in recording a death, the registrar mentioned other members
of the family—perhaps those responsible for reporting the deaths in the first place,
indicating a date and a time of death, and providing a diagnosis of the fatal illness.
The entries provide no signatures of witnesses, and it is possible that no one would
have reported the demise of the Holenko family if it had not been for the last
death, that of the child Volodymyr. Assuming that better records were kept in the
areas in and around large urban centers, and given that this registry exists from
a workers' settlement only six kilometers from Dniprodzerzhynsk, we can only
surmise that the record-keeping in small villages hundreds of kilometers from
large cities must have been haphazard and unreliable. No doubt there were cases in
which the deaths of entire families and people living alone went unregistered.

Moreover, infant mortality in Romankove was severely underestimated. In the
age group from birth to one year, only one death was noted among children up
to the age of one month, whereas three deaths were reported for those between
one and three months old. Among those three to four months old, the number of
deaths was seven. Altogether, there were twenty deaths of children up to a full
year old. According to such statistics, the death rate for those in the first three
months of life was 20 percent of all newborns, that is, twice as low as the average
throughout all Ukraine in the preceding years.[80] Admittedly, these statistics are
not based on a large population and may therefore reflect merely an accidental
divergence. Moreover, the decline in the birth rate could have affected the numbers

of the very youngest (those below the age of two months). Nevertheless, the most probable explanation lies in underestimating deaths among newborns by a factor of at least two or three.

Children below the age of two years accounted for about 23 percent of the total death rate in Romankove in 1933. This rate represents twice that in Ukraine in 1929. Adults ages 23–59 accounted for 25 percent of total deaths and those older than 60, 26 percent. In the whole of Ukraine, the rates were approximately 18 percent for these two demographic groups.[81] In short, the redistribution of the death rate is connected with the decrease in the number of children, the inaccurate registrations of deaths, and the increase in the death rate among the elderly. Undoubtedly a higher number of losses was observed in all age groups, but the elderly and the sick were especially vulnerable at this time.

The registration book for deaths in Romankove suggests that the village's medical aid was practically nonexistent in 1933. Only eleven of 148 people died in the hospital, whereas one died on the job, and 136 died at home. Infants and the elderly, suffering from tuberculosis and enteritis, were evidently treated with primitive home remedies or not treated at all. Although patients in the hospital received professional diagnoses of diseases such as measles, liver cancer, and typhoid fever, those dying at home were diagnosed by relatives or neighbors who used stock phrases: "a weak heart," "coughing and wheezing," "inflammation of the lungs," "chest cold," and, occasionally, "old age" (*starcheskaia nemoshch'*)." There is no doubt that illnesses such as cancer, scarlet fever, diphtheria, and whooping cough claimed many lives and were simply not recognized by those who reported the deaths.

Although they were misdiagnosed, one need not be an experienced physician to understand that what these people did experience—dysentery, diarrhea, bodily emaciation—had one etiology: starvation from the Famine. Few of the elderly, however, are listed in the records as having died from starvation and emaciation; rather their deaths are attributed to "old age." Nevertheless, we can assume that the number of elderly dying from starvation was approximately equal to the number of adult deaths in the age group 23–59, given that the total losses in these groups were at the same percentage—that is, 25 percent. Moreover, we know that the number of deaths in these two age groups during the years 1927–1929 were approximately equal—namely, 18 percent of the total populations of the two groups. In Romankove, some 12 percent of the population is said to have died from bodily emaciation. Deaths attributed to dysentery, diarrhea, and colitis—all a result of the Famine—accounted for 20 percent of the population's decline. These are typical illness of people suffering from famine over a long period of time. In the preceding prosperous years of 1924–1927, in both Ukrainian cities and villages, such digestive illnesses claimed the lives of only 6 percent of the population.[82] In contrast, these illnesses in Romankove accounted for 27 percent of the losses, and the level of the death rate clearly exceeded the norm. In short, we can conclude that the increased death rate from these causes comes to no less than 20 percent.

The Famine increased the loss of population from many other illnesses as well, as people's immune systems were severely weakened. Losses were especially high from upper respiratory infections and pneumonia. According to the demographer Iurii Korchak-Chepurkivs'kyi, in Ukraine the death rate from respiratory illnesses was approximately 5 percent. In Romankove, however, over three times that number died (17 percent), whereas cardiovascular illnesses in the village occurred at about the same percentage as those for the rest of Ukraine (10–11 percent). Let us remember, however, that this rate represents a clear increase in the incidence of actual deaths. Tuberculosis, which in Korchak-Chepurkivs'kyi's survey occupies first place among the various causes of death, held a modest tenth place in Romankove. If in the villages of Ukraine tuberculosis took the lives of more than 10 percent of the population (30 percent from adult groups aged 15–60 years), in Romankove it took only 4 percent and about 10 percent of the workers' age group.[83] Obviously the point here is not that there were fewer losses from tuberculosis in Romankove than in other places. On the contrary, starvation should undoubtedly have increased people's susceptibility to tuberculosis and to death resulting from it. For example, researchers note that during the Famine that occurred in 1918–1921, in the Civil War period, the death rate from tuberculosis increased one and a half times. This Romankove anomaly is explained by assuming that the decreased rate of death from tuberculosis results from increases in death among the population from other causes.

If we compare the death rate in Romankove with that during the Famine years of the Civil War, we find a surprising closeness of data (see table 10). Data from Petrograd has been selected because it was one of the few places where the death rate was calculated fairly accurately.[84] Not only do the basic reasons for population losses coincide, but even their proportions in the general structure of the death rate are similar. This parallel suggests that in both events similar processes were determining the rate of death. The demographer Sergei Novosel'skii points out that the death rate in Petrograd in 1919 surpassed that of 1910–1911 by a factor of three. Romankove likely had the same proportion between the norm of the preceding period and the death rate during the Famine of 1932–1933.

As is evident in table 11, the loss of population in Ukraine in 1927–1936 reached catastrophic proportions.[85] Although 9.05 million people were born in those years, the population actually decreased by 791,000. There were 9.841 million deaths, including 5.1 million from natural causes. In accordance with the age group death rates recorded at the beginning of this period, we can calculate that 3.934 million people perished. It must be noted that the calculations used in constructing table 11 are based on the entire population of Ukraine, both urban and rural, for the entire ten-year period; and they do not present a yearly breakdown of the loss.

Each age group of Ukraine's population lost immense numbers, several in the hundreds of thousands. More men died than women. Of those born before 1927 (i.e., counted in the census of 17 December 1926), approximately one out of every ten died from starvation during the ten years from 1927 to 1936. But by far the largest number died in 1933.

Approximately a third of those included in this population loss were Ukrainian children born between 1926 and 1937. The extremely high infant mortality rate is directly attributable to hunger and the unbearable living conditions. As has been pointed out, not all the deaths occurred from starvation. Weakened by malnutrition, however, people easily succumbed to any of several fatal diseases. Moreover, the increased rate of loss resulted from various campaigns of repression: the annihilation of the kulaks, the arrests of 1930–1931, the destruction of the Ukrainian intelligentsia in 1933–1936, and numerous other blows inflicted by Soviet secret police.

Table 10. Death-specific mortality rates (percentage of total mortality) in Petrograd in 1919 and in Romankove for the second half of 1933.

Causes of Death[a]	Petrograd, 1919	Romankove, 1933
Membranous and catarrhal pneumonia	12.6	16.9
Dysentery	11.9	15.5
Gastrointestinal diseases	9.8	10.8
Starvation	8.8	11.5[b]
Tuberculosis	6.2	4.0
Violent death	5.1	2.0
Typhoid fever	3.8	1.5
Senility	3.4	5.4[b]
Other	38.4	32.4
Total	**100.0**	**100.0**

a. Formulated according to Novosel'skii.
b. Part of the mortality rate from old age [*starcheskaia nemoshch'*] is regarded as death from starvation.

Sources: Sergei A. Novosel'skii, *Demografiia i statistika: Izbr. proizvedeniia* (Moscow, 1978), 110–11; "Book of Civil Records of Deaths in the Village of Romankove in Dnipropetrovsk Oblast," The Archive of the Canadian Institute of Ukrainian Studies, Edmonton, Alberta.

Data is lacking to support an estimate of the losses of specific ethnic groups. We do have evidence, however, that 1.3 million Kazakhs died in the period between 1926 and 1937. Furthermore, we can estimate that 90 percent of those who died in this period in Ukraine were in fact Ukrainians. Including those who lived in Kuban and in other territories of the USSR, the loss of Ukrainians reached as high as 4.1 million. On the whole, the population losses in the USSR during collectivization (1926–1937) total about 8.5 million. About half this number were children.[86]

This loss of children is undoubtedly a result of the worsening conditions in the USSR overall, as residents of both cities and villages received less meat, milk, and bread. The quality of what they did receive also declined. Products that had been quite common grew scarce and were seen as delicacies. Millions of children did not know that eggs, butter, sausage, cottage cheese, sour cream, sugar, and the like even existed. Many never learned. These worsening conditions, of course, affected small children the most.

Table 11. Population Changes in Ukraine, 1927–1937.

Population on December 17, 1926	29,189,000
Number of people born between 1927 and 1937	9,050,000
Decrease	-9,841,000
Attributable to natural causes	-5,100,000
Losses	-3,934,000
of those born before 1927	-2,624,000
of those born after 1927	-1,310,000
Migrations	-807,000
Population on January 1, 1937	**28,398,000**

Note: Iurii A. Korchak-Chepurkovskii, *Izbrannye demograficheskie issledovaniia,* provides a correction for underestimation of the age group 0–2 by 11.9 percent. My calculations contain an adjustment to official data on the birth rate in 1932–1934 and on the decrease in mortality in 1934–1936, with respect to the "norm" as presented in the mortality tables for 1925–1926.

Sources: Iurii A. Korchak-Chepurkovskii, *Izbrannye demograficheskie issledovaniia* (Moscow, 1970), 306–7; S. V. Kul'chyts'kyi and Sergei Maksudov, "Vtraty naselennie Ukraïny vid holodu 1933 [Losses in the population of Ukraine during the Famine of 1933]," *Ukraïns'kyi istorychnyi zhurnal,* no. 2 (1991): 10–19; Sergei Maksudov, "Otsinka vtrat naselennia Ukraïny v roky kolektyvizatsiï [Estimate of population losses in Ukraine during collectivization]," *Filosofs'ka i sotsiolohichna dumka,* no. 4 (1992): 118–31; Sergei Maksudov, "Migratsii v SSSR v 1926–1939 gg. [Migrations in the USSR in 1926–1939]," *Cahiers du monde russe* 40, no. 4 (October–December 1999): 763–96.

Dostoevsky once posed the question of whether it is possible to build a happy future for mankind at the cost of even a single child's suffering. To this question he himself spoke a resounding no. To torment, loot, and kill today for the sake of future well-being should be unthinkable. In Ukraine and elsewhere, the millions of corpses sacrificed for a social and political ideal, however grand or grandiose, led only to new cruelties and suffering that ultimately enveloped the reformers themselves. The architects of that vision discovered to their horror that they had built a great prison, rather than a palace, and that they themselves, both those who created it of their own free will and those who were compelled to do so, were incarcerated in it.

NOTES

*   Tables 6, 7, and 8 reprinted with permission from S. Maksudov, "The Geography of the Soviet Famine of 1933," *Journal of Ukrainian Studies* 8, no. 2 (Winter 1983): 57–58, tables 3, 4, and 5. Tables 5 and 9 adapted with permission from ibid., 56–57, tables 1 and 2. Table 11 adapted with permission from M. Maksudov, "Ukraine's Demographic Losses, 1927–1938," in Roman Serbyn and Bohdan Krawchenko, eds., *Famine in Ukraine, 1932–1933* (Edmonton, 1986): 38, table 1. The author would like to acknowledge the Canadian Institute of Ukrainian Studies for granting permission.

1.   Sergei Maksudov, "Collectivization and Population Losses in Ukraine and the USSR" (Cambridge, Mass., 1984). Some parts of this work were published in Maksudov, *Poteri naseleniia SSSR* (Benson, Vt., 1989), and in various articles. The publications that came out during the last decade confirm the general picture presented in this work and make it possible to arrive at a more accurate figure of population losses in Ukraine.

2.   Iosif V. Stalin, "Itogi pervoi piatiletki: Doklad 7 ianvaria 1933 g.," in *Sochineniia* (Moscow, 1951), 13:191. The Russian measurement system, with corresponding measures in the metric system, is used in this article: 1 pood = 16.38 kg; 1 kg = 2.2046 pounds; 1 centner = 100 kg; 1 ton = 1,000 kg.

3.   Sergei N. Prokopovich, *Narodnoe khoziaistvo SSSR* (New York, 1952), 1:213–15.

4.   *Sobranie zakonov i rasporiazhenii Raboche-krest'ianskogo pravitel'stva Soiuza Sovetskikh Sotsialisticheskikh Respublik*, no. 31 (1932): 190.

5.   Sergei P. Trapeznikov, *Istoricheskii opyt KPSS v osushchestvlenii leninskogo kooperativnogo plana* (Moscow, 1965), 400.

6.   Tsentral'noe statisticheskoe upravlenie SSSR, *Narodnoe khoziaistvo SSSR, 1922–1972: Iubileinyi statisticheskii ezhegodnik* (Moscow, 1972), 216–18; *Sel'skoe khoziaistvo SSSR: Statisticheskii sbornik TsSU* (Moscow, 1960), 27, 86–89.

7.   Kyïvs'kyi derzhavnyi universytet im. T. H. Shevchenka, Institut pidvyshchennia kvalifikatsiï vykladachiv suspil'nykh nauk, and Ukraïns'kyi naukovo-doslidnyi institut ekonomiky i orhanizatsiï sil's'koho hospodarstva im. O. H. Shlikhtera, *Sotsialistychna perebudova i rozvytok sil's'koho hospodarstva Ukraïns'koï RSR*, vol. 1, *1917–1937 rr.* (Kyiv, 1967), 462–63.

8.   Ivan I. Slyn'ko, *Sotsialistychna perebudova i tekhnichna rekonstruktsiia sil's'koho hospodarstva Ukraïny, 1927–1932 rr.* (Kyiv, 1961), 286; Vasyl' I. Hryshko, *Ukraïns'kyi "Holokost," 1933* (New York and Toronto, 1978), 47; Tamara Polishchuk comp., *Chorni zhnyva: Holod 1932–1933 rokiv u Valkivs'komu ta Kolomats'komu raionakh Kharkivshchyny; Dokumenty, spohady, spysky pomerlykh* (Kyiv, 1997), 110–11.

9. F. M. Rudych et al., eds., *Holod 1932–1933 rokiv na Ukraïni: Ochyma istorykiv, movoiu dokumentiv*, comp. R. Ia. Pyrih et al. (Kyiv, 1990), 250–54, 278–79, 296–99.

10. Rudych et al., *Holod 1932–1933 rokiv na Ukraïni*, 260–65, 291–300, 311–14, 334–35; S. V. Kul'chyts'kyi, ed., *Kolektyvizatsiia i holod na Ukraïni, 1929–1933: Zbirnyk dokumentiv i materialiv* (Kyiv, 1992), 563, 567, 577; *Visti VUTsVK* (Kharkiv), 27 December 1932; Slyn'ko, *Sotsialistychna perebudova i tekhnichna rekonstruktsiia*, 297–98.

11. Viktor P. Danilov, ed., *Ocherki istorii kollektivizatsii sel'skogo khoziaistva v soiuznykh respublikakh* (Moscow, 1963), 55.

12. *Sobranie zakonov*, no. 70 (1932): 418; Kul'chyts'kyi, *Kolektyvizatsiia i holod na Ukraïni, 1929–1933* (Kyiv, 1992), 548–49; Polishchuk, *Chorni zhnyva*, 110–11.

13. Oleksa Kalynyk, *Shcho nese z soboiu komunizm? Dokumenty pro rosiis'ko-komunistychnyi teror v Ukraïni* (Munich, 1953), 21–22.

14. Ibid.

15. Rudych et al., *Holod 1932–1933 rokiv na Ukraïni*, 350–70.

16. Iurii A. Moshkov, *Zernovaia problema v gody sploshnoi kollektivizatsii sel'skogo khoziaistva SSSR (1929–1932 gg.)* (Moscow, 1966), 221.

17. Rudych et al., *Holod 1932–1933 rokiv na Ukraïni*, 341–42.

18. *Izvestia TsIK SSSR i VTsIK (Izvestiia Tsentral'nogo ispolnitel'nogo komiteta Soiuza SSR i Vserossiiskogo tsentral'nogo ispolnitel'nogo komiteta sovetov rabochikh krestianskikh i krasnoarmeiskikh deputatov)*, no. 265, 24 September 1932.

19. *Pravda* (Moscow), 15 February 1933.

20. P. Liutarevych, "Tsyfry i fakty pro holod v Ukraïni," *Ukraïns'kyi zbirnyk* 2 (1955): 97. The date of this document is probably incorrect. A similar text can be found in Stalin and Molotov's telegram published in Rudych et al., *Holod 1932–1933 rokiv na Ukraïni*, 238.

21. Liutarevych, "Tsyfry i fakty pro holod v Ukraïni," 97–98.

22. *Novoe russkoe slovo* (New York), 29 March 1963.

23. *Izvestia TsIK SSSR i VTsIK*, no. 218, 8 August 1932.

24. *Sobranie zakonov*, no. 12 (1927): 122–23; no. 50 (1927): 505–6; no. 9 (1931): 104–5.

25. *Sobranie zakonov*, no. 69 (1932): 413; no. 2 (1933): 9.

26. *Sobranie zakonov*, no. 4 (1933): 26.

27. *Sobranie zakonov*, no. 6 (1932): 41; no. 33 (1932): 190–91.

28. *Sobranie zakonov*, no. 79 (1933): 481.

29. *Sobranie zakonov*, no. 14 (1933): 81; no. 4 (1933): 27.

30. Vasilii S. Nemchinov, *Izbrannye proizvedeniia* (Moscow, 1967), 4:331.

31. *Itogi desiatiletiia sovetskoi vlasti v tsifrakh, 1917–1927* (Moscow, 1927), 357.

32. Ibid., 354–60; Moshkov, *Zernovaia problema*, 136.

33. Moshkov, *Zernovaia problema*, 136.

34. Danilov, ed., *Ocherki istorii kollektivizatsii sel'skogo khoziaistva v soiuznykh respublikakh*, 147.

35. Tsentral'noe statisticheskoe upravlenie SSSR, *Narodnoe khoziaistvo SSSR 1922–1972*, 216–18; *Sel'skoe khoziaistvo SSSR*, 27, 86–89, 196, 328–29; Moshkov, *Zernovaia problema*, 226.

36. *Itogi desiatiletiia sovetskoi vlasti v tsifrakh*, 214–19; Moshkov, *Zernovaia problema*, 226.

37. Moshkov, *Zernovaia problema*, 226; Rudych et al., *Holod 1932–1933 rokiv na Ukraïni*, 336; Smolensk Oblast Party Archive, 1917–1938, Records of the All-Union (Russian) Communist Party, Smolensk District [hereafter cited as WKP], file (*delo*) no.162.

38. *Narodnoe khoziaistvo Ukrainy v 1921–1922 godu* (Kharkiv, 1923), viii, 1–15.

39. *Statistika Ukrainy* (Kharkiv), no. 7 (1921): 118; no. 8 (1922), 4–5, 9–41; no. 20 (1922): 2–10, 50–54, 56–59.

40. Aleksandr Asatkin, ed., *Narodne hospodarstvo USRR: Statystychnyi dovidnyk* (Kyiv, 1935), 251–63.

41. Moshkov, *Zernovaia problema*, 128. Many examples of food supplies for workers and other groups are given in E. A. Osokina, *Ierarkhiia potrebleniia: O zhizni liudei v usloviiakh stalinskogo snabzheniia (1928–1935)* (Moscow, 1993).

42. WKP, no. 159.

43. WKP, nos. 128–29.

44. V. I. Fil'kin et al., eds., *Istoriia industrializatsii Severnogo Kavkaza*, vol. 2 *(1933–1941)* (Grozny, 1973), 82–83.

45. WKP, no. 348.

46. WKP, no. 348.

47. Moshkov, *Zernovaia problema*, 136.

48. Asatkin, *Narodne hospodarstvo USRR*, 296–99, 314–15.

49. *Narodnoe khoziaistvo Ukrainy v 1921–1922 godu*, viii, 10–11.

50. *Itogi desiatiletiia sovetskoi vlasti v tsifrakh, 1917–1927*, 354.

51. Iurii Semenko, ed., *Holod 1933 roku v Ukraïni: Svidchennia pro vynyshchuvannia Moskvoiu ukraïns'koho selianstva* (Munich, 1963), 4.

52. Liutarevych, "Tsyfry i fakty pro holod v Ukraïni," 80–98.

53. Dmytro F. Solovei, *Holhota Ukraïny* (Winnipeg, 1953), 1:189; M. Verbyts'kyi, *Naibil'shyi zlochyn Kremlia: Zaplianovanyi shtuchnyi holod v Ukraïni 1932–1933 rokiv* (London, 1952), 83–85; Semenko, *Holod 1933 roku v Ukraïni*, 15.

54. Lev Kopelev, *I sotvoril sebe kumira* (Ann Arbor, 1978), 300–302.

55. Solovei, *Holhota Ukraïny*, 1:184.

56. Verbyts'kyi, *Naibil'shyi zlochyn Kremlia*, 29.

57. Liutarevych, "Tsyfry i fakty pro holod v Ukraïni," 93.

58. Ivan Trifonov, *Ocherki istorii klassovoi bor'by v SSSR, 1921–1937* (Moscow, 1960), 258.

59. Liutarevych, "Tsyfry i fakty pro holod v Ukraïni," 86.

60. Verbyts'kyi, *Naibil'shyi zlochyn Kremlia*, 97.

61. Liutarevych, "Tsyfry i fakty pro holod v Ukraïni," 97.

62. Nikita Sergeevich Khrushchev, *Khrushchev Remembers* (Boston, 1970), 73–74, 109.

63. H. Sova, *Do istoriï bol'shevyts'koï diisnosty (25 rokiv zhyttia ukraïns'koho hromadianyna v SSSR)*, Institute for the Study of the History and Culture of the USSR, Research Materials, series 2, no. 24 (Munich, 1955), 18.

64. Frank Lorimer, *The Population of the Soviet Union: History and Prospects* (Geneva, 1946), 127, 134.

65. Naukove tovarystvo im. Shevchenka (Lviv), *Ukraïns'kyi statystychnyi richnyk, 1936–1937* (Warsaw, 1938), 26–33.

66. Maksudov, "Geography of the Soviet Famine," 52–58.

67. Tsentral'noe statisticheskoe upravlenie, *Itogi Vsesoiuznoi perepisi naseleniia 1959 goda: SSSR* (Moscow, 1962), 54–71, 211–25; *RSFSR* (Moscow, 1963), 62–97; *Ukrainskaia SSR* (Moscow, 1963), 32–43; *Kazakhskaia SSR* (Moscow, 1962), 30–41.

68. M. V. Ptukha, *Vybrani pratsi* (Kyiv, 1971), 446; E. A. Sadvokasova, *Sotsial'no-gigienicheskie aspekty regulirovaniia razmerov sem'i* (Moscow, 1969), 30.

69. William Henry Chamberlain, *The Ukraine: A Submerged Nation* (New York, 1944), 60–61.

70. Solovei, *Holhota Ukraïny*, 1:187.

71. Liutarevych, "Tsyfry i fakty pro holod v Ukraïni," 80–98. The normal death rate of 2 percent would have been somewhat lower in 1929 if we consider as well the decline in the birth rate in the European parts of the USSR, since child mortality is generally far higher than the norm for the remainder of the population. With fewer children being born, the overall death rate should have declined accordingly, making the actual increase in mortality all the more dramatic.

72. Tsentral'ne statystychne upravlinnia, *Statystyka Ukraïny* (Kharkiv), no. 213 (1932), Seriia Demohrafiia 4, no. 10, *Pryrodnyi rukh liudnosty v 1929 r.*, 12–15.

73. Sova, *Do istoriï bol'shevyts'koï diisnosty*, 16.

74. Hryts'ko Siryk, *Fakty i podiï dlia maibutn'oï istoriï Sivershchyny: Moï deiaki zauvahy do "Istoriia mist i sil URSR: Sums'ka oblast',"* Kyiv—1973 (Toronto, 1975), 31–109.

75. Ibid., 36–37, 63–80, 107–9.

76. Kalynyk, *Shcho nese z soboiu komunizm*, 106–12; Book of Civil Records of Deaths in the Village of Romankove in Dnipropetrovsk oblast, covering the second half of 1933. A microfilm copy of this document is on file at the Canadian Institute of Ukrainian Studies, Edmonton.

77. *Istoriia mist i sil URSR: Dnipropetrovs'ka oblast'* (Kyiv, 1973), 365–67.

78. *Statystyka Ukraïny*, no. 213 (1932), *Pryrodnyi rukh liudnosty v 1929 r.*, 12–18.

79. Kalynyk, *Shcho nese z soboiu komunizm*, 106–12.

80. Ptukha, *Vybrani pratsi*, 308–9.

81. Tsentral'ne statystychne upravlinnia, *Statystyka Ukraïny*, no. 213 (1932), *Pryrodnyi rukh liudnosty v 1929 r.*, 12–18.

82. Iurii A. Korchak-Chepurkovskii, *Izbrannye demograficheskie issledovaniia* (Moscow, 1970), 250–61.

83. Ibid.

84. Sergei A. Novosel'skii, *Demografiia i statistika* (Moscow, 1978), 10–11.

85. Maksudov, *Poteri naseleniia SSSR*. See also Maksudov, "Ukraine's Demographic Losses," 27–43; Maksudov, "Migratsii v SSSR v 1926–1939 godakh," *Cahiers du monde russe* 40, no. 4 (October–December 1999), 763–96.

86. Maksudov, "Poteri naseleniia v gody kollektivizatsii," *Zven'ia, istoricheskii al'manakh* (Moscow, 1991–1992), 1:65–112.

The Collectivization Famine in Kazakhstan, 1931–1933

NICCOLÒ PIANCIOLA

For all its magnitude and unprecedented loss of life, the Great Famine of 1932–1933 in Ukraine was not the only, nor the first, famine disaster connected with Stalin's collectivization drive. In the Russian Federation, the largely Ukrainian-inhabited Kuban, the adjacent Don Cossack region, and parts of the Volga region (especially the Volga German areas) were also profoundly affected. The earliest and most disastrous was the experience of Kazakhstan.[1] In fact, as a national group, proportionately the Kazakhs suffered most the consequences of the "revolution from above" in the rural sector: according to the most recent and reliable estimates, S. Maksudov concludes that the number of Kazakh deaths directly attributable to the Famine of 1931–1933 was 1,450,000, or approximately 38 percent of the total population, the highest percentage of any nationality in the USSR.[2]

To understand this catastrophe, its antecedents, and its aftermath in Kazakhstan it is important to consider some characteristics of the region. Traditionally a land of pastoral nomadism, Kazakhstan was yet differentiated from other zones in the USSR where nomad-pastoral peoples lived: it was one of the Asiatic regions of the Russian Empire where the agricultural colonization of Europeans (primarily Russians, Ukrainians, and Germans) on the vast expanses occupied by native peoples had been strongest. In 1916 in the six Kazakh provinces—Turgai, Akmolinsk, Uralsk, Semipalatinsk, Syr Darya and Semirech'e—just under 1.4 million colonists from the European part of the empire were present, nearly a fourth of the total population of the region.[3] Kazakhstan was a Soviet republic (along with Kyrgyzstan and Turkmenistan) in which nomadic or seminomadic herdsmen constituted an exceptionally large percentage of the population: according to data from the Kazakh Bureau of Statistics, in the late 1920s, only 23 percent of Kazakhs were entirely sedentary.[4] The herdsmen did not produce, but did consume, grain. The majority of the native population was composed of herdsmen, only some of whom were nomads, migrating year-round in arid regions or seasonally in the mountain pastures.

In the first historical study specifically on the Famine, Dana Dalrymple pointed out that Kazakhstan, unlike Ukraine and the other areas of the USSR affected by the Famine, was not a breadbasket for the Soviet Union.[5] Northern and eastern Kazakhstan, however, were areas into which Moscow wanted to expand grain cultivation, and, unlike the Central Asian republics, Kazakhstan was included in the Eastern Producer Region, one of the five huge agricultural regions into which the USSR was divided at that time. Moreover, unlike Ukraine and the other affected areas of the USSR, Kazakhstan was a region where between 200,000 and 300,000 "dekulakized" peasants arrived in the period 1930–1934.[6]

In the 1920s Kazakhstan was a peculiar frontier society that had not yet recovered from the 1916–1922 agricultural crisis when hundreds of thousands of Kazakhs died. Northwest Kazakhstan was one of the areas in the USSR struck hardest by the Famine of 1921. The violent methods of requisitioning officially abolished by the New Economic Policy (NEP) continued to be used at least until the harvest of 1922. In addition, recently published archival documents indicate that in 1923 and 1924, a large part of the USSR stretching from Ukraine to the Volga, Siberia, and northern Kazakhstan was hit by a drought that led to the deaths of hundreds of thousands of people. In February 1924, starvation was widespread in many zones in the Aktiubinsk and Kustanai gubernias. The following June, in the Akmolinsk gubernia alone, a census found between 50,000 and 60,000 people suffering from hunger.[7]

To many peasants the state represented forced taxation and military service, and so the Kazakhs remained essentially alienated from the state. The majority of Kazakhs were so poor that they were exempt from taxation and military service. Few had any schooling, and the level of illiteracy among the nomads was one of the highest of any national group in the Soviet Union.

This peculiar frontier society, which was struggling to emerge from the upheavals of 1916–1922, was struck by a second crisis in 1928. The events were characterized not only by the grain requisition crisis but also by a more generalized assault on the Kazakh way of life. This was a campaign to eliminate traditional authority, with the intent to incorporate the Kazakhs into the state governed from Moscow. A full-scale offensive, this process consisted of four stages. In 1928, there was a campaign to requisition the wealth and livestock of the "great *bais*," rich owners of livestock who represented authority and the ownership of the resources of the entire nomad community.[8] Second, young Kazakhs became for the first time subject to the military draft, beginning in the autumn of 1928. (The only prior attempt at mobilizing natives had led to the great revolt of 1916.) Third, the state created a category called "crimes based on tradition" and banned many of the

Kazakhs' cultural practices—a process common to "backward nationalities" in the USSR. Fourth, the region was opened in April 1929 to European colonists.

The breakthrough of 1928 was presented in propaganda as the social revolution that Kazakhstan had been awaiting since the Bolsheviks came to power, the "little October" of which Filipp Goloshchekin, the party head in Kazakhstan, had spoken. But the campaign's targets were not only the rural elite. These shifts in fact went hand in hand with the marginalization and arrests of many formerly important members of the Kazakh nationalist party, Alash Orda, who still held positions in Kazakh institutions, and with a purge inside the Party, in which the Kazakh Bolsheviks opposed to what was happening were removed from their positions.

The 1927–1928 Kazakh campaign to requisition grain was the first example of requisitioning aimed at bringing about collectivization and dekulakization (in this case "debaiization") in the USSR. While it was being carried out, mechanisms of "redistribution of damages" emerged that would lead to the death of over a million Kazakhs. What was officially described as the expropriation of the property of approximately 700 owners of large animal herds acted as a cover for the indiscriminate pillaging of the entire rural Kazakh population.[9]

The same mechanisms can be observed during the collectivization in the winter of 1929–1930. In Kazakhstan, during the first year of the collectivization campaign, the main objective had been the incorporation of European peasants. The areas most involved were therefore the most highly colonized ones, a swath that took in the northern and eastern regions of the republic. The first phase of collectivization followed a pattern common to other regions in the USSR: large-scale revolts, the rapid entry of peasants into the kolkhozes during winter, and their exodus en masse in the spring after Stalin's letter "Dizzy with Success" was published in *Pravda* on 1 March 1930. Although the Kazakhs were not the principal target of the first collectivization drive, they suffered greatly from the grain requisitioning.

After the March retreat, Kazakh officials sought to get a clearer idea of the situation on the ground, especially in the areas where most rebellions had occurred. In April 1930, the Kazakh official E. Ernazarov went to Balkhash, a nomad district where there had been an uprising shortly before. This district, with Lake Balkhash in the north, had a population of approximately 25,000. It was one of the three regions in Alma-Ata oblast that had been officially designated as having "a purely nomad economy" by the commission responsible for defining the dominant agricultural activity in each district, in order to subdivide procurement quotas of grain, meat, and animals. The soviets had been organized there only in 1928, at the time of the first campaigns of forced requisitioning. The district's executive committee's plan called for the requisitioning of 410 tons of grain, an amount it exceeded by an impressive 66 tons. However, as Ernazarov warned Goloshchekin, "the grain and seed were collected at the cost of ruining animal herding; in the district grain was used as currency." Animals were bartered for grain, and the Kazakh herdsmen "were forced to exchange their last cow for grain, in order to observe the dispositions from the local official bodies." As a consequence, the number of animals dropped 35 percent.[10]

Until the spring of 1930, events confirmed what the debaiization campaign had taught regional and national officials two years previously: enforced grain requisitions were carried out at the expense of the Kazakhs. The same practices were followed in setting the grain quotas for 1930–1931. In September 1930, the OGPU reported that the authorities in the Kzyl-Orda district had divided the amount of grain to be delivered among the various zones in the district in such a way that *half* of the district's grain levy would have to be furnished by the Kazalinsk area, one of those classified as having a "purely nomad economy." This decision caused riots and revolts.[11]

The winter of 1930–1931, in fact, saw a new wave of collectivization, this time without the state in any way relenting the following spring. The harvest was even lower than the previous one, while requisitions had been increased from 33 percent to 39.5 percent of the crops gathered. The year 1931 witnessed a turning point also in the policy on the nomads. Faced with growing difficulties in the kolkhoz system, especially the fact that the kolkhozes desperately needed draft animals, authorities decided to have recourse to the livestock the nomads still owned, which was to be used in practice as reserve wealth to shore up the collective system of agriculture that was on the brink of collapse. Meanwhile, between 1930 and 1931, more than 200,000 "dekulakized" peasants (overwhelmingly Russian) had been deported to the region.[12]

During the winter of 1929–1930, along with all-out collectivization and deku-lakization, the "sedentarization of the nomads" had also been decreed, but by the end of 1930, a Moscow commission concluded that the work of sedentarization was at a "standstill." Later, the only work undertaken was the building of barracks of the poorest quality and limited quantity. The nomads viewed sedentarization with great hostility. The herdsmen saw sedentarization as a "trap," devised so that a census could be taken and make it easier to tax and depredate them.[13]

According to the plan, for the end of 1933, some 544,000 people should have been forced to remain in "sedentarization points." Three years later, however, only 70,000 families had been involved,[14] from which the number of those who left the sedentarization points to escape starvation and disease has to be deducted. By concentrating people and animals, the main effect of such "sedentarization points" that were actually formed was to spread disease among humans and animals.

The sole provision carried out for the sedentarization was the construction of housing, which, however, proceeded very slowly because of a shortage of funds and materials and because of the disorganization in transportation. What is more important is that the "sedentarization points" had been chosen without verifying whether they could provide sustenance for animals or even whether there was potable water available for people. Contemporary reports are consistently critical of the choice of these settlements, most of which were located far from pastures and watercourses.[15] In the chaotic conditions that emerged as entire regions were disrupted by revolts against collectivization and as thousands of peasants were uprooted and resettled in the region, Kazakh herdsmen, less valuable for state economic objectives, were marginalized and shunted to the worst land. Even the financing for sedentarization was diverted toward districts where there was a stable Russian agriculture. A fundamental circumstance was the significant difference between the attitude of Slavic officials (the majority in the region) and Kazakh ones. The Slavs' attitude toward sedentarization was basically one of indifference: many local administrators hardly cared about what was happening. Their standard attitude was that it was the Kazakh officials who should be responsible for sedentarizing the Kazakhs. The latter, in many cases, made no attempt to establish "sedentarization points" (which in a time of famine were death traps) but instead sought to convince the nomads to flee Kazakhstan.[16]

Territorially limited famines started to multiply as early as the spring of 1930, the period of huge Kazakh uprisings. Crowds of Slavic peasants, often led by village women, demanded—on occasion successfully—that requisitioned grain be redistributed to the starving.[17] Nevertheless, only with the subsequent requisition and collectivization campaign, launched in late 1930 and early 1931, did the food situation reach the point of no return for the nomads. At the beginning of 1931, the territorial party committee (*kraikom*) of Kazakhstan decided to carry out the final attack on livestock still owned by the pastoralists, among other reasons to feed a kolkhoz sector that had not yet become productive and in which peasants had killed off most of their livestock before being forced to join the collective farms.[18] In 1931, livestock requisitions reached the record level of 68.5 percent of the total number of animals owned by the peasants.[19] Most of the livestock collected had to be sent to feed the cities and to supply the collective farms *outside* Kazakhstan. On 9 September 1931, a resolution of the *kraikom* ordered that 37 percent of the livestock requisition amount should remain inside the republic "with the aim of the speedy reconstruction of the livestock economy of the region, and of the replenishing of the sovkhozes' and kolkhozes' herds."[20] This meant that almost two-thirds of the collected livestock were to be transferred beyond the borders of the republic.

Disorganization in the requisitions process, the lack of forage, and the preference of herdsmen to kill their livestock rather than to surrender them to requisition brigades led to a massive decline in the number of farm animals in the republic. The almost total disappearance of Kazakh livestock was seen as the most serious and least expected of the economic consequences of collectivization in the region. Between 1928 and 1934 Kazakh livestock as a percentage of the Soviet total declined from 18 to 4.5 percent.[21] For the entire USSR between 1928 and 1933, the number of cattle fell by 44 percent, and of sheep and goats by as much as 65 percent;[22] for Kazakhstan the respective figures were 79 percent and 90 percent.[23]

By the autumn of 1931, the Famine was already widespread among nomads, but only in the spring of 1932 did it spread to the European settlers in Kazakhstan. Large numbers of people, devastated by malnutrition, died in epidemics of typhus, scurvy, and smallpox. Cannibalism became widespread. Whereas the famines of 1917–1924 had occurred in different provinces at different times, in the years 1931–1933 the situation was equally tragic throughout Kazakhstan.

Between 1930 and 1934 regional officials had no clear idea of how many people were actually present in the republic. Figures from 1934 showed a decrease since the late 1920s in the total population of approximately 1.7 million people (from 6.5 million to 4.8 million), at a time when the number of people living in cities had nearly tripled. The number of Kazakhs who had died of starvation was not established, nor was the number of refugees who had fled the republic or the number who came back in subsequent years.[24] All that is certain is that entire zones were emptying of their inhabitants.

People began to leave Kazakhstan during the first winter of requisitioning, in 1927–1928; the exodus was to continue in the years to come.[25] People moved to cities and train stations, then fled Kazakhstan to all the surrounding regions: China, Siberia, Central Asia, and the Urals. Two hundred thousand Kazakh herdsmen (less than 10 percent of the Kazakh rural population) fled the republic in 1930.[26] Starting in the autumn of 1931, the emigration wave assumed gigantic proportions: more than 1.5 million rural Kazakhs fled.[27] According to some estimates 200,000 fled to China, whereas another million poured into other Soviet republics. Another commission cited these data: 286,000 families (over a million people) left the republic between 1930 and 1931; 78,000 in 1932, and 31,000 in 1933.[28] The 1931–1932 exodus was the first time refugees left without taking their animals with them and the first time that large numbers of people died. A new term was coined in bureaucratic language to indicate a former herdsman who had lost his livestock and become a refugee—otkochevnik (from kochevnik "nomad"). In the years that followed 400,000 people returned or were forcefully brought back to the republic. The return of Kazakhs from year to year tapered off but continued throughout the 1930s. In 1937, there were still many Kazakhs who had remained in the areas where they had taken refuge during the Famine. The presence of former Kazakh nomads was reported in the Moscow, Stalingrad, Kuibyshev, Saratov and Voronezh regions, and in the Volga German Autonomous Republic. Many of these refugees were "re-deported" to the places from which they had fled. The movement of nomads to neighboring Soviet republics caused enormous problems for the regional officials, who protested vigorously against Goloshchekin and pressed the government to make Kazakhstan stem the flow.[29] In Siberia thefts of livestock by the mass of starving newcomers enflamed tensions between the Siberian population and the refugees, and there were numerous reports of violence against Kazakhs by the Russian population.[30]

The Kazakhs were not the only ones to leave. Many European peasants also sought safety in flight. A report on the Alma-Ata region from October 1933 noted that many European peasants were leaving, moving toward Ukraine and the Northern Caucasus, the regions from which they had originally come and where they had relatives. Other European peasants fled to China.[31]

A further consequence of the situation was the abandonment of children. In Kazakhstan in 1933 there were approximately 61,000 destitute children, either orphans or children abandoned by parents who could no longer feed them.[32] In late 1931 and early 1932, thousands of people had already died in the cities and industrial zones where refugees were concentrated. For example, during the winter, on the site of the copper mining complex on Lake Balkhash, at least 4,000 corpses of Kazakhs were buried in the snow.[33] Thefts by the starving Kazakhs provoked angry reactions from the peasants, who resorted to violence against the former nomads to drive them out of their areas. Widespread rumors convinced many Russians that the Kazakhs were eating Russian children. The threat of epidemics inspired a general terror, further fomenting peasant hostility against the former nomads.[34] The Kazakhs were the first to be fired by sovkhozes and expelled from kolkhozes, whose directors, in a situation of general hardship, chose to dismiss the least skilled and useful workers. Often directors got rid of entire cohorts of workers.[35]

The collapse of agricultural production and animal husbandry, the inability to contain the social crisis triggered by collectivization, and the increasingly insistent protests arriving from the apparatchiks in Kazakhstan, especially from Kazakh officials,[36] convinced Moscow to remove Goloshchekin in January 1933, at the height of the Famine.

Levon Mirzoian, a protegé of Sergei Kirov who held a high position in the Urals, was appointed as Goloshchekin's replacement. The new *kraikom* found a disastrous demographic and economic situation. Half of the Kazakh population was missing (those who survived were coming back into the republic) and the entire livestock-raising economy was destroyed. Although the situation was also difficult in 1933–1934 (cattle figures continued to decrease in 1934, but at a reduced rate), the harvest of 1933 was the first step towards recovery. Already months before, in order to speed up the process of replacing livestock, Moscow had decreed a massive purchase of cattle from China and a liberalization in the owning of livestock. On 17 September 1932, the Party Central Committee in Moscow permitted Kazakh collective farmers to own a private herd. The

Kazkraikom issued a similar resolution on 19 October. The livestock that could be privately owned amounted to 100 sheep and goats and 5 cows. Taking into consideration the scarcity of livestock in the republic at that time, these measures amounted to privatizing *all* the livestock remaining in Kazakhstan.[37] In this way, the state allowed a sort of compromise between a totally collectivized agriculture and traditional livestock breeding. The remaining Kazakhs, now dependent on state distributions of grain and cattle for survival, found a way of living in the collective farms, where in most cases the new kolkhoz brigades proceeded along the old transhumance routes. On 19 December 1934, Mirzoian announced at a convocation of the party branch in Alma-Ata that the number of the head of livestock that could be privately owned would rise to 150 sheep and goats and 7 cows. Meanwhile, Kazakhstan underwent yet another economic-administrative subdivision: this time it was divided into three large economic areas. In the first (animal-raising raions), it would be possible to own the number of animals listed above; in the second (mixed-economy raions), the number was 5 cows and 40 to 50 small animals; in the third (cotton- and grain-growing raions), the number was 2 to 3 oxen, 2 to 3 young pigs and 15 head of sheep and goats.[38]

The way in which the offensive against nomad society was carried out raises three questions: (1) Was depriving the Kazakhs of their means of sustenance planned and, if it was, at what level in the administrative and command apparatus was the decision taken? (2) To what extent did that decision reflect the anti-Kazakh prejudices of local officials and plenipotentiaries, the majority of whom were Slavic? (3) What institutional mechanisms led to the failure of sedentarization and turned that plan into the plunder and marginalization of the nomads?

The logic of the situation naturally led in the direction of plundering the Kazakhs, beyond ethnic tensions (which, however, made the outcome worse), within a system of administration intent on intimidating its underlings, creating shortages at the local level, and extracting the most resources possible from the population. If we examine the logic of relationships of power within the chain of command and the input that came from above, what emerges is the following pattern. The plenipotentiaries or officials in a Kazakh province received orders from Alma-Ata (which had in turn been threatened by Moscow) to collect an unrealistic amount of grain. The Slavic peasants worked the land and grew grain, whereas the herdsmen consumed the grain but did not grow it. Instead they owned large numbers of animals that could be used on land being brought into cultivation in order to increase grain production—all the more necessary since the peasants had killed much of their own livestock during their first winter under collectivization. Given that the consignment quotas were extremely high and the officials were obliged to implement harsh policies, it was preferable to protect as long as possible the grain the peasants had so they would not lack seed for sowing the following year. If this precaution were not taken, there would be no harvest the next year, and the official would be removed for not meeting quotas. If he turned instead to the grain in Kazakh hands, taxing them for an amount of grain that was far higher than what they were suspected to have, this action would force them to sell their animals. The result would have been threefold: more draft animals for farm work; a decrease in the number of animals the Kazakhs owned (in itself a source of continuous conflict with the peasants over pasture rights and the destruction from herds grazing in the peasants' fields); and the Kazakhs' abandoning their nomadic animal herding, a form of economic activity that was not highly productive from the point of view of the state. Under such conditions the impoverished Kazakhs would presumably want to be sedentarized; they would turn into tillers of previously uncultivated land, or might be sent to work in mines and at industrial construction sites; or, more likely, they would simply flee the district and become refugees. In any case, the problem they represented for the official who headed the district would be resolved.

Above and below this intermediate level, there was a variety of strategies: the peasants benefited to some degree by plundering the nomads and competed with them to avoid starvation; the regional officials in Alma-Ata, attempting to satisfy the ever increasing demands from the center, intentionally set into motion the mechanisms for funneling resources away from the nomads, or in any case backed the dynamics operating at the lower levels of the administrative pyramid. The responsibility for the mass deaths that occurred, therefore, hovers somewhere on the border between state and society, where minor officials handled the center's transforming directives for their own ends, in such a way as to redistribute the damage caused by the input from above.

But how well was this input, these orders from the center, understood locally? How did the peripheral institutions decide an order of priority for orders flooding in from Moscow and Alma-Ata? These questions lead us to the third question raised above: why was sedentarization never genuinely attempted?

The impression one gets from reading the documents is that the term "sedentarization" in the years from 1930 to 1934 had two different meanings corresponding to two different periods: the two years from the beginning of 1930 to the end of 1931, and the two years that coincide with the Famine, from the autumn of 1931 to the 1933 harvest. Understood as the settling of nomads in agricultural and animal-raising villages, sedentarization was a low-priority policy in the period 1930–1931, which no local organization actually put into practice and which even official propaganda ignored. During this period the real policies toward the nomads included enforcement of grain and livestock requisitions, and the marginalization of nomads on land of poor quality. Sedentarization existed almost exclusively in bureaucratic documents and official speeches. Local officials fully understood that their first task was to extract grain and economically reinforce the kolkhozes, and that the herdsmen were the social group that contributed the least to these ends.

In the second phase, after the Famine had struck, what began to be called sedentarization was the policy of moving Kazakh refugees (*otkochevniki*) into agricultural and industrial jobs. The prevailing attitude, as it emerges in numerous reports, was indifference toward the nomads, first when sedentarization was being undertaken, then when mass starvation struck. It was surely not because of "excesses" in dealing with the nomads that Goloshchekin was removed from office. These excesses went on for five years, and nearly every year—at the end of every requisition campaign, then at the end of the collectivization campaign—ad hoc commissions issued sterile condemnations. In reality, Goloshchekin thought he could manage the impending social crisis,[39] but failed to protect at least some of the herdsmen's resources from being funneled toward the collective farms and the effort to increase grain production. Livestock died, an appalling famine ensued, and Kazakhstan had to be supplied with grain so that the former nomads could be put to work. For this economic failure, Goloshchekin was removed from his post.

Under the First Five-Year Plan, while the government was implementing policies directed at including Kazakhs within the structures of the Soviet state and at building a Kazakh "nation" incorporated within the community of Soviet nations, the annihilation of part of this same Kazakh "nation" favored by the state's "affirmative action" policies was being carried out. This slaughter was not planned by a totalitarian state that held total control over the chain of command and its peripheral power, but was instead made possible by weak control of the territory by a government whose efforts were dedicated to a chaotic process of industrialization. Mass death, in the case of the Kazakhs, was not an objective the policy makers set out to achieve, but rather the price they were prepared to pay as long as they could achieve the goal of gaining political and economic control over the region. To this end, in local situations in the immense Soviet territory, extracting resources from the population fell most heavily on different social groups on the basis of specific power relations in peripheral societies deeply divided from the social, economic, and cultural points of view.

In the early 1930s the Kazakh refugees found themselves at the lowest rung in the hierarchy of productive usefulness for the state. The herdsmen had become "superfluous" people,[40] deprived of the principal source of wealth they were capable of exploiting, their animals, and rendered ill and vulnerable by a state to which they now by necessity had to turn to for help. They were seen by that state as being even less valuable than the deported kulaks or the "special colonists" abandoned on barren lands or sent to work in vast sovkhozes and in the mines alongside the *otkochevniki*. The animals and lands were expropriated by the state, and the herdsmen were excluded as no longer productive servants from the sphere in which the state might have been interested in their survival.

NOTES

1. The best work on the Famine in Russia proper (Volga, Don, and Kuban regions), with a wide comparative approach, is the recent V. V. Kondrashin and Diana Penner, *Golod: 1932–1933 gody v sovetskoi derevne (na materiale Povolzh'ia, Dona i Kubani)* (Samara, 2002).

2. Sergei Maksudov, "Migratsii v SSSR v 1926–1939 godakh," *Cahiers du monde russe* 40, no. 4 (1999): 770–96.

3. Gulnar Kendirbai, *Land and People: The Russian Colonization of the Kazak Steppe* (Berlin, 2002), 18; Daniel R. Brower, *Turkestan and the Fate of the Russian Empire* (London, 2003), 126–51.

4. That is, they did not move further than half a verst (approximately 0.3 miles) from their winter settlements.

5. Dana G. Dalrymple, "The Soviet Famine of 1932–34," *Soviet Studies* 15, no. 3 (1964): 250–84.

6. In 1930–1931 peasants deported to Kazakhstan arrived from the Middle and Lower Volga (58 percent of the total), Central Black Earth Region (20 percent), Moscow region (6 percent), and Southern Caucasus (2 percent). The remaining 13 percent was formed by "kulaks" and "bais" from inside Kazakhstan. In December 1932 nearly 10,000 Kuban Cossacks were relocated to Kazakhstan, victims of the terror unleashed to fulfill the grain requisitions in their region. In 1933 another 55,000 people were deported to the republic. As is evident from these figures, there were no deportations at this time from Ukraine to Kazakhstan. Data from N. A. Ivnitskii, *Kollektivizatsiia i raskulachivanie (nachalo 30-kh godov)* (Moscow, 1996), 192–94.

7. A. Berelowitch and V. Danilov, eds., *Sovetskaia derevnia glazami VChK-OGPU-NKVD: Dokumenty i materialy,* vol. 2, *1923–1929* (Moscow, 2000), 96, 185, 229, 230, 236, 255.

8. Cf. I. Ohayon, "Du nomadisme au socialisme: Sédentarisation, collectivisation et acculturation des Kazakhs en URSS (1928–1945)" (Ph.D. dissertation, National Institute of Oriental Languages and Civilizations [INALCO], Paris, 2003), 32–105. This work is the best and most thorough study of the end of nomadism in Stalinist Kazakhstan. See also Ohayon, *La sedentarisation des Kazakhs dans L'URSS de Staline: Collectivisation et changement sociale (1928–1945)* (Paris, 2006).

9. Session of the presidium of the Central Committee of the Russian Socialist Federative Soviet Republic (RSFSR), 24 September 1928, Russian State Archive of Social and Political History (hereafter RGASPI), fond 94, opis′ 1, delo 1, listy 680–625 (hereafter fond, op., d., ll.).

10. Report from E. Ernazarov to F. I. Goloshchekin on the situation in the Balkhash

district, 21 April 1930, cited in K. Karazhanov and A. Takenov, eds., *Noveishaia istoriia Kazakhstana: Sbornik dokumentov i materialov (1917–1939 gg.)* (Almaty, 1998), 1:234.

11.　Note from the Plenipotentiary Delegation of the OGPU for Kazakhstan to the Central OGPU on Grain Procurement, 11 September 1930, Tsentral'nyi arkhiv Federal'noi Sluzhby Bezopasnosti Rossiiskoi Federatsii (hereafter TsA FSB), fond 2, op. 8, d. 37, ll. 48–53; cited in V. Danilov, R. Manning, and L. Viola, eds., *Tragediia sovetskoi derevni: Kollektivizatsiia i raskulachivanie; Dokumenty i materialy v 5 tomakh, 1927–1939,* vol. 2, *Noiabr' 1929–Dekabr' 1930* (Moscow, 2000), 603.

12.　L. K. Shotbakova, "Natsional'nyi aspekt pereselencheskoi politiki i korenizatsii v Kazakhstane v 1917–1941 gody" (dissertation, Moscow State University, 1995), 43. In the USSR as a whole, in 1930 and 1931 approximately 1.8 million peasants were exiled from their regions ("first- and second-category kulaks"); of these, those deported to Kazakhstan amounted to 11–14 percent of the total number.

13.　State Archive of the Russian Federation (hereafter GARF), fond A-296, op. 1, d. 450, l. 126 (November 1930).

14.　GARF, fond 6985, op. 1, d. 7, l. 143 (1934).

15.　According to some estimates, only 13 percent of the settlement points had sufficient land and sources of water. See Sh. Mukhamedina, *Istoriia kochevykh i starozhil'cheskikh khoziaistv (Opyt partiino-gosudarstvennoi tsentralizastii khoziaistvennoi zhizni Kazakhstana v 1920–1936 gg.)* (Akmola, 1994), 178.

16.　GARF, fond 6985, op. 1, d. 6, l. 225.

17.　TsA FSB, fond 2, op. 8, d. 709, l. 362 (29 March 1930); and Russian State Archive of the Economy (RGAE), fond 7486, op. 37, d. 132, l. 15-5, cited in Danilov, Manning, and Viola, *Tragediia sovetskoi derevni,* 353, 477–78.

18.　See M. Omarov, *Rasstreliannaia step': Istoriia Adaevskogo vosstaniia 1931 goda po materialam OGPU* (Almaty, 1994), 23, on how this policy was enforced in the Mangishlak raion; see Zh. B. Abylkhozhin, M. K. Kozybaev, and M. B. Tatimov, "Kazakhstanskaia tragediia," *Voprosy istorii,* no. 7 (1989): 61, on the nomad region of Turgai.

19.　Ohayon, "Du nomadisme au socialisme," 226.

20.　Resolution of the Kazkraikom VKP(b) on livestock requisitions, 9 September 1931, RGASPI, fond 17, op. 25, d. 65, l. 22.

21.　See R. W. Davies, M. Harrison, and S. G. Wheatcroft, eds., *The Economic Transformation of the Soviet Union, 1913–1945* (Cambridge, 1994), 289.

22.　Ibid., 113.

23.   GARF, fond 6985, op. 1, d. 4, l. 38; GARF, fond 6985, op. 1, d. 19, l. 105.

24.   GARF, fond 6985, op. 1, d. 16, l. 75.

25.   Emigration was also a frequently used strategy of resistance among the Turkmen:
       see A. L. Edgar, *Tribal Nation: The Making of Soviet Turkmenistan* (Princeton,
       2004), 213–20.

26.   Ohayon, "Du nomadisme au socialisme," 239.

27.   Ibid., 242.

28.   GARF, fond 6985, op. 1, d. 6, l. 224.

29.   Letter from Eikhe, secretary of the *kraikom* of the VKP(b) of Western Siberia,
       to Goloshchekin, secretary of the *kraikom* of the VKP(b) of Kazakstan, cited in
       Karazhanov and Takenov, *Noveishaia istoriia Kazakhstana,* 1:243.

30.   In the raions where the refugees arrived, horse thefts increased twelvefold. See the
       report by the state procurator of the Krai to Eikhe "on the spontaneous movement
       to the Krai of Western Siberia of Kazakhs from the KASSR and on their condition,"
       29 March 1932, in K. Aldazhumanov, et al., eds., *Nasil'stvennaia kollektivizatsiia i
       golod v Kazakhstane v 1931–1933 gg: Sbornik dokumentov i materialov* (Almaty,
       1998), 127.

31.   GARF, fond 6985, op. 1, d. 22, l. 122.

32.   GARF, fond 6985, op. 1, d. 6, l. 34.

33.   From a report to *kraikom* secretary Mirzoian by Narskii, the director of party activity
       in light industry, 3 July 1933, cited in Karazhanov and Takenov, *Noveishaia istoriia
       Kazakhstana,* 266.

34.   Karazhanov and Takenov, *Noveishaia istoriia Kazakhstana,* 266.

35.   Ibid. See also the letter from Turar Ryskulov, vice president of the Sovnarkom of the
       RSFSR, to Stalin, Kaganovich, and Molotov, 9 March 1933, cited in S. Abdiraiymov
       et al., eds., *Golod v kazakhskoi stepi* (Almaty, 1991), 168–69.

36.   As early as August 1931, People's Vice Commissar for Supplies Zeinulla Toregozhin
       had officially criticized the policies of animal requisitioning as one of the principal
       causes of the impoverishment of the nomads, and had been removed from office.
       See N. Nurbaev, "Zhertva kollektivizatsii," *Partiinaia zhizn' Kazakhstana,* no. 8
       (1991): 89. The following year criticism of Goloshchekin increased: on 4 July 1932,
       five Kazakh officials wrote an open letter to Stalin in which they explicitly asked
       for Goloshchekin's removal (Abdiraiymov et al., eds., *Golod v kazakhskoi stepi,*
       128–51) .

37.   This point has been stressed by I. Ohayon, "Du nomadisme au socialisme," 328–32.

38.   Article from *Kazakhstanskaia pravda,* 20 December 1934, GARF, fond 6985, op. 1, d. 9, l. 133.

39.   This crisis was foreseen, as indicated by the fact that at the 1927 Kazakh Party Congress Goloshchekin spoke about a fall in the number of livestock in the passage from the "natural economy" to the "socialist" one.

40.   Matthew Payne, "An Empty Land, a Superfluous People: The Kazakh Steppe and Geographical Visions of the Soviet Regime during Forced Sedentarization, 1928–1934," paper presented at the 35th National Convention of the American Association for the Advancement of Slavic Studies, Toronto, Canada, November 2003.

The 1932–1933 Crisis and Its Aftermath beyond the Epicenters of Famine: The Urals Region

GIJS KESSLER

Studies of the Famine of 1932–1933 have focused primarily on its main epicenters: Ukraine with its highest absolute losses of human life, Kazakhstan with its highest rates of mortality, and the steppe regions of the Don and Kuban to the north of the Caucasus mountain ridge. The current article is an attempt to broaden the perspective on these tragedies by examining the supply crisis of 1932–1933 and its aftermath in a place well outside these areas—the Urals region. Even in this "nonfamine" area death by starvation was ubiquitous in 1932–1933. This underscores the fact that the Famine arose from the general problems created by the Soviet regime's agricultural policies of the preceding years rather than from factors specific to the situation in Ukraine, Kazakhstan, or the North Caucasus. In terms of the imprint it left on rural society, data from the Urals region indicate that during the mid- and late 1930s the rural population attached much greater importance to food and the production of food than it had before. The Famine increased peasants' agrarian orientation, in a sense made them more "peasant," and thus essentially threw them back in time. Placing the Famine in such a wider framework enhances our understanding both of the event itself and of its place in Soviet history.

POCKETS OF FAMINE

What is commonly referred to as the Urals region of Russia covers a vast area on both sides of the north-south ridge that forms the geographical boundary between the European and Asian continents, separating the North European lowlands from the West Siberian plain. At the time of the Famine of 1932–1933 these territories administratively comprised a single Urals province, formed in 1923, which covered an area as large as England, France, Germany, and Italy taken together. In

1934 this vast territory was divided into three new provinces—the Cheliabinsk, Ob-Irtysh, and Sverdlovsk oblasts, the latter of which was split up once more in 1938 to allow for the formation of Perm oblast.[1]

Although best known for its metal industry, in existence since the start of the eighteenth century, the Urals region was also home to agricultural production areas of some importance. In the late 1920s the fertile trans-Ural regions of Ishim, Kurgan, and Shchadrinsk supplied most of the oblast with grain, and even shipped grain, meat, and butter to the European parts of Russia and abroad.[2] The collectivization and industrialization of the 1930s tilted the balance in the regional economy between agriculture and industry firmly to the benefit of the latter, pouring large-scale investment into the existing, outdated metal industry and erecting and developing huge new production facilities.

The industrial boom found its expression in a rapid redistribution of the population. If we leave out the mostly thinly populated northeastern Ob-Irtysh or Tiumen oblast, and consider only the territory covered by the present-day Perm, Sverdlovsk, and Cheliabinsk oblasts, a comparison of the 1926 and 1939 population censuses reveals a growth of the urban population of 279 percent against a total population increase of 129 percent and a decline of the rural population by 13 percent. The urbanization rate increased from 21.9 percent in 1926 to 47.5 percent in 1939. Of the three, the Sverdlovsk oblast was most heavily urbanized in 1939, with just under 60 percent of the population living in towns and urban settlements, against 40 percent and 42 percent respectively in the Perm and Cheliabinsk oblasts.[3]

According to the 1939 population census, ethnic Russians accounted for 89.8 percent of the urban and 86.3 percent of the rural population in the three oblasts.[4] The non-Russian population consisted of Komi in the northwestern Perm oblast, of Tatars in the northwest and of Bashkirs in the southwest, and in the southeast of Kazakhs. Komi, Kazakhs, and Bashkirs were concentrated in rural areas, whereas Tatars were equally represented among the urban and rural populations. The Tatar, Bashkir, and Kazakh populations were part of the larger area of settlement of these nationalities, consisting of the Tatar republic to the west, Kazakhstan to the southeast, and the Bashkir autonomous republic in the southwest, immediately bordering on the Urals oblast. The Bashkir population in particular appears to have been concentrated in the districts adjacent to their national homeland.

As elsewhere, this rapid process of population redistribution was fueled by the destruction of the rural economy and way of life during collectivization. What gave rural departure a particular impulse in the Urals was that procurements already had depleted rural food reserves in 1931, when droughts caused a partial harvest failure in the region. In spite of a decline in grain production by about a third between 1928 and 1932, and a reduction of the livestock herd from 12.7 million to 5.3 million, state procurements rose from 882,000 tons of the 1928 grain harvest to 1,296,100 tons of the 1931 grain harvest, and from 84,200 tons of meat in 1928 to 137,900 tons in 1931.[5] Thus, the deadly scissors of rising procurements and declining production made a relatively early appearance in the region.

In the Famine of 1932–1933 the Urals were not among the hardest-hit areas. Nonetheless, undernourishment and starvation caused significant excess mortality, including several pockets of outright famine. For the year 1933 the number of deaths in the region as a whole exceeded the number of births by a small margin of slightly under four and a half thousand people, thus causing a slight decline of the population in absolute terms, which points to a demographic crisis of some proportion.[6] Because of the bad harvest of 1931, food shortages appeared at a rather early stage, and the supply crisis was a comparatively drawn-out affair. Already in April 1932 the Soviet secret police, the OGPU, reported that in many parts of the region the rural population hovered on the brink of starvation, and the spring sowing of that year took place in a tense and increasingly desperate atmosphere. Things started to turn ugly. Large numbers of horses and other draft animals had perished as a result of the bad harvest of 1931 and the ensuing lack of fodder, or were too emaciated to work. From the Olkhovka and Mokrousovo districts several cases were reported in which the kolkhoz administration forcibly put people to the ploughs for lack of horses, which caused intense resentment. Requisitioning of horses led to sometimes-violent clashes between independent peasant farmers and kolkhozniks involving nightly shoot-outs. In the eastern parts of the province Kazakh horsemen appeared who had fled the forced "denomad-ization" and the terrible famine in their lands. Some of them brought along what remained of their herds and thus bought themselves into local kolkhozes. Others put up their tents in remote areas and organized raids on the surrounding collective farms, stealing livestock and horses. They met with hostility from the local Russian population. In the village of Aleksandrovka a crowd of 20 people, most of them women, lynched two Kazakh horse thieves.[7]

In the towns as well the food situation was grim. In the first four months of 1932 alone worker discontent with food supply sparked seventeen strikes in the region, in the largest of which 580 persons took part.[8] An issue of particular concern was the exclusion of non-working family members from the rationing lists in a number of branches, which caused many workers with families to return to the countryside. Many peasant workers that had left their families behind in the village also returned. Because of the growing food shortages the collective farms often refused to supply the families of kolkhoz members who were working in industry or construction, trying to shift this responsibility to the urban employers of these *otkhodniki,* or migrant workers. These pressures resulted in a partial reversal of the migratory current in 1932, slowly eroding the workforce in those branches that relied most heavily on peasant labor.[9]

It is not exactly clear how the situation developed in the region from the summer of 1932 on. It seems that the harvest saved the day for a while, but what was left of it in the villages after meeting procurements was not everywhere sufficient to carry the population through to the next harvest. In some places people had already run out of grain in December 1932. The first cases of outright starvation and the first Famine-related deaths are reported from January 1933 on, first among children, and then also among adults. One of the better-documented cases is that of a group of several hundred mainly Kazakh workers in the Bredy district in the south of what is now Cheliabinsk oblast, who were fired in a wave of redundancies at local factories and state farms through December 1932 and January 1933, and were subsequently taken off the rationing lists and evicted from enterprise housing. Erecting makeshift huts dug half into the ground and isolating them with hay taken from kolkhoz stables, they tried to keep alive on whatever food they could find, but by the start of February 1933 fifty people had already died, their frozen bodies lying abandoned by the roadside.

From April 1933 on, cases of starvation are reported from an increasing number of districts. In the Turinskaia Sloboda and Brodokalmak districts people on the collective farms were eating rats and livestock that had succumbed. Among the "kulak" deportees working in timber felling in the Sosva village soviet cannibalism occurred, as the deceased were dug up from the graves and partially eaten. In the Poltavskoe and Varna districts in the south deaths from hunger were reported among Kazakh refugees. There appears to have been a noticeably higher incidence of starvation in the Bashkir areas to the southwest, near the border with the Bashkir Autonomous Republic. Especially the Orda district seems to have been badly hit, with a gruesome case of cannibalism recorded as late as July 1933 in which a father killed and ate his four-year-old son. In Sverdlovsk rumors circulated about a terrible epidemic in the Tiumen area that was handled by shooting those that had fallen ill and burning their houses with everything in them. In its dispatches to London the British Embassy in Moscow described this epidemic as an outbreak of the plague, caused by the digging of marmot burrows by peasants in search of the grain stored therein by the animals.[10]

In order to gain better understanding of the geography of famine and starvation in the Urals in those years two sets of data have been plotted on a map of the region (map 1). The first set consists of data on the number of deaths and births in the northern half of the province, the territories that would form the Sverdlovsk province in its 1934–1937 boundaries. The districts (*raiony*) marked in black registered a number of deaths among the rural population in 1933 that exceeded the number of births—a clear indication of famine conditions. Secondly, the shaded areas on the map are districts for which direct evidence of famine or starvation has been found in the archives. The nature of this evidence is indicated for each district on the map. It should be noted immediately that the two sets of data are not mutually exclusive; many of the shaded areas in the southern half of

Map 1. Famine 1932–1933: Urals.

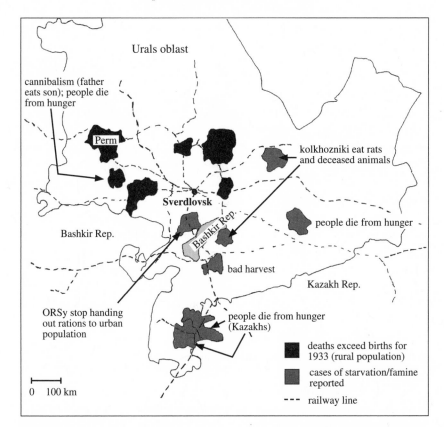

Sources: Rossiiskii gosudarstvennyi arkhiv ekonomiki (RGAE), fond 1562 (TsUNKhU SSSR), op. 329, d. 107, ll. 72r, 72v, 73; Tsentr dokumentatsii obshchestvennykh organizatsii Sverdlovskoi oblasti (TsDOOSO), fond 4 (Uralobkom VKP [b]), op. 11, d. 197, ll. 31, 33–34, 41, 59, 73, 82, 97, 106, 111, 113–15, 130, 132–33.

the province probably had excesses of deaths over births as well, but we simply do not have the demographic data. Along similar lines, direct evidence of famine conditions in the areas indicated in black probably can be located in the archives somewhere, but we just have not come across it.

The map shows a region dotted with pockets of famine, at first glance haphazardly, but with two distinct patterns emerging on closer scrutiny. In the first place most districts hit by famine were located on or near railway lines. Several explanations could be offered for this, the most compelling being that in these areas taking grain and shipping it out was easiest for the procurement brigades. Areas in the vicinity of railway lines must have borne the brunt of procurement campaigns and probably even had to compensate for procurement fallbacks in more remote regions. A second set of explanations centers around the role of railway lines in population displacement. It is well known that in these hungry years people started to move around in search of food, and it can by no means be excluded that in large part the deaths registered in the Urals were in fact people from elsewhere who had succumbed on the road. What is more, these population movements must have facilitated the spread of epidemics among populations already weakened by malnutrition.

The second peculiarity which can be observed from the map is how famine-stricken areas are grouped in a circle around the provincial capital of Sverdlovsk, with no excess mortality or cases of starvation reported for the districts in its immediate vicinity. Without any doubt this reflects the workings of the system of internal passports, specifically of its strict "regime" category, which was introduced in this city in May 1933. As described elsewhere, the issuing of passports and urban residence permits in "regime" areas was a process of social cleansing, in which "undesirable" elements were denied residence and expelled from the areas concerned.[11] Apart from a purge of certain social categories enumerated in a secret protocol to the 1932–1933 passportization decrees, these operations were also specifically aimed at ridding strategic urban centers of peasants in search of food and "hangers-on" to the rationing system.

Passport registration data for Sverdlovsk, given in table 1, reveal the exodus connected to the passportization campaign quite clearly:

Table 1. Passport registration data for Sverdlovsk,
April–June 1933 (absolute figures).

	April	May	June
Arrivals	10,598	5,107	1,436
Arrivals minus departures	4,737	-1,208	-3,129

Source: Gosudarstvennyi arkhiv Rossiiskoi federatsii (GARF), fond a-374 (UNKhU RSFSR), op. 23, d. 235, ll. 256r, 256v, 257r, 257v, 258r, 258v, 259r, 259v.

Whereas April still shows a net migration surplus of 4,373 persons, this trend is sharply reversed in May with the start of passportization. A decline in the number of arrivals and a sharp increase in the number of departures produce a net population outflow, which further deepens in the subsequent month of June.

Persons expelled from "regime" towns during passportization could not settle within a hundred-kilometer zone around these towns, and this is what causes the remarkable "white" circle around Sverdlovsk on map 1. Beyond the hundred-kilometer zone people from elsewhere who had tried to find food in Sverdlovsk and were deported during passportization met with the desperate who were still arriving and finding the town closed. With people streaming into these areas from two sides the pressure on scarce food resources mounted, resulting in starvation and the spread of diseases, finding victims both among the local population and among those who had arrived from elsewhere.

The Famine of 1932–1933 in the Urals was only a shadow of the much greater tragedies that occurred in the main grain-growing regions of Ukraine and the Kuban and in Kazakhstan, but it was a minor affair only in comparison. What perhaps best underlines the severity of the crisis is the fact that the region experienced a net population loss in 1933 due to excess mortality. Although some areas were apparently less affected than others, malnutrition, starvation, and famine occurred throughout the region.

THE SPECTER OF FAMINE AND THE PRODUCTION OF FOOD

Developments in the postfamine countryside are usually viewed in terms of the dichotomy between work on the collective farms and peasant efforts on their private plots. This dichotomy was born out of the supply crisis of 1932–1933. Anxious to prevent a repetition of the Famine, the regime made two important changes to its agricultural policy around the mid-1930s. Together, they were to safeguard food supply to the urban and industrial sector while making the rural population self-sufficient. In February 1935 a new kolkhoz charter was introduced, which unequivocally affirmed the kolkhozniks' right to a private plot and to the individual possession of some livestock.[12] Before, collective farmers had had private plots as well, left over from their individual farms, but now these plots gained legal status and became subject to fixed norms regarding size, which greatly strengthened people's entitlement to them vis-à-vis the kolkhoz administration. In addition, and to make sure that the urban economy would benefit from these concessions, beginning in late 1934 the regime started to stimulate the collective farmers to trade the production of these plots on the market.[13] In order to encourage peasants to use these possibilities, taxation on income derived from household-based agricultural activities was lowered significantly in May 1935.[14]

As Moshe Lewin and M. A. Vyltsan described in their works of the 1970s and 1980s, peasants seized upon this opportunity with fervor and by the late 1930s private plots provided the bulk of agricultural production, with the exception of grain. For collective farmers' households the private plot accounted for between half and three-quarters of total income, depending on the region.[15] Crucial in this remarkable symbiosis between private plot and collective farming was the proviso that peasants were entitled to a private plot and the lower taxes on its produce only for as long as they were kolkhoz members, and, secondly, that peasants were dependent on the kolkhoz for grain. This guaranteed both their kolkhoz membership and, once members, their participation in kolkhoz work, as grain was only paid in remuneration for work. Although a formidable base of subsistence for the peasant household, the private plot alone was not enough for survival, and this was the foundation on which the power of the kolkhoz rested during the second half of the 1930s, rather than on repression as it had during the earlier part of the decade.

Whereas the rise of the private plot was the most conspicuous change in rural life and work following the 1932–1933 crisis, it was accompanied by and indeed partly derived from a more general shift in peasant behavior. It is here that we find the real legacy of the Famine. What happened, basically, was that peasants concentrated their efforts increasingly on the production of food, not only on the private plot, but also on the collective farms. In order to properly understand the nature of this change it is essential to realize that in a peasant economy agricultural activities as such account only for part of a household's activities and income, with nonagricultural activities like crafts and trades, hunting and gathering, or wage labor providing supplementary income during the slack agricultural season.[16] Particularly in Russia, with its short agricultural season, the role of nonagricultural side earnings had always been pronounced and col-lectivization did not fundamentally alter this situation, at least not in these early decades.[17] Collective farm work simply did not provide the rural population with a sufficient income and this made engagement in off-farm activities a condition sine qua non for survival.

Particularly during the first half of the decade, when the private plot offered fewer possibilities for offsetting an insufficient kolkhoz income and industry craved for labor, peasant involvement in nonagricultural activities ran high. It would require a serious effort to compile a consistent body of data from rural household budgets to properly analyze trends in the importance of nonagricultural income for the rural population, but available statistics indicate the direction of change. Table 2 presents data on the contribution of nonagricultural side earnings to household income from surveys of peasant household budgets from 1925/26, 1931 and 1939.

Data for 1931 and 1939 are for the Urals region, whereas for 1925/26 all-Union data are given as well as data for the two categories into which agricultural areas in Russia are usually grouped—the grain-consuming and grain-producing regions. Most of the Urals was a grain-consuming region, but some areas belonged to the category of grain-producing regions. Data for 1925/26 and 1939 are based on a sample of the rural population as a whole, while data for 1931 cover only those collective farmers who had belonged to the stratum of "middle peasants" before entering the kolkhoz. Although these data are far from ideally comparable,

Table 2. Non-agricultural side earnings and peasant incomes, 1925–1939.

	1925–1926	1931	1939
Percent of total household income			
Grain-consuming regions	22.5	--	--
Grain-producing regions	12.7	--	--
USSR	13.2	--	--
Urals region	--	36.0	10.0

Source: Data for 1925–1926 and 1932 taken from, respectively, V. P. Danilov, "Krest'ianskii otkhod na promysly v 20-kh godakh," *Istoricheskie zapiski* 94 (1974): 99–100; GARF, fond r-5446 (SNK SSSR), op. 13a, d. 1263, l. 9. Data for 1939 calculated by author from GARF, fond a-374, op. 22, d. 368, ll. 1–2.

they nonetheless allow for some conclusions. No matter which data we take for 1925/26, the trend is always one of an increased reliance on nonagricultural side earnings in 1931 as compared to the mid-1920s, and a subsequent decline of their role in the peasant economy over the period 1931–1939. If we compare the 1939 figures to the 1925/26 USSR average the decline is minimal, but, considering the economic profile of the region, the comparison should rather be to the 1925/26 figures for the grain-consuming regions. This would mean that by the end of the 1930s the share of peasant income from nonagricultural work had decreased to half of what it had been in the mid-1920s.

Despite the inadequacies of the data, the trend is clear—by the end of the 1930s peasants in the Urals were much more deeply involved in agriculture proper than they had been on the eve of collectivization and in its immediate aftermath. Figures on marketing, moreover, indicate that this involvement in agriculture was primarily consumption-oriented. Figure 1 below shows the percentages of household income in kind that was retained or marketed during the periods January–June and July–December 1939.[18] Income in kind comprised both the production of the private plot and the payments in grain and other crops received from the kolkhozes.

As we can see, only a minor part of this income in kind was subsequently marketed: about a quarter during the first half of the year, and slightly under a fifth during the second half of the year. The rest was consumed on the farm.

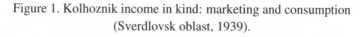

Figure 1. Kolhoznik income in kind: marketing and consumption
(Sverdlovsk oblast, 1939).

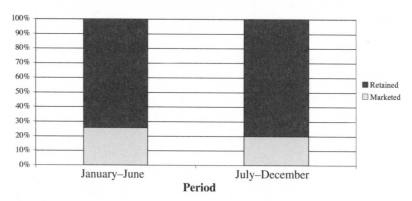

These findings make the peasants' zealous efforts on their private plots appear in a somewhat different light than the more familiar data on their share in the supply of food to the urban sector that we have referred to above. These were not people working for the market, but people doing all they could to supply themselves with what they needed to avoid the situation they had found themselves in during the crisis of 1932–1933. Food and the provisioning of food must have been the paramount concern in the countryside of the mid- and late 1930s, by comparison to which all other considerations were secondary. The reaction of the rural population to the supply problems of 1936–1937 is telling in this respect. When grain reserves started to run out in the Sverdlovsk oblast toward the spring of 1937, panic seized the villages and peasants traveled en masse to the towns to buy bread. Trains arrived full of peasants with huge sacks, which they filled with bread, emptying one shop after another. As the NKVD later reported, in some districts this influx of peasant buyers had been triggered by attempts on the part of the authorities to retain available reserves for the urban population by suspending the sale of bread in the rural areas.[19]

CONCLUSION

Having looked at the Famine of 1932–1933 through the prism of a region that was not at its epicenter, and having traced its echoes in this region through the mid- and late 1930s, some broader observations can be made regarding the place of the Famine in the Soviet history of the interwar period. In the first place it becomes ever clearer how intimately connected famine and collectivization were. The 1932–1933 Famine was the logical, if perhaps not inevitable, outcome of the agricultural policies adopted by the Stalinist leadership at the end of the 1920s, which aimed at extracting maximum amounts of grain and other produce from the agricultural sector without investment to increase productivity. Moreover, at the same time they threw the whole sector in disarray by a violent, ill-conceived and chaotic forced collectivization of agricultural producers. As the example of the Urals eloquently demonstrates, this set of policies alone was enough to produce famine and starvation within three years. In regions where further complicating factors were added in, like the "denomadization" in Kazakhstan or the anti-nationalist campaign in Ukraine, it produced mass famine.[20]

A second observation concerns the consequences of the Famine. Evidence for the Urals region confirms in this respect what common sense would suggest: food and the provisioning of food became a number one concern and for some perhaps even an obsession. One of the consequences was that the rural population increasingly concentrated its efforts on agriculture, primarily on the private plot, but also in the collective farms. In a certain sense, after the crisis of 1932–1933 the rural world turned inwards, retreated onto the private plot, and became more peasantlike. After the exodus from the village during the early years of collectivization, the urban and the rural worlds to a certain extent drifted apart again during the mid- and late 1930s. The main link was, of course, trade. The fragile foundation it rested on was the private plot.

NOTES

1. B. V. Lichman and V. D. Kamynin, eds., *Istoriia Urala,* vol. 2, *XX vek* (Ekaterinburg, 1998), 90–122; *Sverdlovskaia oblast' pered vyborami v mestnye sovety deputatov trudiashchikhsia* (Sverdlovsk, 1939), 3.

2. *Sverdlovskaia iarmarka 1928 g. i putevoditel' po g. Sverdlovsku: Spravochnik* (Sverdlovsk, 1928), 46–47; Uralplan and Uraloblispolkom, *Sel'sko-khoziaistvennye raiony Ural'skoi oblasti* (Sverdlovsk, 1928), 41–48, 56.

3. Calculated by author from V. B. Zhiromskaia, ed., *Vsesoiuznaia perepis' naseleniia 1939 goda: Osnovnye itogi; Rossiia* (Petersburg, 1999), 24–26.

4. Calculated by author from Iu. A. Poliakov, ed., *Vsesoiuznaia perepis' naseleniia 1939 goda: Osnovnye itogi* (Moscow, 1992), 63–65.

5. Cf. I. E. Plotnikov, "Kak likvidirovali kulachestvo na Urale," *Otechestvennaia istoriia,* no. 4 (1993): 166; Ural'skoe oblastnoe upravlenie narodno-khoziaistvennogo ucheta, *Sotsialisticheskoe stroitel'stvo Urala za 15 let* (Sverdlovsk, 1932), 52–53.

6. 62,442 deaths were registered against 57,966 births. Cf. G. E. Kornilov, ed., *Letopis' ural'skikh dereven': Tezisy dokladov regional'noi nauchno-prakticheskoi konferentsii* (Ekaterinburg, 1995), 93–94.

7. Russian State Archive of the Economy (RGAE), fond 7486 (NKZ SSSR), op. 37s, d. 236, ll. 33–35; d. 239, ll. 18–19, 25–27; Documentation Center of Public Organizations of Sverdlovsk Oblast (TsDOOSO), fond 4 (Ural'skii obkom VKP [b]), op. 10, d. 234, l. 124; d. 235, ll. 142–43.

8. E. Osokina, *Za fasadom "stalinskogo izobiliia": Raspredelenie i rynok v snabzhenii naseleniia v gody industrializatsii, 1927–1941* (Moscow, 1998), 126.

9. On the reduction of the urban workforce, see State Archive of Sverdlovsk Oblast (GASO), fond r-241 (Uralplan), op. 2, d. 2002, ll. 89–95. On the refusal of kolkhozes to supply the families of *otkhodniki,* see GASO, fond r-922 (Uralkolkhozsoiuz), op. 1, d. 147, ll. 124, 159, 177.

10. TsDOOSO, fond 4 (Uralobkom VKP [b]), op. 11, d. 197, ll. 31, 59, 73, 82, 100, 106, 111, 113–15, 130, 132–33. On the rumors of the epidemic in Tiumen, see TsDOOSO, fond 161 (Sverdlovskii gorkom VKP [b]), op. 1, d. 107, ll. 15–16. For the British Embassy report see Marco Carynnyk, Lubomyr Y. Luciuk, and Bohdan S. Kordan, eds., *The Foreign Office and the Famine: British Documents on Ukraine and the Great Famine of 1932–1933* (Kingston, Ont., 1988), 257.

11. Cf. G. C. Kessler, "The Passport System and State Control over Population Flows in the Soviet Union, 1932–1940," *Cahiers du monde russe* 42, nos. 2–4 (2001): 485–86.

12. *Sobranie zakonov i rasporiazhenii Raboche-krest'ianskogo pravitel'stva SSSR (SZ SSSR)*, 1935, no. 11, art. 82.

13. I. E. Zelenin, "Byl li kolkhoznyi neonep?" *Otechestvennaia istoriia*, no. 2 (1994): 114.

14. *Istoriia kolkhoznogo prava: Sbornik zakonodatel'nykh materialov SSSR i RSFSR, 1917–1958 gg.*, vol. 1, *1917–1936* (Moscow, 1959), 454–55.

15. Moshe Lewin, "The Kolkhoz and the Russian Muzhik," chap. 7 in *The Making of the Soviet System: Essays in the Social History of Interwar Russia* (London, 1985); M. A. Vyltsan, *Zavershaiushchii etap sozdaniia kolkhoznogo stroia (1935–1937 gg.)* (Moscow, 1978), 198–207.

16. An appropriate concept for describing and understanding the complementarity of different economic activities in the household economy is that of the labor cycle. Cf. Jan Lucassen, *Migrant Labour in Europe, 1600–1900: The Drift to the North Sea* (London and Wolfeboro, N.H., 1987).

17. G. C. Kessler, "The Peasant and the Town: Rural-Urban Migration in the Soviet Union, 1929–40" (Ph.D. thesis, European University Institute, Florence, 2001). See esp. chaps. 2 and 4.

18. State Archive of the Russian Federation (GARF), fond a-374 (UNKhU RSFSR), op. 22, d. 388, ll. 1–2.

19. TsDOOSO, fond 161 (Sverdlovskii gorkom VKP [b]), op. 1, d. 969, ll. 17, 22, 25–27, 81–88.

20. On the "denomadization" in Kazakhstan and the connection between the Famine and antinationalist policies in Ukraine, see, respectively, the contributions by Niccolò Pianciola in this volume and Terry Martin, "The National Interpretation of the 1933 Famine," chap. 7 of *The Affirmative Action Empire: Nations and Nationalism in the Soviet Union, 1923–1939* (Ithaca, N.Y., 2001).

The Holodomor and Memory[*]

GEORGE G. GRABOWICZ

To fathom the Holodomor, the Ukrainian Great Famine of 1932–1933, one has to invoke more than one's ability to reason. For a moment, one has to overcome the denial and the rationalizations that so often anesthetize us to reality and invoke the imagination, and then, armed by it, to peer into the heart of darkness. For only the imagination, the source not only of creativity but also our sense of humanity, can help us adequately conceive the dimensions of this horror.

In Auschwitz (Oświęcim) the imagination is moved by the death camp itself and by its museum, with its horrific display cases that show the accumulated belongings and traces of countless victims, the heaps of eyeglasses and prosthetic devices, of children's shoes and human hair. In Yad Vashem there also is a museum and a great monument of grief where one can see hundreds of photographs, thousands of personal items, and some two million Pages of Testimony, and hear the continuous reading of the names of those who perished. In Ukraine there is nothing of the kind—neither a museum where one can actualize memory and give voice to grief, nor exhibits, nor a generally known narrative of the events, nor even a preliminary register of those who perished. Until very recently, in the collective national memory of Ukraine (we are not speaking here of the scholars and the historians, and not of the diaspora either) the Holodomor was also absent—or so it appeared on the surface.

But there is still the imagination. At the beginning of the preface to his *Harvest of Sorrow*, Robert Conquest notes that the number of victims of the Holodomor can be roughly calculated thus: every letter in the text of his book of some 350 pages would stand for twenty or so victims! But this multiplication factor is not

[*] A Ukrainian-language version of this article appeared as "Holodomor i pam'iat'," *Krytyka*, no. 12 (December 2003): 10–13.

entirely transparent; it is far better to find a one-to-one relationship. So how could we more accurately imagine, say, five million victims? (As we know, the demographic reconstructions of the Holodomor place the number of victims at between four or five million to seven million, or indeed more.) These numbers somehow defy concretization. In 1933 that would have been between a fifth and a quarter of the entire Ukrainian rural population, or something like the combined populations of Sweden, Norway, and Denmark at that time. Although this, too, hardly presents a concrete image—for how can we imagine the entire population of one, or indeed several, Scandinavian countries? Except that if they were to be suddenly depopulated, we can hardly imagine that the world would be ignorant of this fact. So imagine then that the page you are reading is a field the size of an acre and every letter is a grave, thus presenting a small village cemetery of about 2,700 people. (In fact, however, the victims were usually buried into compacted, many-leveled pits—as the poet Pavlo Tychyna alluded to in his macabre and yet officially sanctioned 1933 poem "The Party Leads" [*Partiia vede*].) Each page of this book would be such a cemetery, and in order to arrive at the figure of five million one would have to have thirteen books such as this.

These are the bare numbers. But the victims were not anonymous numbers but people, and each person—man, woman, and child—had a name and a personal history. How many times was the entire repertoire of Ukrainian names exhausted?

In Washington, D.C., there is the Vietnam Veterans Memorial, which contains on its black granite surface the names of the American servicemen who fell in that war. One always sees people there touching the names, as if to come nearer to the shadows of the fallen. And whether searching for a name or not, one always sees reflection in the black granite—an intended fusion of past and present. There are about 58,260 names inscribed on that wall—about one-hundredth of the number of Holodomor victims. Each of the two walls of the Memorial is seventy-five meters long, rising at the highest point to three meters. If one were to erect a similar monument to the victims of the Holodomor, it would have to be several city blocks long and several stories high. But the names one would have to inscribe are mostly missing: we know of only one in a hundred, or one in a thousand.

And then one can try to imagine that death by hunger, its pain and its duration. And the circumstances of that final solution of the peasant problem—that is, the circumstances, the tactics and strategy of the "Great Peasant War" that the Soviet Union conducted against its own rural population.[1] And however much one's "normal" instincts rebel at evoking them—for who needs these images of horror, should not the dead bury the dead and the living go on with their lives?—the extermination, the brutality of the perpetrators, the mass psychoses, the cannibalism, the horror of it all, should perhaps be imagined, if only for a moment—for without it the Famine becomes an abstraction, an even paler shadow of what it was. All of these people had been alive, and what took their lives was as concrete as they: mass murder, state terror, genocide. The dimensions of the crime are conveyed by demographic statistics and through ever-increasing documentary evidence. The fabric, the circumstances of the crime are attested by the memory of witnesses, by documents and photographs and even some films, and subsequently by literary and artistic works that bore witness to what occurred. But this is only a fragment of the picture, for wherever possible the evidence was systematically destroyed and covered up. The very mention of the Holodomor was subject to severe punishment in the Soviet Union, and the preservation of memory occurred almost entirely without an institutional base. One can easily imagine that if the Soviet Union had flourished instead of collapsing, it all could have been forgotten. And yet the Holodomor was not forgotten, and the attention paid to it during this anniversary becomes an additional guarantee of the survival of its memory.

I

As so much in Ukrainian history, the Famine of 1932–1933 requires broad contextualization and concerted rethinking, and the present volume is a step in that direction. The heart of the matter is in Ukraine, a nation in the very process of establishing its identity. While efforts by historians to address the Holodomor began on the eve of independence (1989–1990) and became more intense immediately afterwards,[2] and while the official Ukrainian government position recognized it as a genocide even before the Orange Revolution, it is only as a result of that sea change that genuine, ongoing, and officially sanctioned efforts were made by the Yushchenko administration to inscribe the Holodomor into the consciousness of Ukraine's citizens and of world opinion. On each of these fronts these efforts are encountering both understanding and resistance. In Ukraine, recognition of the Holodomor as a genocide and perhaps *the* defining moment for the Ukrainian nation in the twentieth century is strongly resisted by that considerable segment of the population that still identifies with the Soviet past. In terms of world opinion (assuming, of course, that that metaphor is somehow meaningful), the process of recognizing the Holodomor is impeded by a range of factors: state policy (most starkly the resistance by a Russia determined to lay claim to the entire Soviet legacy and its great-power status to also admit that part of that legacy is a genocide against the Ukrainian nation); the attendant realpolitik, where good relations with various centers of power clearly take precedence over deciding on ethical issues and historical rights and wrongs; and, not least of all, a numbing of world opinion in the face of multifarious calamities and atrocities. In the last several decades, after all, the world has witnessed genocides in Cambodia (1975–1978), in Iraq against the Kurds (1986–1989), in Rwanda (1993), in former Yugoslavia (especially Bosnia, 1995) and the ongoing one (since 2003) in Darfur in the Sudan. A number of these were, or still remain, not recognized as genocides by various countries or by the UN.[3] And how many remember the genocide perpetrated by the Indonesian military in East Timor in 1999 after a UN-sponsored referendum on independence?

In light of this, the passivity (if not complete indifference) of world opinion is not singular. Still, as argued by Alain Besançon and Andrea Graziosi, the silence of specifically the West to this calamity is as eloquent as it is deplorable.[4] In some measure this reflects geopolitical realities and the consensus (or stasis) they subtend. Thus, the majority of Western historians began to seriously consider the Famine only after the collapse of the Soviet Union (the acceptance of it as the Holodomor, as a Famine-Genocide, is still ongoing). Underlying it were ideological or cryptoideological premises; for example, the dominant or mainstream predisposition to consider collectivization as a necessary function of the Soviet Union's modernization, and indeed to see the Soviet Union itself as a country like most other countries—with certain peculiarities, to be sure, but a "normal" country nonetheless. Scholarship, after all, like any other intellectual activity, has its phases, fashions, hypes, and periods of blindness or deafness. We are thus dealing with large intellectual processes and attendant schemata of prioritization, interpretation, and political correctness. For Besançon the basis for the invisibility of the Holodomor in the eyes of many in the West, particularly for the intellectuals of the Left, and particularly in France, is ideological schematism—where Nazi terror and genocide somehow conceal from view the Bolshevik version of the same.[5] Contributing to this, of course, was also Soviet disinformation and propaganda, supported by communist sympathizers outside the Soviet Union. As a result, the Ukrainian Holodomor was for a long time (and in some smaller measure still is) surrounded not only by the inertia of ignorance, but also by a reflexive denial of its very existence. On the most evident level this is now associated with the name of Walter Duranty, the *New York Times* correspondent who, while reporting from the Soviet Union in 1932–1933, denied the existence of any famine, specifically in Ukraine; Duranty later received a Pulitzer prize for his uncritical reporting from Moscow in 1931. The prize still has not been revoked. As we shall see, he is not the last of the deniers.

The fiftieth anniversary of the Great Famine was duly observed in the emigration (soon to be reconceived as the diaspora)—and, of course, it was only there that it could be observed. This anniversary, as Frank Sysyn has summarized it, stimulated four more or less coordinated projects: (1) through the Toronto-based (created in 1983) Famine Research Committee (now the Ukrainian Canadian Research and Documentation Centre) efforts were begun for making and then disseminating and popularizing the film *Harvest of Despair: The 1932–33 Famine in Ukraine* (1985; directed by Slavko Novytski, produced by Yurij Luhovy and Slavko Novytski); (2) in 1986 with the financial support of the Ukrainian National Association and with the academic stewardship of the Ukrainian Research Institute of Harvard University there appeared the already mentioned monograph, *Harvest of Sorrow* by Robert Conquest; (3) 1985 also saw the creation of the U.S. Congress Commission on the Ukraine Famine, with James Mace as staff director; and (4) in 1988 an international commission for studying the Holodomor was also founded.[6] At that time the Ukrainian Canadian scholars Roman Serbyn and Bohdan Krawchenko were also active as researchers and organizers of scholarly investigations of the Holodomor.[7]

II

A key response to the Holodomor, beginning with the Soviets, was that of denial.[8] As Henry R. Huttenbach notes at the outset of his article in *Studies in Comparative Genocide*, this is a structural component: "Denial has become an integral part of genocide; not to take this aspect into consideration is to fail to comprehend a major component of the dynamics of extermination."[9]

Although much has been studied (particularly the activities of Duranty),[10] a comprehensive examination of the course and concrete instances of Holodomor denial is still to appear. In the West this has been partially done in Conquest's book, in the catalogue of the Harvard exhibit of December 1983–February 1984, in Marco Carynnyk's study in the above-noted Canadian Institute of Ukrainian Studies collection of 1986, and in Sysyn's 1999 article.[11] The denial is ongoing, however, and hardly confined to the 1930s. In 1987, in response to the efforts of the Ukrainian diaspora there appeared in the publishing house of the Communist Party of Canada a book by a Canadian journalist Douglas Tottle entitled *Fraud, Famine and Fascism: The Ukrainian Genocide Myth from Hitler to Harvard*,[12] and a year later the New York newspaper *Village Voice* published an article by Jeff Coplon, "In Search of a Soviet Holocaust: A 55-Year-Old Famine Feeds the Right."[13] Common to both of them is the thesis that the Holodomor never occurred (there may have been a famine, but it never had the dimensions that are imputed, and it was caused by drought) and that efforts at observing it come from collaborators with Nazism and fascism; Conquest is a bad scholar in the pay of these same Ukrainian collaborators-nationalists-anticommunists. In contrast to Tottle, Coplon cites several academics (Moshe Lewin, Roberta Manning) who also reject Conquest's book and his thesis of the Holodomor as genocide.[14]

These, however, were the journalists, and in the case of Tottle, unabashed apologists for the Soviets. More telling—and deplorable—were the efforts of academics and intellectuals, which continue to this day. Judging by Internet publications, the discussion between those who assert and those who deny the Holodomor does not abate. In the course of the last several years these discussions have taken place in such forums as "H-Russia" and "artukraine"; among the deniers were Mark Tauger, Grover Furr, Arch Getty, and others; rebutting them were James Mace, Taras Kuzio, Bohdan Krawchenko, David Marples, and others. It was evident that professional qualifications and even (albeit seldom) a correct tone were no assurance against intellectual and moral blindness; and to this we shall return. Virtual space, moreover, also makes time virtual, and these debates can be accessed as if they were occurring today.[15]

For its part, Ukraine also provided an interesting instance of virtual time—and its own peculiar variant of Holodomor denial. In 1983 Ukraine did indeed observe a major anniversary—but it was not of the Holodomor, of course. What it did observe and celebrate was the 1,500th anniversary of the founding of Kyiv. (The Ninth International Congress of Slavists, which took place in Kyiv in 1983, was still showing the effects of that celebratory buzz: new monuments, new publications, new tourist paraphernalia, and so on.) In Kyiv today there are still stories about how celebrated Ukrainian academics from the Academy of Sciences bargained with their even more celebrated Moscow colleagues to wangle this anniversary and this very "round" date; and if Moscow would not agree to 2,000 years (the sum initially asked), then 1,500 would also do. The only question remaining is what happened in 483 AD? And precisely 483, and not 473, or 493, or indeed 583? For what do we know, in fact, about the fifth century, and wherefrom this sudden confidence about the founding date of Kyiv? To be sure, there is no need to strain one's reasoning powers or one's imagination. As Omeljan Pritsak, then director of HURI, put it as soon as the date and the celebration were announced, the fictional date as to the founding of Kyiv was designed to mask the very real, fiftieth anniversary of the Holodomor. And the fraud was itself typically Soviet: instead of memory and mourning, not to speak of expiation, the population was offered an augmented dose of amnesia in the guise of more triumphalism and yet another effort to cement the "eternal unity" of the Ukrainian and Russian peoples.[16]

III

At present, most troubling for many is the conceptual frame for seeing the Holodomor, in effect the question of whether it legally and formally meets the criteria of genocide. The question of whether it really occurred, or whether it may have been the result of acts of nature, drought, and so on, is no longer debatable. Arguably, the great majority of informed and decent people and a broad range of institutions and governments, precisely those who articulate "world opinion," accept the fact that a man-made famine did occur in Ukraine in 1932–1933. But for some, mass murder is not the same as genocide, and applying this term to the Famine of 1932–1933 is somehow not politically correct, almost a form of double-dealing. While not at all equivalent to the denials noted above, it is a qualification, which may in turn become demurral or indeed de facto denial. In some measure it models the thinking of the academics noted earlier—not, to be sure, of such as Tottle or Coplon. Characteristically, it applies to people who hardly see themselves as deniers of the Holodomor; to the contrary, they see themselves as sympathetic, if somehow more objective.

A telling example—precisely because it involves researchers and scholars whose commitment to fairness and accuracy and underlying sympathy to the victims of the Holodomor is not in question, and because at the time (five years ago) the matter was seen as considerably more questionable than now—is an exchange of views on the Internet portal of Deutsche Welle on the eve of a joint German-Ukrainian conference in Lüneburg, Germany (19–20 December 2003) on precisely the topic of "Was the Holodomor of 1932–1933 a Genocide?"[17] In the internet article/press release the reporter puts that very question to one of the participants, Prof. Wilfried Jilge of the Center for the Study of the History and Culture of East Central Europe: "In discussions around the Holodomor in Ukraine one hears ever more often the term *genocide*. In your opinion, how justified is this usage?" Professor Jilge's answer is classic in its academic and diplomatic correctness:

> What I cannot claim is that this was a genocide specifically targeted against the Ukrainian people. That is to say, did the Bolsheviks, the Center clearly intend to destroy the Ukrainian nation? I would answer cautiously: in order to claim that I would need more documentary evidence. Instances of famine were also noted in Kazakhstan and in the German-settled areas of the Volga region. But there is no doubt that the famine in Ukraine assumed particularly brutal form and caused serious demographic results. In any case, the problem is much too deep and complex to be formulated in one thesis.[18]

For purposes of full correctness, Deutsche Welle also gives the floor to a Ukrainian participant, Prof. Stanislav Kul′chyts′kyi. For him,

> the fact that this was a genocide is absolutely evident. Although it is difficult to prove. On the basis of documentation one can only confirm the techniques for the organization of the Famine. The technique was simple: all food products were confiscated and from January 1933 to July—that is, to the next harvest—the peasants were left with nothing. This was, indeed, a genocide according to both national and class criteria. According to the class criterion in that the blow was against peasants. And according to the national criterion: these were Ukrainian peasants, citizens of the Ukrainian SSR. And the Ukrainian republic, at least formally, was a country. And in order not to allow the possible development of separatism, Stalin, as was his custom, applied preventive repressions against the peasants in Ukraine

and in Kuban. And although Kuban was part of the Russian Federation, its population, according to the census of 1926, was two-thirds Ukrainian.[19]

Kul'chyts'kyi's argument should have been persuasive to his German colleagues, but one can hardly be certain. The very terms employed, "specifically targeted," "clearly intended," "documentary evidence"—these are recurring topoi—project a high standard of intentionality and evidence. For, at first glance, there are no Soviet documents analogous to the train schedules to Auschwitz or the minutes of the Wannsee conference where the Hitler regime planned the Final Solution.[20] But, as we see from the earlier work of Terry Martin and Iurii Shapoval and Valerii Vasyl'iev, and now of several other researchers, there is considerable and mounting documentary evidence about the planning and the unmistakable intentionality of the Holodomor.[21] In this context the traditional reservations, of which the above exchange is a telling, if altogether politically correct instance, begin to appear in a somewhat different light.

IV

The real issue, arguably, lies not in these concerns, but in a broader and more inclusive perception of the phenomenon of genocide itself.

The concept of genocide has its history and its historical setting, but without a contextualization of its origins, and particularly the gamut of mass murder to which it is now being applied with an increasingly clear international consensus, it may become merely schematic. More essential, therefore, than the original juridical definition may be the dynamics of its development, its evolution in the course of the entire genocidal twentieth century, and its function in the future. The literature on genocide is massive, and it has been swelled in the course of the last few years by the work of a growing number of scholars and whole programs and institutes. To recapitulate it is no easy task; one can only hope to give a general outline of the subject.[22] In relation to the Holodomor, indeed the Holodomor-as-genocide, the issue has now also drawn scholarly attention, especially since this has become the official position of Ukraine and part of an official campaign to have the United Nations and the international community recognize it as such.[23]

The term "genocide" itself was first proposed by the Jewish-Polish jurist Raphael Lemkin in 1944 to describe the destruction of whole national, racial, or ethnic groups by Axis powers during the Second World War.[24] On 9 December 1948, the UN adopted a Genocide Convention with the following definition:

> In the present Convention, genocide means any of the following acts com-
> mitted with intent to destroy, in whole or in part, a national, ethnical, racial
> or religious group as such:

(a)   Killing members of the group;

(b)   Causing serious bodily or mental harm to members of the group;

(c)   Deliberately inflicting on the group conditions of life calculated to bring about its physical destruction in whole or in part;

(d)   Imposing measures intended to prevent births within the group;

(e)   Forcibly transferring children of the group to another group.[25]

From the beginning, scholars and critics have been quick to point out that on the insistence of the Soviet Union (and Great Britain, which also supported this) the Convention fails to mention the possibility that victims of genocide may also be "political and other groups"; clearly, for a Stalinist Soviet Union that was not an acceptable definition. Obviously, this also distorted the very meaning and purpose of the Convention. As Eric Weitz notes, according to this approach, "if the Khmer Rouge were to come before an international tribunal, the indictment of genocide could be leveled only because of their treatment of Vietnamese, Muslims, or other minorities in Cambodia, but not for the vast repressions carried out against Khmer city dwellers and the educated elite."[26]

A second moment in the Convention that continually elicits criticism is the criterion of intentionality, of the concerted planning of a genocide. But as scholars and researchers argue, the presence of such intentionality is notoriously difficult to prove for genocidal regimes that characteristically and consistently hide their deeds and their motivations.[27] As with the genocide denial noted above, this can well be seen as a structural feature of genocide, and the search for the "smoking gun" of unambiguous "intent" may well be an impossible task, if not a distraction. Much more productive, as Helen Fein argues, is to focus on the consistency of action and our ability to make necessary discriminations.[28] For Israel W. Charny, the component of intentionality is altogether irrelevant:[29] for what is the relevance of the motivational nuances of the killers for the hundreds of thousands or millions of victims?

It seems clear that the Holocaust is paradigmatic in our thinking about genocide. And there is no doubt that in its dimensions, planning, ruthlessness, comprehensiveness (the Nazis were intent on destroying Jews wherever they may have been), the utilization of all the resources of the state (industrial, bureaucratic, communicational, even academic), this genocide does stand out.[30] It is significant, however, that among the most dedicated and authoritative of scholars dealing with the Holocaust are also those who insist that it should not overshadow or diminish other genocides, but indeed help in making them more comprehensible. Thus in his article on "Uniqueness of a Case of Genocide" that follows the article on the Ukrainian Genocide (i.e., the Holodomor) in volume 2 of the *Encyclopedia of Genocide*, Alan S. Rosenbaum writes of the deplorable competition that emerges at times from a comparative treatment of genocides—particularly in social or political contexts:

To argue for the uniqueness of any one type of genocide, despite persuasive historical arguments for the uniqueness of various aspects of every genocide, has invited an unseemly display of claims and counterclaims asserting the moral primacy of one genocide over another. One example of this spasm of competitive victimization is the attempt by some authorities to downgrade a given genocide by assigning it a lesser category of importance such as "massacre," thereby denying its pertinent similarities to known cases of genocide. [The author is not referring to "genocidal massacre" which is a term for genocide, but on a smaller scale, but to "massacre" as *not-genocide.—*Ed.] This is the case where Turkish authorities seek to rewrite or marginalize the Armenian Genocide.[31]

Perhaps the most eloquent and persuasive, comprehensive, and resonant with experience and moral authority is the position of the already-mentioned Israel W. Charny, Executive Director of the Institute on the Holocaust and Genocide in Jerusalem, author of numerous books on genocide and editor of the above-noted *Encyclopedia of Genocide*. He begins his important article "Toward a Generic Definition of Genocide" with this unambiguous recasting of the definition of genocide from a legalistic, UN Convention–driven (and hence intrinsically politicized and ultimately "mentalist") to one that is empirical, sociological, and humanist:

The definition of genocide adopted in law and by professional social scientists must match the realities of life, so that there should be no situation in which thousands and even millions of defenseless victims of mass murder do not "qualify" as victims of genocide. Insofar as there is ever a major discrepancy between the reality of masses of dead people and our legal-scholarly definitions it is the latter which must yield and change.[32]

Charny dedicates his *Genocide: A Critical Bibliographic Review* "to all those who oppose with uncompromising integrity any and all instances of mass murder, massacre, genocide" and then, as part of the dedication, appends this personal avowal:

I am deeply opposed to all definitional battles between scholars who would claim that "only" a given form of vicious massacre is "truly" genocide, with the resulting implication that the mass murders of other human beings, that for one reason or another do not qualify for the pure-form definition, are not deserving of the same intellectual or moral status. I suggest that a concept of *genocide* refer to *all* instances of mass deaths of people, of which one especially heartbreaking type *is intentional genocide*, which is to be defined as the willful attempt to destroy all or substantial numbers of a given ethnic/religious/national political/ (or whatever basis for defining) given people.[33]

His altogether inclusive, generic understanding of genocide also proceeds to draw essential distinctions between the different kinds of motivations, purposes and, yes, moral stances in the genocide debates. The core of the matter is "definitionalism," which he proceeds to define

> as a damaging style of intellectual inquiry based on perverse, fetishistic involvement with definitions to the point at which the reality of the subject under discussion is "lost," that is, no longer experienced emotionally by the scholars conducting the inquiry, to the point that the real enormity of the subject no longer guides or impacts on the deliberations. The discussions about whether a given massacre or mass murder can be considered genocide are often emotionless, argumentative, and superrational, and one senses that the motivations and meta-meanings of the discussion often are based on intellectual competition and the claims to scholarly fame of the speakers rather than on genuine concern for the victims. The predominant intellectual goal of most participants in these definitional turf battles over what is and is not genocide is generally to exclude unfavored categories from the field.
>
> For me, the passion to exclude this or that mass killing from the universe of genocide, as well as the intense competition to establish the exclusive "superiority" or unique form of any one genocide, ends up creating a fetishistic atmosphere in which the masses of bodies that are not to be qualified for the definition of genocide are dumped into a conceptual black hole, where they are forgotten.[34]

V

The conceptualization of the Holodomor precisely as a genocide; as mass murder perpetrated by a criminal and, as in so many of its actions (the other Soviet famines, especially the Kazakh, the Great Terror, the deportations of whole peoples, Katyn), a habitually genocidal state against its defenseless citizenry; as a politically motivated action against the very vitality of the Ukrainian nation and its core social group, the peasantry—all this is a process well under way, both in Ukraine and in the world at large. When one surveys the academic scene and more broadly "world opinion" on this matter at the time of the fiftieth anniversary of the Holodomor in 1983 and compares it to the one that obtains now, the movement of recognition stands out as something remarkable and inexorable. Rapidly accumulating research, reflected in this volume in the studies of Andrea Graziosi and Hennadii Boriak, augmented by the recent work of such Ukrainian scholars as Stanislav Kul'chyts'kyi, and summarized and "inventoried" in such comprehensive works as *The Historiography of Genocide*, is making an incontrovertible case for the premeditated, intentional nature of the Holodomor, a genocide against a people, intending to "deal a crushing blow," as the Stalinist strategy conceived it, against the Ukrainian nation—both the backbone, the peasantry, and the intelligentsia and elites.[35] As such it reflects and fulfills even the narrowly drawn terms or conditions of the original 1948 UN Genocide Convention. Within the confines of that paradigm the "definitionalist" debates will continue, along with the ongoing search for an ever more "smoking" gun and for clearer instances of the letter and spirit of genocidal intent on the part of the perpetrators; and they will be augmented, alas, by various forms of both innocent and not-so-innocent denial.[36] But as the above discussion has shown, both the massive evidence of the crime and the very nature of the changing field of genocide studies make this rather moot: the Holodomor is now generally seen for what it is—and always was.

But as with every genocide, it, too, has its unique horror. It inheres not only in its immense dimension, those hundreds of hectares of corpses, and not only in the fact that of all the major genocides of the genocidal twentieth century this was one of the longest in reaching the awareness of the international community (the Armenian genocide, to be sure, has been denied from the very beginning, above all by the Turkish authorities, but it has also been widely recognized for what it was—from the beginning—by much of the world). The core of the matter is that in the case of the Holodomor there not only was no punishment or expiation, no clear—until the most recent of times—formulation of the crime itself before the tribunal of world opinion, but the fact that for over half a century the great majority of the Ukrainian people, under the Soviets, lived in a country where the killers and their political descendants were their leaders, and remained their ruling elite. After the Second World War and the Holocaust the Nazi regime and its perpetrators—not just in the eyes of their victims, but for the world at large—were formally and symbolically judged and punished, and became a synonym of evil. The Turkish genocide against the Armenians was not punished, and the Turkish authorities, and much of the Turkish population, and many others as well, including various presumably bona fide scholars, still deny that genocide, but the world in large measure condemns it, and the Armenians as a nation were never obliged to express praise and love for their killers. That fate, however, befell the Ukrainians, and the wages of that collective spiritual crippling—which is precisely one of the core definitions of genocide—are altogether obvious. To this day a large number of the Ukrainian polity denies the Holodomor and professes solidarity with and allegiance to its perpetrators and their spiritual descendants. The treatment of this collective and defining trauma is an ongoing process—and a major task facing Ukraine and indeed the region as well.

NOTES

1. Cf. Andrea Graziosi, *The Great Soviet Peasant War: Bolsheviks and Peasants, 1917–1933* (Cambridge, Mass., 1996).

2. See the article in this volume by Hennadii Boriak; also Boriak, "The Publication of Sources on the History of the 1932–1933 Famine-Genocide: History, Current State, and Prospects," *Harvard Ukrainian Studies* 25, no. 3–4 (Fall 2001): 167–86; Wilfried Jilge, "Holodomor und Nation: Der Hunger im ukrainischen Geschichtsbild," in "Vernichtung durch Hunger: Der Holodomor in der Ukraine und der UdSSR," special issue, *Osteuropa* 12 (2004): 147–63.

3. Thus the United States did not recognize the Rwanda genocide as such; it recognizes the one in Darfur—but the UN does not recognize it. France is still broadly condemned for not recognizing the genocide in Rwanda, and indeed for supporting the perpetrators; see "France 'Should be Charged' for Rwanda Genocide," *afrol News*, 6 April 2005, http://www.afrol.com/articles/16082 (accessed 8 October 2008).

4. Alen Bezanson [Alain Besançon], "Retrospektyva bezpam'iatstva," *Krytyka*, no. 12 (December 2003): 20–22; Andrea Gratsiozi [Graziosi], "Usvidomliuvannia Holodomoru," *Krytyka*, no. 12 (December 2003): 18–20.

5. Bezanson, "Retrospectyva bezpam'iatstva"; Alain Besançon, *Le Malheur du siècle: Sur le communisme, le nazisme, et l'unicité de la Shoah* (Paris, 1998). The issue of Nazi and communist crimes is also discussed in Stéphane Courtois, introduction to *The Black Book of Communism: Crimes, Terror, Repression*, trans. Jonathan Murphy and Mark Kramer, 1–31 (Cambridge, Mass., 1999).

6. See Frank E. Sysyn, "The Ukrainian Famine of 1932–3: The Role of the Ukrainian Diaspora in Research and Public Discussion," in *Studies in Comparative Genocide*, ed. Levon Chorbajian and George Shirinian, 182–215 (London and New York, 1999), here 189.

7. See, for example, Roman Serbyn and Bohdan Krawchenko, eds., *Famine in Ukraine, 1932–1933* (Edmonton, 1986).

8. In tracing it, Sysyn also notes the attempt by the Soviet authorities to dissuade the director and coworkers of the Ukrainian Research Institute from engaging in this project; see Sysyn, "The Ukrainian Famine of 1932–3," 190, 206–7n22.

9. Huttenbach illustrates this thesis on the basis of the genocides of the Armenians at the beginning of the century, later the Jews and the Roma and the Croatian Serbs during World War II; see Henry R. Huttenbach, "The Psychology and Politics of Genocide Denial: A Comparison of Four Case Studies," in Chorbajian and Shirinian, *Studies in Comparative Genocide*, 216–29. One should also note that this study includes the work of the Turkish historian Taner Akçam, "The Genocide of the Armenians and the Silence of the Turks," which focuses in particular on the deep and institutionalized denial by Turkey and most Turks of the Armenian genocide.

10.   See S. J. Taylor, *Stalin's Apologist: Walter Duranty, the New York Times's Man in Moscow* (New York, 1990).

11.   See Oksana Procyk, Leonid Heretz, and James E. Mace, comps., *Famine in the Soviet Ukraine, 1932–1933: A Memorial Exhibition, Widener Library, Harvard University* (Cambridge, Mass., 1986); Marco Carynnyk, "Blind Eye to Murder: Britain, the United States and the Ukrainian Famine of 1933," in Serbyn and Krawchenko, *Famine in Ukraine 1932–1933*, 109–38; Sysyn, "The Ukrainian Famine of 1932–3."

12.   Douglas Tottle, *Fraud, Famine and Fascism: The Ukrainian Genocide Myth from Hitler to Harvard* (Toronto, 1987). Sysyn also examines a book by the Ukrainian Canadian communist Petro Kravchuk (*Our History: The Ukrainian Labour-Farmer Movement in Canada, 1907–1991* [Toronto, 1996]), which reveals the role of Kyiv authorities in the publication of Tottle's book; see Sysyn, "The Ukrainian Famine of 1932–3," 211–12n39.

13.   Jeff Coplon, "In Search of a Soviet Holocaust: A 55-Year-Old Famine Feeds the Right," *Village Voice*, 12 January 1988.

14.   Sysyn, "The Ukrainian Famine of 1932–3," 212n40.

15.   Search, for example, the websites H-Russia, http://www.h-net.org/˜russia/; and "The Great Famine-Genocide in Soviet Ukraine, 1932–1933 (Holodomor)," ArtUkraine. com, http://www.artukraine.com/famineart.index.htm (accessed 8 October 2008).

16.   As to the mechanisms applied in the Stalin era to ensure acquiescence and amnesia, see Dmytro Zlepko, "'Alles ist wunderbar': Der Holodomor aus der Sicht der Zeitgenossen," in "Vernichtung durch Hunger: Der Holodomor in der Ukraine und der UdSSR," special issue, *Osteuropa* 12 (2004): 192–203.

17.   See Liubomyr Petrenko, "Chy buv holodomor u 1932/33 rokakh henotsy-dom?" DW-WORLD.DE, 8 December 2003, http://www.dw-world.de/dw/ article/0,2144,2477273,00.html (accessed 1 October 2008).

18.   Ibid. All translations from the Ukrainian text are my own.

19.   Ibid.

20.   See Eric D. Weitz, *A Century of Genocide: Utopias of Race and Nation* (Princeton, 2003), 130–31; also Christopher R. Browning, *The Origins of the Final Solution: The Evolution of Nazi Jewish Policy, September 1939–March 1942* (Lincoln, Neb., 2004).

21.   Teri Martyn [Terry Martin], "Pro kozhnoho z nas dumaie Stalin . . . ," *Krytyka*, no. 12 (December 2003): 14–18; and esp. Iurii Shapoval and Valerii Vasyl'iev, *Komandyry velykoho holodu: Poïzdky V. Molotova i L. Kahanovycha v Ukraïnu ta na Pivnichnyi Kavkaz, 1932–1933 rr.* (Kyiv, 2001). See also Stanislav Kul'chyts'kyi,

Holodomor 1932–1933 rr. iak genotsyd: Trudnoshchi usvidomlennia (Kyiv 2008), esp. chap. 4, "Genotsyd: Stalins'kyi zadum ta ioho vykonannia," 228–83; Ruslan Pyrih, ed., *Holodomor 1932–1933 rokiv v Ukraïni: Dokumenty i materialy* (Kyiv, 2007); and Liudmyla Hrynevych, ed., *Kolektyvizatsiia sil's'koho hospodarstva ta Holodomor 1932–1933 rokiv v Ukraïni: Khronika podii v 4-okh knyhakh* (Kyiv, forthcoming).

22. See Dan Stone, ed., *The Historiography of Genocide* (Basingstoke, 2008); and Samuel Totten, William S. Parsons, and Israel W. Charny, eds., *Century of Genocide: Eyewitness Accounts and Critical Views* (New York, 1997).

23. See, for example, Viktor Yushchenko's opinion piece "Holodomor," *Wall Street Journal*, 27 November 2007, available at http://www.president.gov.ua/en/news/8296. html; the then Minister for Foreign Affairs of Ukraine Borys Tarasiuk's official statement at the sixtieth session of the UN General Assembly, 18 September 2005, http://www.mfa.gov.ua/mfa/en/publication/content/4521.htm (both sites accessed 15 October 2008); the earlier version of this article, Hryhorii Hrabovych, "Holodomor i pam'iat'"; and a more recent overview, Andrii Portnov, "Teoriia henotsydu pered vyklykom Holodomoru," *Krytyka*, no. 5 (May 2008): 11–13.

24. Raphael Lemkin, *Axis Rule in Occupied Europe: Laws of Occupation, Analysis of Government, Proposals for Redress* (Washington, D.C., 1944); see also Frank Chalk, "Redefining Genocide," in *Genocide: Conceptual and Historical Dimensions*, ed. George J. Andreopoulos, 47–63 (Philadelphia, 1994).

25. United Nations, Convention on the Prevention and Punishment of the Crime of Genocide, 9 December 1948; cited in Chalk, "Redefining Genocide," 48.

26. Weitz, *A Century of Genocide*, 9.

27. See George J. Andreopoulos, "The Calculus of Genocide," introduction to *Genocide: Conceptual and Historical Dimensions*, 7.

28. Thus, "although the borderlines between genocide and 'democide' in the Soviet Union are unclear, we do have case studies of the destruction of nations that fit the Convention definition of genocide: the Ukrainians in 1932–33 decimated by man-made famine, and the deportations of suspect peoples during and after World War II in conditions that caused almost half to die." Helen Fein, "Genocide, Terror, Life Integrity, and War Crimes: The Case for Discrimination," in Andreopoulos, *Genocide: Conceptual and Historical Dimensions*, 95–107, here 99.

29. Andreopoulos, "The Calculus of Genocide," 7; see Israel W. Charny, "Toward a Generic Definition of Genocide," in Andreopoulos, *Genocide: Conceptual and Historical Dimensions*, 64–94.

30. See, for example, Yehuda Bauer, "Comparison of Genocides," in Chorbajian and Shirinian, *Studies in Comparative Genocide*, 31–43; and Alan S. Rosenbaum, "Uniqueness of a Case of Genocide," in *Encyclopedia of Genocide*, ed. Israel W. Charny, vol. 2, 567–71 (Santa Barbara, 1999).

31.   Rosenbaum, "Uniqueness of a Case of Genocide," 569; italics and ed. note in original.

32.   Charny, "Toward a Generic Definition of Genocide," 64.

33.   See dedication page (v) of *Genocide: A Critical Bibliographic Review*, ed. Israel W. Charny, vol. 2 (London, 1991); italics in original.

34.   Charny, "Toward a Generic Definition of Genocide," 91–92.

35.   See Kul′chyts′kyi, *Holodomor 1932–1933 rr. iak genotsyd*, esp. 262–83 and the discussion there of the tactic of a "crushing blow" (*sokrushitel′nyi udar*).

36.   See the studies by Israel W. Charny on the phenomenon of genocide denial, e.g., "The Psychology of Denial of Known Genocides," in *Genocide: A Critical Bibliographic Review*, 2:3–37, esp. 23; "Innocent Denials of Known Genocides: A Further Contribution to a Psychology of Denial of Genocide," *Human Rights Review* 1, no. 3 (April–June 2000): 15–39; and esp. "The Psychological Satisfaction of Denials of the Holocaust or Other Genocides by Non-Extremists or Bigots, and Even by Known Scholars," *Idea: A Journal of Social Issues* 6, no. 1 (2001), http://www.ideajournal.com/articles.php?id=27 (accessed 1 October 2008). Particularly striking in the latter article is Charny's analysis of the "Relationship Between 'Innocent' and Malevolent Denial," as illustrated by the writings of Profs. Bernard Lewis and Ernst Nolte, with reference to the Armenian genocide and the Holocaust, respectively.

Index

abortion, 81, 82
All-Ukrainian Central Executive Committee (VUTsVK), 26
All-Ukrainian Union of Agricultural Collectives, 27
Archive of the President of the Russian Federation, 25
archives, 1991 opening of, 2, 22
Armenian genocide, 142, 146n36
Auschwitz, 131

Belarusians, 7, 9
Besançon, Alain, 134
black lists (*chernye doski*), 35, 54, 56, 64
Bokan', Mykola, 35
Boriak, Hennadii, 141
Bosnia, 133
Burckhardt, Jacob, 13

Cambodia, 133. *See also* Khmer Rouge
Canadian Institute of Ukrainian Studies, 53, 135
cannibalism, 28, 37, 108, 120
Carr, E. H., 14n4
Carynnyk, Marco, 135
census of 1959, 80–87
Central Archive of the Federal Security Service (FSB) of Russia, 25
Communist Party of Ukraine (KP[b]U), 8, 26, 27, 56
Central State Archives of Public Organizations (TsDAHO), 26
Central State Archives of Supreme Bodies of Power and Government (TsDAVO), 26
Chamberlain, William Henry, 84
Charny, Israel W., 139, 140–41
Cherkasy oblast, 82
Chernihiv and Chernihiv oblast, 71, 73, 82
Chubar, Vlas, 29

collectivization, 5, 53, 55, 94, 105–7, 118, 126–27. *See also* dekulakization
Conquest, Robert, 2, 131
Coplon, Jeff, 135
Cossacks, 7
Council of People's Commissars of the Ukrainian SSR (RNK), 26
Crimea oblast, 31, 82

Danilov, Viktor, 3, 26
Darfur, 133
Davies, R. W., 3
dekulakization, 7, 36, 86–88, 105. *See also* collectivization
demographic data on the Famine
    death records, 89–91
    geographic distribution of victims, 8
    infant mortality, 90–91, 93, 94
    number of victims, 6, 10, 132
    population losses, 80–94, 108
denomadization, 5, 11, 106–7, 110–12, 118, 127
disease, 77, 91–92
Dnipropetrovsk oblast, 75, 82, 86, 88
documentary evidence of the Famine
    All-Union level, 24–26
    archival, regional, 37; archival, state, 24–29
    criminal case proceedings, 28, 37
    destruction of, 22, 29, 38–39
    falsification of, 22, 33, 90–91
    foreign, 29, 120
    local level, 28–29
    personal accounts, 29, 75–80
    photographs, 35–37, 49n34, 76
    press accounts, 35
    publication of, 22, 30–31, 37–38
    republic level, 26–28
    vital statistics registers, 24, 33–35, 38. *See also* demographic data
Donbas, 73, 75